L. (Luise) Mühlbach

Queen Hortense

A Historical Romance

L. (Luise) Mühlbach

Queen Hortense
A Historical Romance

ISBN/EAN: 9783744693776

Printed in Europe, USA, Canada, Australia, Japan

Cover: Foto ©Thomas Meinert / pixelio.de

More available books at **www.hansebooks.com**

Edition De Luxe

Queen Hortense

An Historical Romance

By

Louisa Mühlbach

Translated from the German by

Chapman Coleman

The Chesterfield Society

London - New York

CONTENTS.

BOOK I.

DAYS OF CHILDHOOD AND OF THE REVOLUTION.

BOOK II.

THE QUEEN OF HOLLAND.

iv CONTENTS.

QUEEN HORTENSE.

BOOK I.

DAYS OF CHILDHOOD AND OF THE REVOLUTION.

CHAPTER I.

DAYS OF CHILDHOOD.

" ONE moment of bliss is not too dearly bought with death," says our great German poet, and he may be right; but a moment of bliss purchased with a long lifetime full of trial and suffering is far too costly.

And when did it come for her, this "moment of bliss?" When could Hortense Beauharnais, in speaking of herself, declare, "I am happy? Now, let suffering and sorrow come upon me, if they will; I have tasted felicity, and, in the memories it has left me, it is imperishable and eternal!"

Much, very much, had this daughter of an empress and mother of an emperor to endure.

In her earliest youth she had been made familiar with misfortune and with tears; and in her later life, as maiden, wife, and mother, she was not spared.

1

A touchingly-beautiful figure amid the drama of the Napoleonic days was this gentle and yet high-spirited queen, who, when she had descended from the throne and had ceased to be a sovereign, exhausted and weary of life, found refuge at length in the grave, yet still survived among us as a queen—no longer, indeed, a queen of nations, but the Queen of Flowers.

The flowers have retained their remembrance of Josephine's beautiful daughter; they did not, like so many of her own race, deny her when she was no longer the daughter of the all-powerful emperor, but merely the daughter of the "exile." Among the flowers the lovely Hortense continued to live on, and Gavarni, the great poet of the floral realm, has reared to her, as Hortensia, the Flower Queen, an enchanting monument, in his "*Fleurs Animées.*" Upon a mound of Hortensias rests the image of the Queen Hortense, and, in the far distance, like the limnings of a half-forgotten dream, are seen the towers and domes of Paris. Farther in the foreground lies the grave of Hortense, with the carved likeness of the queenly sister of the flowers. Loneliness reigns around the spot, but above it, in the air, hovers the imperial eagle. The imperial mantle, studded with its golden bees, undulates behind him, like the train of a comet; the dark-red ribbon of the Legion of Honor, with the golden cross, hangs around his neck, and in his beak he bears a full-blooming branch of the crown imperial.

It is a page of world-renowned history that this charming picture of Gavarni's conjures up before us—

an historical pageant that sweeps by us in wondrous fantastic forms of light and shadow, when we scan the life
of Queen Hortense with searching gaze, and meditate
upon her destiny. She had known all the grandeur and
splendor of earth, and had seen them all crumble again to
dust. No, not all! Her ballads and poems remain, for
genius needs no diadem to be immortal.

When Hortense ceased to be a queen by the grace of
Napoleon, she none the less continued to be a poetess
"by the grace of God." Her poems are sympathetic and
charming, full of tender plaintiveness and full of impassioned warmth, which, however, in no instance oversteps
the bounds of womanly gentleness. Her musical com-
positions, too, are equally melodious and attractive to
the heart. Who does not know the song, "*Va t'en,
Guerrier*," which Hortense wrote and set to music, and
then, at Napoleon's request, converted into a military
march? The soldiers of France once left their native
land, in those days, to the sound of this march, to carry
the French eagles to Russia; and to the same warlike
harmony they have marched forth more recently, toward
the same distant destination. This ballad, written by
Hortense, survived. At one time everybody sang it,
joyously, aloud. Then, when the Bourbons had returned,
the scarred and crippled veterans of the *Invalides*
hummed it under their breath, while they whispered
secretly to each other of the glory of *La Belle France*,
as of a beautiful dream of youth, now gone forever.

To-day, that song rings out with power again through

France, and mounts in jubilee to the summit of the column on the Place Vendôme. The bronze visage of the
emperor seems to melt into a smile as these tremulous
billows of melody go sweeping around his brow, and the
Hortensias on the queen's grave raise dreamingly their
heads of bloom, in which the dews of heaven, or the tears
of the departed one, glisten like rarest gems, and seem to
look forth lovingly and listen to this ditty, which now for
France has won so holy a significance—holy because it is
the master-chant of a religion which all men and all
nations should revere—the "religion of our memories."
Thus, this "*Va t'en, Guerrier*," which France now sings,
resounds over the grave of the queen, like a salute of
honor over the last resting-place of some brave soldier.

She had much to contend with—this hapless and
amiable queen—but she ever proved firm, and ever retained one kind of courage that belongs to woman—the
courage to smile through her tears. Her father perished
on the scaffold; her mother, the doubly-dethroned empress, died of a broken heart; her step-father, the Emperor Napoleon, pined away, liked a caged lion, on a lone
rock in the sea! Her whole family—all the dethroned
kings and queens—went wandering about as fugitives
and pariahs, banished from their country, and scarcely
wringing from the clemency of those to whom *they* had
been clement, a little spot of earth, where, far from the
bustle and intercourse of the world, they might live in
quiet obscurity, with their great recollections and their
mighty sorrows. Their past lay behind them, like a glit-

tering fairy tale, which no one now believed; and only the present seemed, to men and nations, a welcome reality, which they, with envenomed stings, were eager to brand upon the foreheads of the dethroned Napoleon race.

Yet, despite all these sorrows and discouragements, Hortensia had the mental strength not to hate her fellow-beings, but, on the contrary, to teach her children to love them and do good to them. The heart of the dethroned queen bled from a thousand wounds, but she did not allow these wounds to stiffen into callousness, nor her heart to harden under the broad scars of sorrow that had ceased to bleed. She cherished her bereavements and her wounds, and kept them open with her tears; but, even while she suffered measureless woes, it solaced her heart to relieve the woes and dry the tears of others. Thus was her life a constant charity; and when she died she could, like the Empress Josephine, say of herself, "I have wept much, but never have I made others weep."

Hortense was the daughter of the Viscount de Beau-harnais, who, against the wishes of his relatives, married the beautiful Josephine Tascher de la Pagerie, a young creole lady of Martinique. This alliance, which love alone had brought about, seemed destined, nevertheless, to no happy issue. While both were young, and both inexperienced, passionate, and jealous, both lacked the strength and energy requisite to restrain the wild impulses of their fiery temperaments within the cool and tranquil bounds of quiet married life. The viscount was too young to be not merely a lover and tender husband,

but also a sober counsellor and cautious instructor in the
difficult after-day of life; and Josephine was too innocent, too artless, too sportive and genial, to avoid all those
things that might give to the watchful and hostile family
of her husband an opportunity for ill-natured suspicions,
which were whispered in the viscount's ear as cruel cer-
tainties. It may readily be conceived, then, that such a
state of things soon led to violent scenes and bitter grief.
Josephine was too beautiful and amiable not to attract
attention and admiration wherever she went, and she was
not yet *blasée* and hackneyed enough to take no pleasure
in the court thus paid to her, and the admiration so universally shown her, nor even to omit doing her part to
win them. But, while she was naive and innocent at
heart, she required of her husband that these trifling outside coquetries should not disquiet him nor render him
distrustful, and that he should repose the most unshaken
confidence in her. Her pride revolted against his suspicions, as did his jealousy against her seeming frivolity;
and both became quite willing, at last, to separate, notwithstanding the love they really bore each other at the
bottom of their hearts, had not their children rendered
such a separation impossible. These children were a son,
Eugene, and a daughter, Hortense, four years younger
than the boy. Both parents loved these children with
passionate tenderness; and often when one of the stormy
scenes at which we have hinted took place in the presence of the young people, an imploring word from Eugene or a caress from little Hortense would suffice to

reconcile their father and mother, whose anger, after all, was but the result of excessive attachment.

But these domestic broils became more violent with time, and the moment arrived when Eugene was no longer there to stand by his little sister in her efforts to soothe the irritation of her parents. The viscount had sent Eugene, who was now seven years of age, to a boarding-school; and little Hortense, quite disheartened by the absence of her brother, had no longer the means or the courage to allay the quarrels that raged between her parents, but would escape in terror and dismay, when they broke out, to some lonely corner, and there weep bitterly over a misfortune, the extent of which her poor little childish heart could not yet estimate.

In the midst of this gloomy and stormy period, the young viscountess received a letter from Martinique. It was from her mother, Madame Tascher de la Pagerie, who vividly depicted to her daughter the terrors of her lonely situation in her huge, silent residence, where there was no one around her but servants and slaves, whose singularly altered and insubordinate manner had, of late, alarmed the old lady, and filled her with secret apprehensions for the future. She, therefore, besought her daughter to come to her, and live with her, so that she might cheer the last few years of her mother's existence with the bright presence of her dazzling youth.

Josephine accepted this appealing letter from her mother as a hint from destiny; and, weary of her domestic wrangles, and resolved to end them forever, she took her little daughter, Hortense, then scarcely four years old, and with her sailed away from France, to seek beyond the ocean and in her mother's arms the new happiness of undisturbed tranquillity.

But, at that juncture, tranquillity had fled the world. The mutterings and moanings of the impending tempest could be heard on all sides. A subterranean rumbling was audible throughout all lands; a dull thundering and outcry, as though the solid earth were about to change into one vast volcano — one measureless crater — that would dash to atoms, and entomb, with its blazing lava-streams and fiery cinder-showers, the happiness and peace of all humanity. And, finally, this terrific crater did, indeed, open and hurl destruction and death on all sides, over the whole world, uprooting, with demoniac fury, entire races and nations, and silencing the merry laugh and harmless jest with the overpowering echoes of its awful voice!

This volcano was the revolution. In France, the first and most fearful explosion of this terrific crater occurred, but the whole world shook and heaved with it, and, on all sides, the furious masses from beneath overflowed on the surface, seeking to reverse the order of things and place the lowest where the highest had been. Even away in Martinique this social earthquake was felt, which had already, in France, flung out the bloody guillotine from its relentless crater. This guillotine had become the altar of the so-called enfranchisement of nations, and upon this altar the intoxicated, unthinking masses offered up to their new idol those who, until then, had been their lords and masters, and by whose death they now believed that they could purchase freedom for evermore.

"Egalité! fraternité! liberté!" Such was the battle-cry of this howling, murdering populace. Such were the three words which burned in blood-red letters of fire above the guillotine, and their mocking emblem was the glittering axe, that flashed down, to sever from their bodies the heads of the aristocrats whom, in spite of the new religion represented in those three words, they would not recognize as brethren and equals, or admit to the freedom of life and of opinion. And this battle-cry of the murderous French populace had penetrated as far as Martinique, where it had aroused the slaves from their sullen obedience to the point of demanding by force that participation in freedom, equality, and brotherhood, that had so long been denied them. They, at last, rose everywhere in open insurrection against their masters, and the firebrands which they hurled into the dwellings of the whites served as the bridal torches to their espousal of liberty.

The house of Madame Tascher de la Pagerie was one of the abodes in which these firebrands fell.

One night Josephine was awakened by the blinding light of the flames, which had already penetrated to her chamber. With a shriek of terror, she sprang from her bed, caught up little Hortense in her arms from the couch where the child lay quietly slumbering, wrapped

2

her in the bedclothes, and rushed, in her night-attire, from the house. She burst, with the lion-like courage of a mother, through the shouting, fighting crowds of soldiers and blacks outside, and fled, with all the speed of mortal terror, toward the harbor. There lay a French vessel, just ready to weigh anchor. An officer, who at that moment was stepping into the small boat that was to convey him to the departing ship, saw this young woman, as, holding her child tightly to her bosom, she sank down, with one last despairing cry, half inanimate, upon the beach. Filled with the deepest compassion, he hastened to her, and, raising both mother and child in his arms, he bore them to his boat, which then instantly put out from land, and bounded away over the billows with its lovely burden.

The ship was soon reached, and Josephine, still tightly clasping her child to her breast, and happy in having saved this only jewel, climbed up the unsteady ladder to the ship's decks. Until this moment all her thoughts remained concentrated upon her child, and it was only when she had seen her little Hortense safely put to bed in the cabin and free from all danger—only after she had fulfilled all the duties of a mother, that the woman revived in her breast, and she cast shamed and frightened glances around her. Only half-clad, in light, fluttering night-clothes, without any other covering to her beautiful neck and bosom than her superb, luxuriant hair, which fell around her and partly hid them, like a thick black veil, stood the young Viscountess Josephine de Beauharnais, in the midst of a group of gazing men!

However, some of the ladies on the ship came to her aid, and, so soon as her toilet had been sufficiently improved, Josephine eagerly requested to be taken back to land, in order that she might fly to her mother's assistance.

But the captain opposed this request, as he was unwilling to give the young fugitive over to the tender mercies of the assassins who were burning and massacring ashore, and whose murderous yells could be distinctly heard on board of the vessel. The entire coast, so far as the eye could reach, looked like another sea—a sea, though, of flame and smoke, which shot up its leaping billows in long tongues of fire far against the sky. It was a terrible, an appalling spectacle; and Josephine fled from it to the bedside of her little sleeping daughter. Then, kneeling there by the couch of her child, she uplifted to heaven her face, down which the tears were streaming, and implored God to spare her mother.

But, meanwhile, the ship weighed anchor, and sped farther and farther away from this blazing coast.

Josephine stood on the deck and gazed back at her mother's burning home, which gradually grew less to her sight, then glimmered only like a tiny star on the distant horizon, and finally vanished altogether. With that last ray her childhood and past life had sunk forever in the sea, and a new world and a new life opened for both mother and child. The past was, like the ships of Cor-

tez, burned behind her; yet it threw a magic light far
away over into her future, and as Josephine stood there
with her little Hortense in her arms, and sent her last
farewell to the island where her early days had been
spent, she bethought her of the old mulatto-woman who
had whispered in her ear one day :

"You will go back to France, and, ere long after
that, all France will be at your feet. You will be
greater there than a queen."

CHAPTER II.

THE PROPHECY.

It was toward the close of the year 1790 that Josephine, with her little daughter, Hortense, arrived in
Paris and took up her residence in a small dwelling.
There she soon received the intelligence of the rescue
of her mother, and of the re-establishment of peace in
Martinique. In France, however, the revolution and the
guillotine still raged, and the banner of the Reign of
Terror—the red flag—still cast its bloody shadow over
Paris. Its inhabitants were terror-stricken ; no one knew
in the evening that he would still be at liberty on the
following day, or that he would live to see another sun-
set. Death lay in wait at every door, and reaped its
dread harvest in every house and in every family. In
the face of these horrors, Josephine forgot all her earlier

griefs, all the insults and humiliations to which she had been subjected by her husband; the old love revived in her breast, and, as it might well be that on the morrow death would come knocking at her own door, she wished to devote the present moment to a reconciliation with her husband, and a reunion with her son.

But all her attempts in this direction were in vain. The viscount had felt her flight to Martinique to be too grave an injury, too great an insult, to be now willing to consent to a reconciliation with his wife. Sympathizing friends arranged a meeting between them, without, however, previously informing the viscount of their design. His anger was therefore great when, on entering the parlor of Count Montmorin, in response to that gentleman's invitation, he found there the wife he had so obstinately and wrathfully avoided. He was about to retire hastily, when a charming child rushed forward, greeted him tenderly in silvery tones, and threw herself into his arms. The viscount was now powerless to fly; he pressed his child, his Hortense, to his heart, and when the child, with a winning smile, entreated him to kiss her mamma as he had kissed her; when he saw the beautiful countenance of Josephine wet with tears; when he heard his father's voice saying, "My son, reconcile yourself with my daughter! Josephine is my daughter, and I would not call her so if she were unworthy," and when he saw his handsome son, Eugene, gazing at him wistfully, his head resting on his mother's shoulder, his heart relented. Leading little Hortense by the hand, he stepped forward to his wife, and, with a loud cry of joy and a blissful greeting of love, Josephine sank on his bosom.

Peace was re-established, and husband and wife were now united in a closer bond of love than ever before. The storms seemed to have spent their rage, and the heaven of their happiness was clear and cloudless. But this heaven was soon to be overcast with the black shadow of the revolution.

Viscount Beauharnais, returned by the nobility of Blois to the new legislative body, the Estates-General, resigned this position, in order to serve his country with his sword instead of his tongue. With the rank of adjutant-general, he repaired to the Army of the North, accompanied by Josephine's blessings and tears. A dread premonition told her that she would never see the general again, and this premonition did not deceive her. The spirit of anarchy and insurrection not only raged among the people of Paris, but also in the army. The aristocrats, who were given over to the guillotine in Paris, were also regarded with distrust and hatred in the army, and Viscount Beauharnais, who, for his gallantry on the battle-field of Soissons, had been promoted to the position of commanding general, was accused by his own officers of being an enemy of France and of the new order of things. He was arrested, taken back to Paris, and thrown into the prison of the Luxembourg, where so many other victims of the revolution lay in confinement.

The sad intelligence of her husband's misfortune soon reached Josephine, and aroused her love to energetic action in his behalf. She mentally vowed to liberate her husband, the father of her children, or to die with him. She courageously confronted all dangers, all suspicions, and was happy when she found him in his prison, where she visited him, whispering words of consolation and hope in his ear.

But at that time love and fidelity were also capital crimes, and Josephine's guilt was twofold: first, because she was an aristocrat herself, and secondly, because she loved and wept for the fate of an aristocrat, and an alleged traitor to his country. Josephine was arrested and thrown into the prison of St. Pelagie.

Eugene and Hortense were now little better than orphans, for the prisoners of the Luxembourg and St. Pelagic, at that time, only left their prisons to mount the scaffold. Alone, deprived of all help, avoided by all whom they had once known and loved, the two children were threatened with misery, want, and even with hunger, for the estate of their parents had been confiscated, and, in the same hour in which Josephine was conducted to prison, the entrances and doors of their dwelling were sealed, and the poor children left to find a sheltering roof for themselves. But yet they were not entirely helpless, not quite friendless, for a friend of Josephine, a Madame Holstein, had the courage to come to the rescue, and take the children into her own family.

But it was necessary to go to work cautiously and wisely, in order to avoid exciting the hatred and vengeance of those who, coming from the scum of the people, were now the rulers of France. An imprudent word, a look, might suffice to cast suspicion upon, and render up to the guillotine, this good Madame Holstein, this courageous friend of the two children. It was in itself a capital crime that she had taken the children of the accused into her house, and it was therefore necessary to adopt every means of conciliating the authorities. It was thought necessary that Hortense should, in company with her protectress, attend the festivals and patriotic processions, that were renewed at every decade in honor of the one and indivisible republic, but she was never required to take an active part in these celebrations. She was not considered worthy to figure among the daughters of the people; she had not yet been forgiven for being the daughter of a viscount, of an imprisoned *ci-devant*. Eugene had been apprenticed to a carpenter, and the son of the viscount was now often seen walking through the streets in a blouse, carrying a board on his shoulder or a saw under his arm.

While the children of the accused were thus enjoying temporary security, the future of their parents was growing darker and darker, and not only the life of the general, but also that of his wife, was now seriously endangered. Josephine had been removed from the prison of St. Pelagie to that of the Carmelites, and this brought her a step nearer the scaffold. But she did not tremble for herself, she thought only of her children and her husband; she wrote affectionate letters to the former, which she bribed her jailer to forward to their destination, but all her efforts to place herself in communication with her husband were abortive. One day she received the fearful intelligence that her husband had just been conducted before the revolutionary tribunal. Josephine waited for further intelligence in an agony of suspense. Had this tribunal acquitted her husband, or had it condemned him to death? Was he already free, or was he free in a higher sense—was he dead? If he were free, he would have found means to inform her of the fact; and if he were dead, his name would certainly have been mentioned in the list of the condemned. In this agony of suspense, Josephine passed the long day. Night came, but brought no rest for her and her companions in misery —the other occupants of the prison—who also looked death in the face, and who watched with her throughout the long night.

The society assembled in this prison was brilliant and select. There were the Dowager Duchess de Choiseul, the Viscountess de Maille, whose seventeen-years-old daughter had just been guillotined; there was the Marquise de Créqui, the intellectual lady who has often been called the last marquise of the *ancien régime*, and who in her witty memoirs wrote the French history of the eighteenth century as viewed from an aristocratic standpoint. There was Abbé Téxier, who, when the revolutionists threatened him with the lantern, because he had refused to take the oath of allegiance to the new constitution, replied: "Will you see any better after having hung me to the lantern?" And there was yet another, a M. Duvivier, a pupil of Cagliostro, who, like his master, could read the future, and with the assistance of a decanter full of water and a " dove," that is, an innocent young girl of less than seven, could solve the mysteries of fate.

To him, to the Grand Cophta, Josephine now addressed herself after this day of dread uncertainty, and demanded information of the fate of her husband.

In the stillness of the night the gloomy, desolate hall of the prison now presented a strange aspect. The jailer, bribed with an assignat of fifty francs, then worth only forty sous, however, had consented that his little six-years-old daughter should serve the Grand Cophta as "dove," and had made all other preparations. A table stood in the middle of the hall, on which was a decanter filled with clear, fresh water, around which were three candles in the form of a triangle, and placed as near the decanter as possible, in order that the dove should be able to see the better. The little girl, just aroused from sleep and brought from her bed in her night-gown, sat on a chair close to the table, and behind her stood the earnest, sombre figure of the Grand Cophta. Around the table stood the prisoners, these duchesses and marquises, these ladies of the court of Versailles who had preserved their aristocratic manners in the prison, and were even here so strictly observant of etiquette, that those of them who had enjoyed the honor of the *tabou-ret* in the Tuileries, were here accorded the same precedence, and all possible consideration shown them.

On the other side of the table, in breathless suspense, her large, dark eyes fastened on the child with a touching expression, stood the unhappy Josephine, and, at some distance behind the ladies, the jailer with his wife.

Now the Grand Cophta laid both hands on the child's head and cried in a loud voice, "Open your eyes and look!"

The child turned pale and shuddered as it fixed its gaze on the decanter.

"What do you see?" asked the Grand Cophta. "I want you to look into the prison of General Beauharnais. What do you see?"

"I see a little room," said the child with vivacity. "On a cot lies a young man who sleeps; at his side stands another man, writing on a sheet of paper that lies on a large book."

"Can you read?"

"No, citizen. Now the man cuts off his hair, and folds it in the paper."

"The one who sleeps?"

"No, the one who was just now writing. He is now writing something on the back of the paper in which he wrapped the hair; now he opens a little red pocket-book, and takes papers out of it; they are assignats, he counts them and then puts them back in the pocket-book. Now he rises and walks softly, softly."

"What do you mean by softly? You have not heard the slightest noise as yet, have you?"

"No, but he walks through the room on tiptoe."

"What do you see now?"

"He now covers his face with his hands and seems to be weeping."

"But what did he do with his pocket-book?"

"Ah, he has put the pocket book and the package with the hair in the pocket of the coat that lies on the sleeping man's bed."

"Of what color is this coat?"

"I cannot see, exactly; it is red or brown, lined with blue silk and covered with shining buttons."

"That will do," said the Grand Cophta; "you can go to bed, child."

He stooped down over the child and breathed on her forehead. The little girl seemed to awaken as from a trance, and hurried to her parents, who led her from the hall.

"General Beauharnais still lives!" said the Grand Cophta, addressing Josephine.

"Yes, he still lives," cried she, sadly, "but he is preparing for death." *

Josephine was right. A few days later Duchess d'Anville received a package and a letter. It was sent to her by a prisoner in La Force, named De Legrois. He had occupied the same cell with General Beauharnais and had found the package and the letter, addressed to the duchess, in his pocket on the morning of the execution of the general.

* This scene is exactly as represented by the Marquise de Créqui, who was present and relates it in her memoirs, vol. vi., p. 238.

In this letter the general conjured Duchess D'Anville to deliver to Josephine the package which contained his hair and his last adieus to wife and children.

This was the only inheritance which General Beauharnais could bequeath to his Josephine and her unhappy children!

Josephine was so agitated by the sight of her husband's hair and his last fond words of adieu, that she fainted away, a stream of blood gushing from her mouth.

Her companions in misfortune vied with each other in giving her the most tender attention, and demanded of the jailer that a physician should be called.

"Why a physician!" said the man, indifferently. "Death is the best physician. He called the general to-day; in a few days he will restore to him his wife."

This prophecy was almost verified. Josephine, scarcely recovered from her illness, received her citation from the Tribunal of Terror. This was the herald of certain death, and she courageously prepared for the grave, troubled only by thoughts of the children she must leave behind.

A fortunate and unforeseen occurrence saved her. The men of the revolution had now attained the summit of their power, and, as there was no standing still for them, they sank into the abyss which themselves had digged.

The fall of Robespierre opened the prisons and set at liberty thousands of the already condemned victims of the revolution.

Viscountess Josephine left her prison; she was restored to liberty, and could now hasten to her children, but she came back to them as a poor widow, for the seals of the "one and indivisible republic" were on hers and her children's property as well as on that of all other aristocrats.

CHAPTER III.

CONSEQUENCES OF THE REVOLUTION.

FRANCE drew a breath of relief; the Reign of Terror was at an end, and a milder and more moderate government wielded the sceptre over the poor land that had so lately lain in the agonies of death. It was no longer a capital offence to bear an aristocratic name, to be better dressed than the *sans-culottes*, to wear no Jacobin-cap, and to be related to the emigrants. The guillotine, which had ruled over Paris during two years of blood and tears, now rested from its horrid work, and allowed the Parisians to think of something else besides making their wills and preparing for death.

Mindful of the uncertainty of the times, the people were disposed to make the most of this release from the fear of immediate death, and to enjoy themselves to the utmost while they could.

They had so long wept, that they eagerly desired to laugh once more; so long lived in sorrow and fear, that they now ardently longed for amusement and relaxation. The beautiful women of Paris, who had been dethroned by the guillotine, and from whose hands the reins had been torn, now found the courage to grasp these reins again, and reconquer the position from which the storm-wind of the revolution had hurled them.

Madame Tallien, the all-powerful wife of one of the five directors who now swayed the destinies of France; Madame Récamier, the friend of all the eminent and distinguished men of that period; and Madame de Staël, the daughter of Necker, and the wife of the ambassador of Sweden, whose government had recognized the republic—these three ladies gave to Paris its drawing-rooms, its reunions, its *fêtes*, its fashions, and its luxury. All Paris had assumed a new form, and, although the Church had not yet again obtained official recognition, the belief in a Supreme Being was already re-established. Robespierre had already been bold enough to cause the inscription, "There is a Supreme Being," to be placed over the altars of the churches that had been converted into "Temples of Reason." Yes, there is a Supreme Being; and Robespierre, who had first acknowledged its existence, was soon to experience in himself that such was the case. Betrayed by his own associates, and charged by them with desiring to make himself dictator, and place himself at the head of the new Roman-French Republic as a new Cæsar, Robespierre fell a prey to the Tribunal of Terror which he himself had called into existence. While engaged in the Hôtel de Ville in signing death-sentences which were to furnish fresh victims to the guillotine, he was arrested by the Jacobins and National Guards, who had stormed the gates and penetrated into the building, and the attempt to blow out his brains with his pistol miscarried. Bleeding, his jaw shattered by the bullet, he was dragged before Fouquier-Tainville to receive his sentence, and to be conducted thence to the scaffold. In order that the proceeding should be attended with all formalities, he was, however, first conducted to the Tuileries, where the Committee of Public Safety was then sitting in the chamber of Queen Marie Antoinette. Into the bedchamber of the queen whom Robespierre had brought to the scaffold, the bleeding, half-lifeless dictator was now dragged. Like a bundle of rags he was contemptuously thrown on the large table that stood in the middle of the room. But yesterday Robespierre had been enthroned at this table as almighty ruler over the lives and possessions of all Frenchmen; but yesterday he had here issued his decrees and signed the death-sentences, that lay on the table, unexecuted. These papers were now the only salve the ghastly, groaning man could apply to the wound in his face, from which blood poured in streams. The death-sentences signed by himself now drank his own blood, and he had nothing but a rag of a tricolor, thrown him by a compassionate *sans-culotte*, with which to bind up the great, gaping wound on his head. As he sat there in the midst of the blood-saturated papers, bleeding, groaning, and complaining, an old National Guard, with outstretched arms, pointing to this ghastly object, cried: "Yes, Robespierre was right. There is a Supreme Being!"

This period of blood and terror was now over; Robespierre was dead; Théroigne de Méricourt was no longer the Goddess of Reason, and Mademoiselle Maillard no longer Goddess of Liberty and Virtue. Women had given up representing divinities, and desired to be themselves again, and to rebuild in the drawing-rooms of the capital, by means of their intellect and grace, the throne which had gone down in the revolution.

Madame Tallien, Madame Récamier, and Madame de Staël, reorganized society, and all were anxious to obtain admission to their parlors. To be sure, these entertainments and reunions still wore a sufficiently strange and fantastic appearance. Fashion, which had so long been compelled to give way to the *carmagnole* and red cap, endeavored to avenge its long banishment by all manner of caprices and humors, and in doing so assumed a political, reactionary aspect. *Coiffures à la Jacobine* were now supplanted by *coiffures à la victime* and *au repentir*. In order to exhibit one's taste for the fine arts, the draperies of the statues of Greece and ancient Rome were now worn. Grecian *fêtes* were given, at which the black soup of Lycurgus was duly honored, and Roman feasts which, in splendor and extravagance, rivalled those of Lucullus. These Roman feasts were particularly in vogue at the palace of Luxembourg, where the directors of the republic had now taken up their residence, and where Madame Tallien exhibited to the new French society the new wonders of luxury and fashion. Too proud to wear the generally-adopted costume of the Gre-

3

cian republic, Madame Tallien chose the attire of the
Roman patrician lady ; and the gold-embroidered purple
robes, and the golden tiara in her black, shining hair,
gave to the charming and beautiful daughter of the republic the magnificence of an empress. She had also
drawn around her a splendid court. All eagerly pressed
forward to pay their respects to and obtain the good
will of the mighty wife of the mighty Tallien. Her
house was the great point of attraction to all those who
occupied prominent positions in Paris, or aspired to such.
While in the parlors of Madame Récamier, who, despite
the revolution, had remained a zealous royalist, the past
and the good time of the Bourbons were whispered of,
and witty and often sanguinary *bon mots* at the expense
of the republic uttered—while in Madame de Staël's parlors art and science had found an asylum—Madame Tallien and court lived for the present, and basked in the
splendor with which she knew how to invest the palace
of the dictators of France.

In the mean while, Viscountess Josephine Beauharnais had been living, with her children, in quiet retirement, a prey to sad memories. A day came, however,
when she was compelled to tear herself from this last
consolation of the unhappy, the brooding over the sorrows and losses of the past, or see her children become
the victims of misery and want. The time had come
when she must leave her retirement, and step, as a petitioner, before those who had the power to grant, as a
favor, that which was hers by right, and restore to her, at

least in part, her sequestered estate. Josephine had known Madame Tallien when she was still Madame de Fontenay, and it now occurred to her that she might assist her in her attempt to recover the inheritance of her father. Madame Tallien, the "Merveilleuse de Luxembourg," also called by her admirers, "Notre-dame de Thermidor," felt much flattered at being called on by a real viscountess, who had filled a distinguished position at the court of King Louis. She therefore received her with great amiability, and endeavored to make the charming and beautiful viscountess her friend. But Josephine found that estates were more easily lost than recovered. The republic, one and indivisible, was always ready to take, but not to give; and, even with the kindly offices of Madame Tallien freely exerted in her behalf, it was some time before Josephine succeeded in recovering her estate. In the mean time, she really suffered want, and she and her children were compelled to bear the hardships and mortifications which poverty brings in its train. But true friends still remained to her in her misery; friends who, with true delicacy, furnished her with the prime necessities of life—with food and clothing for herself and children. In general, it was characteristic of this period that no one felt humiliated by accepting benefits of this kind from his friends. Those who had lost all had not done so through their own fault; and those who had saved their property out of the general wreck could not attribute their fortune to their own merit or wisdom, but merely to chance. They therefore consid-

ered it a sacred duty to divide with those who had been
less fortunate; and the latter would point with pride
to the poverty which proved that they had been true to
themselves and principle, and accept what friendship
offered. This was the result of a kind of community
of property, to which the revolution had given birth.
Those who had possessions considered it their duty to
divide with those who had not, and the latter regarded
this division rather as a right than as a benefit conferred.

Josephine could, therefore, accept the assistance of
her friends without blushing; she could, with propriety,
allow Madame de Montmorin to provide for the ward-
robe of herself and daughter; and she and Hortense
could accept the invitation of Madame Dumoulin to dine
with her twice a week. There, at Madame Dumoulin's,
were assembled, on certain days, a number of friends,
who had been robbed of their fortunes by the storms of
the revolution. Madame Dumoulin, the wife of a rich
army-contractor, gave these dinners to her friends, but
each guest was expected to bring with him his own
white-bread. White-bread was, at that time, considered
one of the greatest dainties; for, there being a scarcity
of grain, a law had been proclaimed allotting to each sec-
tion of Paris a certain amount of bread, and providing
that no individual should be entitled to purchase more
than two ounces daily. It had, therefore, become the
general custom to add the following to all invitations :
" You are requested to bring your white bread with
you," for the reason that no more than the allotted two

ounces could be had for money, and that amount cost the purchaser dearly.* Josephine, however, had not even the money to buy the portion allowed her by law. An exception to this rule was, however, made in favor of Josephine and Hortense; and at Madame Dumoulin's dinners the hostess always provided white bread for them, and for them alone of all her guests. Viscountess Beauharnais was soon, however, to be freed from this want. One day when she had been invited by Madame Tallien to dinner, and had walked to the palace with Hortense, Tallien informed her that the government had favorably considered her petition, and was willing to make some concessions to the widow of a true patriot who had sealed his devotion to principle with his blood; that he had procured an ordinance from the administration of domains, pursuant to which the seals were at once to be removed from her furniture and other personal property, and that the republic had remitted to her, through him, an order on the treasury for her relief, until the sequestration of her landed estates should be annulled, which he expected would soon take place.

Josephine found no words in which to express her thanks. She pressed her daughter to her heart and cried out, her face bathed in tears: "We shall at last be happy! My children shall no longer suffer want!" This time the tears Josephine shed were tears of joy, the first in long years.

* Mémoires de Monsieur de Bourrienne sur Napoleon, etc., vol. L, p. 80.

Care and want were now over. Josephine could now give her children an education suitable to their rank; she could now once more assume the position in society to which her beauty, youth, amiability, and name entitled her. She no longer came to Madame Tallien's parlor as a suppliant, she was now its ornament, and all were eager to do homage to the adored friend of Madame Tallien, to the beautiful and charming viscountess. But Josephine preferred the quiet bliss of home-life in the circle of her children to the brilliant life of society; she gradually withdrew from the noisy circles of the outer world, in order that she might, in peaceful retirement, devote herself to the cultivation of the hearts and minds of her promising children.

Eugene was now a youth of sixteen years, and, as his personal security no longer required him to deny his name and rank, he had left his master's carpenter-shop, and laid aside his blouse. He was preparing himself for military service under the instruction of excellent teachers, whom he astonished by his zeal and rare powers of comprehension. The military renown and heroic deeds of France filled him with enthusiasm; and one day, while speaking with his teacher of the deeds of Turenne, Eugene exclaimed with sparkling eyes and glowing countenance: "I too will become a gallant general, some day!"

Hortense, now a girl of twelve years, lived with her mother, who was scarcely thirty years old, in the sweet companionship of an elder and younger sister. They were inseparable companions; Nature had given Hor-

tense beauty with a lavish hand; her mother gave to this
beauty grace and dignity. Competent teachers instructed
her daughter's intellect, while the mother cultivated her
heart. Early accustomed to care and want, this child had
not the giddy, thoughtless disposition usually characteristic of girls of her age. She had too early gained an in-
sight into the uncertainty and emptiness of all earthly magnificence, not to appreciate the littleness of those things
upon which young girls usually place so high an estimate.
Her thoughts were not occupied with the adornment of
her person, and she did not bend her young head beneath the yoke of capricious fashion: for her, there were
higher and nobler enjoyments, and Hortense was never
happier than when her mother dispensed with her attend-
ance at the entertainments at the house of Madame Tallien
or Madame Barras, and permitted her to remain at home,
to amuse herself with her books and harp in a better and
more useful, if not in a more agreeable manner, than she
could have done in the brilliant parlors to which her
mother had repaired. Early matured in the school of
experience and suffering, the girl of twelve had acquired
a womanly earnestness and resolution, and yet her noble
and chaste features still wore the impress of childhood,
and in her large blue eyes reposed a whole heaven of
innocence and peace. When she sat with her harp at
the window in the evening twilight, the last rays of the
setting sun gilding her sweet countenance, and surrounding as with a halo her beautiful blond hair, Josephine
imagined she saw before her one of those angel-forms of

innocence and love which the poet and painter portray. In a kind of trance she listened to the sweet sounds and melodies which Hortense lured from her harp, and accompanied with the silvery tones of her voice, in words composed by herself, half-childish prayer, half rhapsody of love, and revealing the most secret thoughts of the fair young being who stood on the threshold of womanhood, bidding adieu to childhood with a blissful smile, and dreaming of the future.

CHAPTER IV.

GENERAL BUONAPARTE.

WHILE Josephine de Beauharnais, after the trials of these long and stormy years, was enjoying blissful days of quiet happiness and repose, the gusts of revolution kept bursting forth from time to time in fits of fury, and tranquillity continued far from being permanently restored. The clubs, those hot-beds of the revolution, still exercised their pestilential influence over the populace of Paris, and stirred the rude masses incessantly to fresh paroxysms of discontent and disorder.

But already the man had been found who was to crush those wild masses in his iron grasp, and dash the speakers of the clubs down into the dust with the flashing master-glance of his resistless eye.

That man was Napoleon Buonaparte. He was hardly

twenty-nine years of age, yet already all France was talking of him as a hero crowned with laurels, already had he trodden a brilliant career of victory. As commander of a battalion he had performed prodigies of valor at the recapture of Toulon; and then, after being promoted to the rank of general, had gone to the army in Italy on behalf of the republic. Bedecked with the laurels of his Italian campaign, the young general of five-and-twenty had returned to France. There, the government, being still hostile and ill-disposed toward him, wished to remove him from Paris, and send him to La Vendée as a brigadier-general. Buonaparte declined this mission, because he preferred remaining in the artillery service, and, for that reason, the government of the republic relieved him of his duties and put him on half-pay.

So, Buonaparte remained in Paris and waited. He waited for the brilliant star that was soon to climb the firmament for him, and shed the fulness of its rays over the whole world. Perhaps, the secret voices which whispered in his breast of a dazzling future, and a fabulous career of military glory, had already announced the rising of his star.

So Buonaparte lived on in Paris, and waited. He there passed quiet, retired, and inactive days, associating with a few devoted friends only, who aided him, with delicate tact, in his restricted circumstances. For Buonaparte was poor; he had lost his limited means in the tempests of the revolution, and all that he possessed consisted of the laurels he had won on the battle-field, and his half

pay as a brigadier-general. But, like the Viscountess
de Beauharnais, Napoleon had some true friends who
deemed it an honor to receive him as a guest at their
table, and also, like Josephine, he was too poor to bring
his wheaten loaf with him to the dinners that he attended, as was then the prevailing custom. He often
dined, in company with his brother Louis, at the house
of his boyhood's friend Bourrienne, and his future secretary was at that time still his host, favored of the gods.
The young general, instead of, like his brother, bringing
his wheaten loaf, brought only his ration, which was rye-
bread, and this he always abandoned to his brother Louis,
who was very fond of it, while Madame Bourrienne took
care that he should invariably find his supply of white
bread at his plate. She had managed to get some flour
smuggled into Paris from her husband's estate, and had
white-bread made of it secretly, at the pastry-cook's.
Had this been discovered, it would inevitably have prepared the way for all of them to the scaffold.

Thus, then, young General Buonaparte, or, as he subsequently wrote the name himself, " Bonaparte," passed
quiet days of expectation, hoping that, should the exist-
ing government, so hostile to him, be suppressed by another, his wishes might be at last fulfilled. These wishes
were, by the way, of a rather unpretending character.
" If I could only live here quietly, at Paris," he once
remarked to his friend Bourrienne, " and rent that pretty
little house yonder, opposite to my friends, and keep a
carriage besides, I should be the happiest of men ! "

He was quite seriously entertaining the idea of rent-ing the "pretty little house" in common with his uncle Fesch, afterward the cardinal, when the important events that soon shook Paris once more prevented him, and the famous 13th Vendémiaire, 1795, again summoned the young general away from his meditations to stern prac-tical activity. It was on that day, the 13th Vendémiaire (October 5th), that there came the outburst of the storm, the subterranean rumblings of which had been so long perceptible. The sections of Paris rose against the Na-tional Convention which had given France a new consti-tution, and so fixed it that two thirds of the members of the Convention should reappear in the new legislative body. The sections of Paris, however, were prepared to accept the new constitution only when it provided that the legislative body should spring from fresh elections entirely. The Convention, thus assailed in its ambitious hankering for power, was resolved to stand its ground, and called upon the representatives who commanded the armed forces, to defend the republic of their creation. Barras was appointed the first general commanding the Army of the Interior, and Bonaparte the second. It was not long before a ferocious conflict broke out in the streets between the army and the insurgent sections. At that time the populace were not always so ready, as they have been since then, to tear up the pavements for barri-cades, and the revolters, put to flight by the terrible fire and the fierce onset of the artillery, made the Church of St. Roch and the Palais Royal their defensive points; but

they were driven from them also; the struggle in the
streets recommenced, and streams of blood had to flow
ere it was over.

After the lapse of two days order was restored, and
Barras declared to the triumphant National Convention
that the victory over the insurgents was chiefly due to
the comprehensive and gallant conduct of General Bonaparte.

The National Convention, as a token of gratitude,
conferred upon the latter the permanent position of second general of the Army of the Interior, which had been
allotted to him temporarily, only on the day of peril.
From that moment, Bonaparte emerged from obscurity;
his name had risen above the horizon !

He now had a position, and he could better comprehend the whispering voices that sang within his bosom
the proud, triumphant song of his future career. He
was now already conscious that he had a shining goal before his gaze—a goal to which he dared not yet assign a
title, that flitted about him like a dazzling fairy tale, and
which he swore to make reality at last.

One day, there came to the headquarters of the young
general-in-chief a young man who very pressingly asked
to see him. Bonaparte had him admitted, and the dignified form, the courageous, fiery glance, the noble, handsome countenance of the stranger, at once prepossessed
him in the young man's favor, and he forthwith questioned him in gentle, friendly tones, concerning the object
of his visit.

"General," said the young man, "my name is Eugene Beauharnais, and I have served the republic on the Rhine. My father was denounced before the Committee of Public Safety as a *suspect*, and given over to the Revolutionary Tribunal, who had him murdered, three days before the fall of Robespierre."

"Murdered!" exclaimed Bonaparte, in threatening tones.

"Yes, general, murdered!" repeated Eugene, with resolution. "I come now to request, in the name of my mother, that you will have the kindness to bring your influence to bear upon the committee, to induce them to give me back my father's sword. I will faithfully use it in fighting the enemies of my country and defending the cause of the republic."

These proud and noble words called up a gentle, kindly smile to the stern, pale face of the young general, and the fiery flash of his eyes grew softer.

"Good! young man, very good!" he said. "I like this spirit, and this filial tenderness. The sword of your father—the sword of General Beauharnais—shall be restored to you. Wait!"

With this, he called one of his adjutants, and gave him the necessary commands. A short time only had elapsed, when the adjutant returned, bringing with him the sword of General Beauharnais.

Bonaparte himself handed it to Eugene. The young man, overwhelmed with strong emotion, pressed the weapon—the sole, dear possession of his father—to his lips and to his heart, and tears of sacred emotion started into his eyes.

Instantly the general stepped to his side, and his slender white hand, which knew so well how to wield the sword, and yet was as soft, as delicate, and as transparent as the hand of a duchess, rested lightly on Eugene's shoulder.

"My young friend," said he, in that gentle tone which won all hearts to him, "I should be very happy could I do anything for you or your family."

Eugene gazed at him with an expression of childish amazement. "Good general!" he managed to say; "then mamma and my sister will pray for you."

This ingenuousness made the general smile ; and, with a friendly nod, he desired Eugene to offer his respects to his mother, and to call upon him soon again.

This meeting of Eugene and General Bonaparte was the commencement of the acquaintanceship between Bonaparte and Josephine. The sword of the guillotined General Beauharnais placed an imperial crown upon the head of his widow, and adorned the brows of his son and his daughter with royal diadems.

CHAPTER V.

THE MARRIAGE.

A few days after this interview between Bonaparte and Eugene, Josephine met Bonaparte at one of the brilliant *soirées* given by Barras, the first general-in-chief. She asked Barras to introduce her to the young general, and then, in her usual frank manner, utterly the opposite of all prudery, yet none the less delicate and decorous, extending her hand to Bonaparte, she thanked him, with the tender warmth of a mother, for the friendliness and kindness he had manifested to her son.

The general looked with wondering admiration at this young and beautiful woman, who claimed to be the mother of a lad grown up to manhood. Her enchanting face beamed with youth and beauty, and a sea of warmth and passion streamed from her large, dark eyes, while the gentle, love-enticing smile that played around her mouth revealed the tender feminine gentleness and amiability of her disposition. Bonaparte had never mastered the art of flattering women in the light, frivolous style of the fashionable coxcomb ; and when he attempted it his compliments were frequently of so unusual and startling a character that they might just as well contain an affront as a tribute of eulogy.

"Ah! ah! How striking that looks!" he once said, while he was emperor, to the charming Duchess de Chevreuse. "What remarkable red hair you have!"

"Possibly so, sire," she replied, "but this is the first time that a man ever told me so."

And the duchess was right; for her hair was not red, but of a very handsome blond.*

To another lady, whose round, white arms pleased him, he once said : "Ah, good Heavens, what red arms you have!" Then, again, to another : "What beautiful hair you have; but what an ugly head-dress that is! Who could have put it up for you in such ridiculous style?"

Bonaparte, as I have said, did not know how to compliment women with words; but Josephine well understood the flattering language that his eyes addressed to her. She knew that she had, in that very hour, conquered the bold young lion, and she felt proud and happy at the thought; for the unusually imposing appearance of the young hero had awakened her own heart, which she had thought was dead, to livelier palpitations.

From that time forth they saw each other more frequently, and, ere long, Josephine heard from Bonaparte's own lips the glowing confession of his love. She reciprocated it, and promised him her hand. In vain her powerful friends, Tallien and Barras, endeavored to dissuade her from marrying this young, penniless general; in vain did they remind her that he might be killed in the very next battle, and that she might thus again be

* The Duchess de Chevreuse was shortly afterward banished to Tours, because she refused to serve as a lady of honor to the Queen of Spain.

left a reduced widow. Josephine shook her handsome curls, with a peculiar smile. Perhaps she was thinking of the prophecy of the negress at Martinique; perhaps she had read in the fiery glances of Bonaparte's eye, and on his broad, thoughtful brow, that he might be the very man to bring that prophecy to its consummation; perhaps she loved him ardently enough to prefer an humble lot, when shared with him, to any richer or more brilliant alliance. The representations of her friends did not frighten her away, and she remained firm in her determination to become the wife of the young general, poor as he was. Their wedding-day was fixed, and both hastened with joyous impatience to make their modest little preparations for their new housekeeping establishment. Yet Bonaparte had not been able to complete his dream of happiness; he possessed neither house nor carriage, and Josephine, too, was without an equipage.

Thus both of them often had to content themselves with going on foot through the streets, and it may be that, in this halcyon period of their felicity, they regarded the circumstance rather as a favor than as a scurvy trick of Fortune. Their tender and confidential communications were not disturbed by the loud rattle of the wheels, and they were not obliged to interrupt their sweet interchange of sentiment while getting into and out of a vehicle. Arm-in-arm, they strolled together along the promenades, he smiling proudly when the passers-by broke out in spontaneous exclamations of delight at Josephine's beauty, and she happy and exultant

4

as she overheard the whispered admiration and respect with which the multitude everywhere greeted Bonaparte, as she pressed with the general through the throng.

One day, Bonaparte accompanied the viscountess on a visit to Ragideau, the smallest man but the greatest lawyer in Paris. He had been the business attorney of the Beauharnais family for a long time, and Josephine now wished to withdraw from his hands, for her own disposal, a sum of money belonging to her that had been deposited with him. Bonaparte remained in the anteroom while Josephine went into the adjoining apartment, which was Ragideau's office.

"I have come to tell you that I am going to marry again," said Josephine, with her winning smile, to Ragideau.

The little attorney gave a friendly nod, as he replied : "You do well, and I congratulate you with all my heart, viscountess, for I am satisfied that you have made no other than a worthy choice."

"Undoubtedly, a very worthy choice," exclaimed Josephine, with the proud and happy look of a person really in love. "My future husband is General Bonaparte !"

The little great man (of a lawyer) fairly started with alarm. "How?" said he, "You!—the Viscountess Beauharnais, you—marry this little General Bonaparte, this general of the republic, which has already deposed him once, and may depose him again to-morrow, and throw him back into insignificance?"

Josephine's only reply was this: "I love him."

"Yes, you love him, now," exclaimed Ragideau, warmly. "But you are wrong in marrying him, and you will, one day, rue it. You are committing a folly, viscountess, for you want to marry a man who has nothing but his hat and his sword."

"But who also has a future," said Josephine, gayly, and then, turning the conversation, she began to speak of the practical matters that had brought her thither.

When her business with the notary had been concluded, Josephine returned to the anteroom where Bonaparte was waiting for her. He came, smiling, to meet her, but, at the same moment, he gave the notary, who was with her, so fierce and wrathful a glance that the latter shrank back in consternation. Josephine also remarked that Bonaparte's countenance was paler that day than usual, and that he was less communicative and less disposed to chat with her; but she had already learned that it was not advisable to question him as to the cause of his different moods. So, she kept silent on that score, and her cheerfulness and amiability soon drove away the clouds that had obscured the general's brow.

The nuptials of Bonaparte and Josephine followed, on the 9th of March, 1796, and the witnesses, besides Eugene and Hortense, Josephine's children, were Barras, Jean Lemarois, Tallien, Calmelet, and Leclerq. The marriage-contract contained, along with the absolutely requisite facts of the case, a very pleasant piece of flattery for Josephine, since, in order to establish an equality of ages between the two parties, Bonaparte had him-self put down a year older, and Josephine four years younger, than they really were. Bonaparte was not, as the contract states, born on the 5th of February, 1768, but on the 15th of August, 1769; and Josephine not, as the document represents, on the 23d of July, 1767, but on the 23d of June, 1763.*

Josephine acknowledged this gallant act of her young spouse in queenly fashion, for she brought him, as her wedding-gift, his appointment to the command of the Italian army, which Barras and Tallien had granted to her, at her own request.

But, before the young bridegroom repaired to his new scene of activity, there to win fresh laurels and re-nown, he passed a few happy weeks with his lovely wife and his new family, in the small residence in the Rue Chautereine, which he had purchased a short time before his marriage, and which Josephine had fitted up with that elevated and refined good taste that had always distinguished her.

One-half of Bonaparte's darling wish was at length fulfilled. He had his house, which was large enough to receive his friends. There was now only a carriage to be procured in order to make the general the "happiest of men."

But, as the wishes of men always aspire still farther the farther they advance, Bonaparte was no longer con-

* Bourrienne, vol. i, p. 350.

tent with the possession of a small house in Paris. He now wanted an establishment in the country also.

"Look me up a little place in your beautiful valley of the Yonne," he wrote about this time to Bourrienne, who was then living on his property near Sens; "and as soon as I get the money, I will buy it. Then I will retire to it. Now, don't forget that I do not want any of the national domains." *

As for the carriage, the peace of Campo Formio brought the victorious General Bonaparte a magnificent team of six gray horses, which was a present to the general of the French Republic from the Emperor of Austria, who did not dream that, scarcely ten years later, he would have him for a son-in-law.

These superb grays, however, were—excepting the laurels of Arcola, Marengo, and Mantua, the only spoils of war that Bonaparte brought back with him from his famous Italian campaign—the only gift which the general had not refused to accept.

It is true that the six grays could not be very conveniently hitched to a simple private carriage, but they had an imposing look attached to the gilded coach of state in which, a year later, the first consul made his solemn entry into the Tuileries.

* Bourrienne, vol. i, p. 102.

CHAPTER VI.

JOSEPHINE, now the wife of General Bonaparte, had
but a few weeks in which to enjoy her new happiness,
and then remained alone in Paris, doubly desolate, because she had to be separated, not only from her husband, but from her children. Eugene accompanied his
young step-father to Italy, and Hortense went as a pupil
to Madame Campan's boarding-school. The former, lady-
in-waiting to Queen Marie Antoinette, had, at that time,
opened an establishment for the education of young
ladies, at St. Germain, and the greatest and most eminent families of newly-republicanized France liked to
send their daughters to it, so that they might learn from
the former court-lady the refined style and manners of
old royalist times.

Hortense was, therefore, sent to that boarding-school,
and there, in the society of her new Aunt Caroline—the
sister of Bonaparte, and afterward Queen of Naples—and
the young Countess Stephanie Beauharnais, her cousin,
passed a few happy years of work, of varied study, and
of youthful maiden-dreams.

Hortense devoted herself with iron diligence, and untiring enthusiasm, to her studies, which consisted, not
only in the acquisition of languages, in music, and drawing, history and geography, but still more in the master-
ing the so-called *bon ton* and that aristocratic *savoir vivre*

of which Madame Campan was a very model. While Hortense was thus receiving instruction on the harp from the celebrated Alvimara, in painting from Isabey, dancing from Coulon, and singing from Lambert, and was playing on the stage of the amateur theatre at the boarding-school the parts of heroines and lady-loves; while she was participating in the balls and concerts that Madame Campan gave, in order to show off the talent of her pupils to the friends she invited; while, in a word, Hortense was thus being trained up to the accomplishments of a distinguished woman of the world, she did not dream how useful all these little details, so trivial, apparently, at the time, would one day be to her, and how good a thing it was that she had learned to play parts at Madame Campan's, and to appear in society as a great lady.

Meanwhile, Josephine was passing days of gratified pride and exulting triumph at Paris, for the star of her hero was ascending, brighter and brighter in its effulgence, above the horizon; the name of Bonaparte was echoing in louder and louder volume through the world, and filling all Europe with a sort of awe-inspired fear and trembling, as the sea becomes agitated when the sun begins to rise. Victory after victory came joyfully heralded from Italy, as ancient states fell beneath the iron tread of the victor, and new ones sprang into being. The splendid old Republic of Venice, once the terror of the whole world, the victorious Queen of the Adriatic, had to bow her haughty head, and her diadem fell in fragments at the feet of her triumphant conqueror. The lion of

St. Mark's no longer made mankind tremble at his angry roar, and the slender monumental pillars on the Piazzetta were all that remained to the shattered and fallen Venetian Republic of her conquests in Candia, Cyprus, and the Morea. But, from the dust and ashes of the old commonwealth, there arose, at Bonaparte's command, a new state, the Cisalpine Republic, as a new and youthful daughter of the French Republic; and, when the last Doge of Venice, Luigi Manin, laid his peaked crown at the feet of Bonaparte, and then fainted away, another Venetian, Dandolo, the son of a family that had given Venice the greatest and most celebrated of her doges, stepped to the front at the head of the new republic— that Dandolo of whom Bonaparte had said that he was "a man."

"Good God!" exclaimed Bonaparte one day to Bourrienne, "how seldom one meets *men* in the world! In Italy there are eighteen millions of inhabitants, but I have found only two *men* among them all—Dandolo and Melzi." *

But, while Bonaparte was despairing of *men*, in the very midst of his victories, he cherished the warmest, most impassioned love for his wife, to whom he almost daily wrote the tenderest and most ardent letters, the answers to which he awaited with the most impatient longing.

Josephine's letters formed the sole exception to a very unusual and singular system that Bonaparte had adopted

* Bourrienne, vol. i, p. 139.

during a part of his campaign in Italy. This was to leave all written communications, excepting such as came to him by special couriers, unread for three weeks. He threw them all into a large basket, and opened them only on the twenty-first day thereafter. Still, General Bonaparte was more considerate than Cardinal Dubois, who immediately consigned *all* the communications he received to the flames, *unread,* and—while the fire on his hearth was consuming the paper on which, perchance, was written the despairing appeal of a mother, imploring pardon for her son ; of a disconsolate wife, beseeching pity for her husband ; or the application of an ambitious statesman, desiring promotion—would point to them with a sardonic smile, and say, " There's *my* correspondence ! " Bonaparte, at least, gave the letters a perusal, three weeks after they reached him, indeed ; but those three weeks saved him and his secretary, Bourrienne, much time and labor, for, when they finally went to work on them, time and circumstances had already disposed of four fifths of them, and thus only one fifth required answers—a result that made Bonaparte laugh heartily, and filled him with justifiable pride in what he termed his " happy idea."

Josephine's letters, however, had not an hour or a minute to wait ere they were read. Bonaparte always received them with his heart bounding with delight, and invariably answered them, in such impassioned, glowing language as only his warm southern temperament could suggest, and contrasted with which even Josephine's missives seemed a little cool and passionless.

Ere long Bonaparte ceased to be satisfied with merely getting letters from his Josephine. He desired to have her, in person, with him ; and hardly had the tempest of war begun to lull, ere the general summoned his beloved to his side at Milan. She obeyed his call with rapture, and hastened to Italy to join him. Now came proud days of triumph and gratified affection. All Italy hailed Bonaparte as the conquering hero ; all Italy did homage to the woman who bore his name, and whose incomparable fascination and amiability, gracefulness and beauty, won all hearts. Her life now resembled a magnificent, glorified, triumphal pageant ; a dazzling fairy festival ; a tale from the " Arabian Nights " that had become reality, with Josephine for its enchanted heroine, sparkling with stars, and gleaming with golden sunshine.

CHAPTER VII.

VICISSITUDES OF DESTINY.

RESPLENDENT was the triumphal procession with which Bonaparte made his proud entry into Paris, on his return from Italy. In the front court-yard of the Luxembourg, the palace occupied by the *Corps Législatif*, was erected a vast amphitheatre, in which sat all the high authorities of France ; in the centre of the amphitheatre stood the altar of the country, surmounted by three gigantic statues, representing Freedom, Equality, and Peace.

As Bonaparte stepped into this space, all the dense crowd that occupied the seats of the amphitheatre rose to their feet, with uncovered heads, to hail the conqueror of Italy, and the windows of the palace were thronged with handsomely dressed ladies, who waved welcome to the young hero with their handkerchiefs. But suddenly this splendid festival was marred by a serious mischance. An officer of the Directory, who, the better to satisfy his curiosity, had clambered up on the scaffolding of the right-side wing of the palace, then undergoing extension, fell from it, and struck the ground almost at Napoleon's feet. A shout of terror burst almost simultaneously from a thousand throats, and the ladies turned pale and shrank back, shuddering, from the windows. The palace, which a moment before had exhibited such a wealth of adornment in these living flowers, now stood there bare, with empty, gaping casements. A perceptible thrill ran through the ranks of the *Corps Législatif*, and here and there the whisper passed that this fall of an officer portended the early overthrow of the Directory itself, and that it, too, would soon, like the unfortunate victim of the accident, be lying in its death agonies at the feet of General Bonaparte.

But the Directory, nevertheless, hastened to give the victor of Arcola new *fêtes* every day ; and when these *fêtes* were over, and Bonaparte, fatigued with the speeches, the festivities, the toasts, etc., would be on his way returning homeward, there was the populace of Paris, who beset his path in crowds, to greet him with hearty cheers;

and these persistent friends he had to recognize, with
smiles and shakings of the hand, or with a nod and a
pleasant glance.

A universal jubilee of delight had seized upon the
French. Each individual saw in Bonaparte renown and
greatness reflected on himself. Every one regarded him
as the most brilliant impersonation of his own inner per-
sonality, and, therefore, felt drawn toward him with a
sort of reverential exultation.

Josephine gave herself up with her whole soul to the
enjoyment of these glorious occasions. While Bonaparte,
almost completely overwhelmed and disturbed, could have
held aloof from these ovations of the people of Paris,
they, on the contrary, filled the heart of his wife with
pride and joy. While in the theatre, he shrank back,
abashed, behind his wife's chair when the audience, learn-
ing his presence, filled their noisy plaudits and clamored
to have a glimpse at him, Josephine would thank the
crowd on his behalf with a bewitching smile, and eyes
swelling with tears for this proof of their regard, which
to her seemed but a natural and appropriate tribute to
her Achilles, her lion-hearted hero. But Bonaparte did
not allow himself to be blinded by these demonstrations;
and one day, when popular enthusiasm seemed as though
it would never end, and the crowd were untiring in their
cries of " *Vive Bonaparte !* " while Josephine turned her
face toward him, glowing with delight, and called out,
exultingly—"See, how they love you, these good people
of Paris ! " he replied, with an almost melancholy expres-

sion, "Bah ! the crowd would be just as numerous and noisy if they were conducting me to the scaffold ! "

However, these festivals and demonstrations at length subsided, and his life resumed its more tranquil course.

Bonaparte could now once more spend a few secluded days of rest and calm enjoyment in his (by this time more richly-decorated) dwelling in the Rue Chautereine, the name of which the city authorities had changed to *Rue de la Victoire*, in honor of the conqueror at Arcola and Marengo. He could, after so many battles and triumphs, afford to repose a while in the arms of love and happiness.

Nevertheless, this inactivity soon began to press heavily on his restless spirit. He longed for new exploits, for fresh victories. He felt that he was only at the commencement, and not at the end of his conquering career; he constantly heard ringing in his ears the notes of the battle-clarion, summoning him to renewed triumphs and to other paths of glory. Love could only delight his heart, but could not completely satisfy it. Repose he deemed but the beginning of death.

" If I remain here inactive any longer, I am lost," said he. " They retain the resemblance of nothing whatever in Paris ; one celebrity blots out another in this great Babylon ; if I show myself much oftener to the public, they will cease to look at me, and if I do not soon undertake something new, they will forget me."

And he did undertake something new, something unprecedented, that filled all Europe with astonishment.

He left the shores of France with an army to conquer, for the French Republic, that ancient land of Egypt, on whose pyramids the green moss of long-forgotten ages was flourishing.

Josephine did not accompany him. She remained behind in Paris ; but she needed consolation and encouragement to enable her to sustain this separation, which Bonaparte himself had confessed to her might be just as likely to last six years as six months. And what could afford better consolation to a heart so tender as Josephine's than the presence of her beloved daughter ? She had willingly given up her son to her husband, and he had accompanied the latter to Egypt, but her daughter remained, and her she would not give up to any one, not even to Madame Campan's boarding-school.

Besides, the education of Hortense was now completed. She who had come to St. Germain as a child, left the boarding-school, after two years' stay, a handsome, blooming young lady, adorned with all the charms of innocence, youth, grace, and refinement.

Although she was now a young lady of nearly sixteen, she had retained the thoughts and ways of her childhood. Her heart was as a white sheet of paper, on which no profane hand had ventured to write a mortal name. She loved nothing beyond her mother, her brother, the fine arts, and flowers. She entertained a profound but speech-less veneration for her young step-father. His burning gaze made her uneasy and timorous ; his commanding voice made her heart throb anxiously ; in fine, she reverenced him with adoring but too agitated an impression of awe to find it possible to love him. He was for her at all times the hero, the lord and master, the father to whom she owed implicit obedience, but she dared not love him; she could only look up to and honor him from a distance.

Hortense loved nothing but her mother, her brother, the fine arts, and flowers. She still looked out, with the expectant eyes of a child, upon the world which seemed so beautiful and inviting to her, and from which she hoped yet to obtain some grand dazzling piece of good fortune without having any accurate idea in what it was to consist. She still loved all mankind, and believed in their truth and rectitude. No thorn had yet wounded her heart; no disenchantment, no bright illusion dashed to pieces, had yet left its shadow on that clear, lofty brow of transparent whiteness. The expression of her large blue eyes was still radiant and undimmed, and her laugh was so clear and ringing, that it almost made her mother sad to hear it, for it sounded to her like the last echo of some sweet, enchanting song of childhood, and she but too well knew that it would soon be hushed.

But Hortense still laughed, still sang with the birds, rivalling their melodies; the world still lay before her like an early morning dream, and she still hoped for the rising of the sun.

Such was Hortense when her mother took her from Madame Campan's boarding-school, to accompany her to the baths of Plombières. But there it was that Hortense came near experiencing the greatest sorrow of her life, in nearly losing her mother.

She was with Josephine and some other ladies in the drawing-room of the house they occupied at Plombières. The doors facing the balcony were open, to let in the warm summer air. Hortense was sitting by the window, painting a nosegay of wild flowers, that she had gathered with her own hands on the hills of Plombières. Josephine found the atmosphere of the room too close, and invited some ladies to step out with her upon the balcony. A moment afterward there was heard a deafening crash, followed by piercing shrieks of terror; and when Hortense sprang in desperate fright to the front entrance, she found that the balcony on which her mother and the other ladies had stood had disappeared. Its fastenings had given way, and they had been precipitated with it into the street. Hortense, in the first impulse of her distress and horror, would have sprung down after her beloved mother, and could only be held back with the greatest difficulty. But this time fate had spared the young girl, and refrained from darkening the pure, unclouded heaven of her youth. Her mother escaped with no other injury than the fright, and a slight wound on her arm, while one of the ladies had both legs broken.

Josephine's time to die had not yet come, for the prophecy of the fortune-teller had not yet been fulfilled. Josephine was, indeed, the wife of a renowned general, but she was not yet " something more than a queen."

CHAPTER VIII.

BONAPARTE'S RETURN FROM EGYPT.

BONAPARTE had got back from Egypt. His victory at Aboukir had adorned his brows with fresh laurels, and all France hailed the returning conqueror with plaudits of exulting pride. For the first time, Hortense was present at the festivities which the city of Paris dedicated to her step-father; for the first time she saw the homage that men and women, graybeards and children alike, paid to the hero of Italy and Egypt. These festivities and this homage filled her heart with a tremor of alarm, and yet, at the same time, with joyous exultation. In the midst of these triumphs and these ovations which were thus offered to her second father, the young girl recalled the prison in which her mother had once languished, the scaffold upon which the head of her own father had fallen; and frequently when she glanced at the rich gold-embroidered uniform of her brother, she reminded him with a roguish smile of the time when Eugene went in a blue blouse, as a carpenter's apprentice, through the streets of Paris with a long plank on his shoulder.

These recollections of the first terrible days of her youth kept Hortense from feeling the pride and arrogance of good fortune, preserved to her her modest, unassuming tone of mind, prevented her from entertaining any overweening or domineering propensity in her day of prosperity, or from seeming cast down and hopeless

5

when adversity came. She never lulled herself with the idea of good fortune that could not pass away, but her remembrances kept her eyes wide open, and hence, when misfortune came, it did not take her by surprise, but found her armed and ready to confront it.

Nevertheless, she drank in the pleasure of these prosperous days in full draughts, delighted as she was to see the mother, of whom she was so fond, surrounded by such a halo of glory and gratified love; and in the name of her murdered father she thanked General Bonaparte with double fervor, from the bottom of her heart, for having been the means of procuring for her mother, who had suffered so deeply in her first wedded life, so magnificent a glow of splendor and happiness in her second marriage.

In the mean while, new days of storm and tumult were at hand to dispel this brief period of tranquil enjoyment. A fresh revolution convulsed all France, and, ere long, Paris was divided into two hostile camps, burning to begin the work of mutual annihilation. On one side stood the democratic republicans, who looked back with longing regret to the days of terrorism and bloodshed, perceiving, as they did, that tranquillity and pro tracted peace must soon wrest the reins of power from their grasp, and therefore anxiously desiring to secure control through the element of intimidation. This party declared that liberty was in danger, and the Constitution threatened; they summoned the *sans-culottes* and the loud-mouthed republicans of the clubs to the armed de-

fence of the imperilled country, and pointed with menacing hands at Bonaparte as the man who wished to
overthrow the republic, and put France once more in the
bonds of servitude.

On the other side stood the discreet friends of the
country, the republicans by compulsion, who denounced
terrorism, and had sworn fidelity to the republic, only
because it was under this reptile disguise alone that they
could escape the threatening knife of the guillotine.   On
this side were arrayed the men of mind, the artists and
poets who hopefully longed for a new era, because they
knew that the days of terror and of the tyrannical democratic republic had brought not merely human beings,
but also the arts and sciences, to the scaffold.   With
them, too, were arrayed the merchants and artisans, the
bankers, the business-men, the property-owners, all of
whom wanted to see the republic at least established
upon a more moderate and quiet foundation, in order to
have confidence in its durability and substantial character, and to commence the works of peace with a better
assurance of success.   And at the head of these moderate
republicans stood Bonaparte.

The 18th Brumaire of the year 1798 was the decisive
day.   It was a fearful struggle that then began afresh—a
struggle, however, in which little blood was spilt, and
not men but principles were slaughtered.

The Council of Elders, the Council of the Five
Hundred, the Directory, and the Constitution of the year
III., fell together, and from the ruins of the bloody and

ferocious democratic republic arose the moderate, rational republic of the year 1798. At its head were the three consuls, Bonaparte, Cambacères, and Lebrun.

On the day following, the 18th Brumaire, these three consuls entered the Luxembourg, amid the plaudits of the people, and slept, as conquerors, in the beds of the Directory of yesterday.

From that day forward a new world began to take shape, and the forms of etiquette which, during the ascendency of the democratic republic, had slunk away out of sight into the darkest recesses of the Luxembourg and the Tuileries, began to reappear, slowly and circumspectly, 'tis true, in broad daylight. People were no longer required, in accordance with the spirit of equality, to ignore all distinctions of condition and culture, by the use of the words "citizen" and "citizeness;" or, in the name of brotherhood, to endure the close familiarities of every brawling street ruffian; or, in the name of liberty, to let all his own personal liberty and inclination be trampled under foot.

Etiquette, as I have said, crept forth from the dark corners again; and the three consuls, who had taken possession of the Luxembourg, whispered the word "monsieur" in each other's ears, and greeted Josephine and her daughter, who were installed in the apartments prepared for them in the palace on the next day, with the title of "madame." Yet, only a year earlier, the two words "monsieur" and "madame" had occasioned revolt in Paris, and brought about bloodshed. A year earlier, General Augereau had promulged the stern order of the day in his division, that, "whoever should use the word 'monsieur' or 'madame,' orally or in writing, on any pretext whatever, should be deprived of his rank, and declared incapable of ever again serving in the army of the republic." *

Now, these two proscribed words made their triumphant entry, along with the three consuls, into the palace of the Luxembourg, which had been delivered from its democratic tyrants.

Josephine was now, at least, "Madame" Bonaparte, and Hortense was "Mademoiselle" Beauharnais. The wife of Consul Bonaparte now required a larger retinue of servants, and a more showy establishment. Indeed, temerity could not yet go so far as to speak of the *court* of Madame Bonaparte and the *court ladies* of Mademoiselle Hortense; they had still to be content with the limited space of the diminutive Luxembourg, but they were soon to be compensated for all this, and, if they still had to call each other *monsieur* and *madame*, they could, a few years later, say "your highness," ". your majesty," and "monseigneur," in the Tuileries.

The Luxembourg Palace was soon found to be too small for the joint residence of the three consuls, and too confined for the ambition of Bonaparte, who could not brook the near approach of the other two men who shared the supreme control of France with him. Too small it was also for the longings that now spoke with

* Bourrienne, vol. i., p. 229.

ever louder and stronger accents in his breast, and
pushed him farther and farther onward in this path of
splendor and renown which, at first, had seemed to him
but as the magic mirage of his dreams, but which now
appeared as the glittering truth and reality of his waking
hours. The Luxembourg was then too small for the
three consuls, but they had to go very circumspectly and
carefully to work to prepare the way to the old royal
palace of the Bourbons. It would not do to oust the
representatives of the people, who held their sessions
there, too suddenly; the distrustful republicans must not
be made to apprehend that there was any scheme on foot
to revolutionize France back into monarchy, and to again
stifle the many-headed monster of the republic under a
crown and a sceptre. It was necessary, before entering
the Tuileries, to give the French people proof that men
might still be very good republicans, even although they
might wish to be housed in the bedchamber of a king.

Hence, before the three consuls transferred their
quarters to the Tuileries, the royal palace had to be transformed to a residence worthy of the representatives of
the republic. So, the first move made was to set up a
handsome bust of the elder Brutus—a war-trophy of Bonaparte's, which he had brought with him from Italy—
in one of the galleries of the Tuileries; and then David
had to carve out some other statues of the republican
heroes of Greece and Rome and place them in the saloons. A number of democratic republicans, who were
defeated and exiled on the 13th Vendémiaire, were per-

mitted to return to France, and news of the death of WASHINGTON, the noblest and wisest of all republicans, arriving just at that time, Bonaparte ordered that the whole army should wear the badge of mourning for ten days. Black bands were worn on the arm, and sable streamers waved from the standards, in honor of the deceased republican hero.

However, when these ten days were past, and France and her army had sufficiently expressed their regret, the three consuls entered the Tuileries through the grand portal, on the two sides of which towered aloft two liberty-poles that still bore the old inscription of the republic of 1792. On the tree to the right was the legend " August 10, 1792," and on the one to the left, " Royalty in France is overthrown and will never rise again." It was between these two significant symbols that Bonaparte first strode into the Tuileries. It was a very long and imposing procession of carriages which moved that day toward the palace, through the streets of the capital. They only lacked the outward pomp and magnificence which rendered the latter *fêtes* of the empire so remarkable. With the exception of the splendid vehicle in which the three consuls rode, and which was drawn by the six grays presented by the Emperor of Austria, there were but few good equipages to be seen. France of the new day had not had the opportunity to build any state-coaches, and those of old France had been too shamefully misused to admit of their ever serving again ; for it would be out of the question to employ, in this solemn

procession of the three consuls, the state-carriages of the
old aristocracy, that had served as the vehicles in which
the democratic republic had transported dead dogs to
their place of deposit. Such had been the fact in the
September days of the year 1793.

The unclaimed dogs of the fugitive or slaughtered
aristocracy at that time wandered without masters, by
thousands, through the streets and slaked their thirst
with the blood which flowed down from the guillotine
and dyed the ground with the purple of the new system
of popular liberty.

The smell of the fresh blood and the ghastly suste-
nance which the guillotine yielded them had restored the
animals to their original savage propensities, and hence
those who had been so fortunate as to escape the murderous axe of the *sans-culottes* had now to apprehend the
danger of falling a victim to the sharp teeth of these
wild blood-hounds ; and as the ferocious brutes knew no
difference between aristocrats and republicans, but fell
upon both with equal fury, it became necessary, at last,
to annihilate these new foes of the republic. So, the
Champs Élysées were surrounded with troops, and the
dogs were driven into the Rue Royale and the Place
Royale, where they were mowed down by musketry.
On that one day the dead carcasses of more than three
thousand dogs lay about in the streets of Paris, and there
they continued to fester for three days longer, because a
dispute had arisen among the city officials as to whose
duty it was to remove them. At length the Convention

undertook that task, and intrusted the work to representative Gasparin, who was shrewd enough to convert the removal of the dead animals into a republican ceremony. These were the dogs of the *ci-devants* and aristocrats that were to be buried, and it was quite proper, therefore, that they should receive aristocratic honors.

Gasparin, acting upon this idea, caused all the coaches of the fugitive and massacred aristocracy to be brought from their stables, and the carcasses of the dogs were flung into these emblazoned and escutcheoned vehicles of old France. Six grand coaches that had belonged to the king opened the procession, and the tails, heads, bodies and legs of the luckless quadrupeds could be seen behind the glittering glass panels heaped together in wild disorder.*

After this public canine funeral celebration of the one and indivisible republic, the gilded state-coaches could not be consistently used for any human and less mournful occasion, and hence it was that the consular procession to the Tuileries was so deficient in carriages, and that public hacks on which the numbers were defaced had to be employed.

With the entry of Bonaparte into the Tuileries the revolution was at an end. He laid his victorious sword across the gory, yawning chasm which had drunk the blood of both aristocrats and democrats; and of that sword he made a bridge over which society might pass

* Mémoires of the Marchioness de Créqui, vol. viii., p. 10.

from one century to the other, and from the republic to the empire.

As Bonaparte was walking with Josephine and Hortense through the Diana Gallery on the morning after their entry into the Tuileries, and was with them admiring the statuary he had caused to be placed there, both of the ladies possessing much artistic taste, he paused in front of the statue of the younger Brutus, which stood close to the statue of Julius Cæsar. He gazed long and earnestly at both of the grave, solemn faces; but, suddenly, as though just awaking from a deep dream, he sharply raised his head, and, laying his hand with an abrupt movement upon Josephine's shoulder, as he looked up at the statue of Brutus with blazing, almost menacing glances, said in a voice that made the hearts of both the ladies bound within their bosoms:

"It is not enough to be in the Tuileries: one must remain there. And whom has not this palace held? Even street thieves and conventionists have occupied it! Did not I see with my own eyes how the savage Jacobins and cohorts of *sans-culottes* surrounded the palace and led away the good King Louis XVI. as a prisoner! Ah! never mind, Josephine; have no fear for the future! Let them but dare to come hither once more!"*

And, as Bonaparte stood there and thus spoke in front of the statues of Brutus and Julius Cæsar, his voice re-echoed like angry thunder through the long gallery,

* Bourrienne, vol. vi., p. 3.

and made the figures of the heroes of the dead republic tremble on their pedestals.

Bonaparte lifted his arm menacingly toward the statue of Brutus, as though he would, in that fierce republican who slew Cæsar, challenge all republican France, whose Cæsar and Augustus in one he aspired to be, to mortal combat.

The revolution was closed. Bonaparte had installed himself in the Tuileries with Josephine and her two children. The son and daughter of General Beauharnais, whom the republic had murdered, had now found another father, who was destined to avenge that murder on the republic itself.

The revolution was over!

BOOK II.

THE QUEEN OF HOLLAND.

CHAPTER I.

A FIRST LOVE.

With the entry of Bonaparte into the Tuileries, the revolution closed, and blissful days of tranquillity and gay festivity followed. Josephine and Hortense were the cynosure of all these festivals, for they were, likewise, the animating centre whence the grace and beauty, the attractive charm, and the intellectual significance of them all, proceeded.

Hortense was passionately fond of dancing, and no one at "the court of Josephine" tripped it with such gracefulness and such enchanting delicacy as she. Now, as the reader will observe, people already began to speak of the "court" of Madame Bonaparte, the powerful wife of the First Consul of France. Now, also, *audiences* were held, and Josephine and Hortense already had a court retinue who approached them with the same subserviency and humility as though they had been princesses of the blood.

Madame Bonaparte now rode with her daughter through the streets of Paris in a richly-gilded coach, under a military escort, and wherever the populace caught a glimpse of them they greeted the wife and daughter of the first consul with applauding shouts.

Bonaparte's coachmen and servants had now a livery, and made their appearance in green coats with gold embroidery and galloons. There were chamberlains and lackeys, grooms and outriders; splendid dinners and evening parties were given, and the ambassadors of foreign powers were received in solemn audience; for, now, all the European states had recognized the French Republic under the consulate, and, as Bonaparte had concluded peace with England and Austria, these two great powers also sent envoys to the court of the mighty consul.

Instead of warlike struggles, the Tuileries now witnessed contentions of the toilet, and *powder or no powder* was one of the great questions of etiquette in which Josephine gave the casting vote when she said that "every one should dress as seemed best and most becoming to each, but yet endeavor to let good taste pervade the selection."

For some time, meanwhile, Hortense had participated with less zest than formerly in the amusements and parties of the day; for some time she had seemed to prefer being alone more than in previous years, and held herself aloof in the quiet retirement of her own apartments, where the melancholy, tender, and touching melodies

which she drew from her harp in those lonely hours
seemed to hold her better converse than all the gay and
flattering remarks that she was accustomed to hear in
her mother's grand saloons.

Hortense sought solitude, for to solitude alone could
she confide what was weighing on her heart; to it alone
could she venture to confess that she was in love, and
with all the innocent energy, all the warmth and absolute
devotion of a first attachment. How blissful were those
hours of reverie, of expectant peering into the future,
which seemed to promise the rising of another sun of
happiness to her beaming gaze! For this young girl's
passion had the secret approbation of her mother and
her step-father, and both of them smilingly pretended
not to be, in the least degree, aware of the tender understanding that subsisted between Hortense and General
Duroc, Bonaparte's chief adjutant; only that, while Josephine took it to be the first tender fluttering of a
young girl's heart awaking to the world, Bonaparte as-
cribed a more serious meaning to it, and bestowed earnest thought upon the idea of a union between Hortense
and his friend. He was anxious, above all other things,
to give Duroc a more important and imposing status, and
therefore sent him as ambassador to St. Petersburg, to
convey to the Emperor Alexander, who had just ascended his father's throne, the congratulations and good
wishes of the First Consul of France.

The poor young lovers, constantly watched as they
were, and as constantly restrained by the rules of an eti-

quette which was now becoming more and more rigid, had not the consolation accorded to them of exchanging even one last unnoticed pressure of the hand, one last tender vow of eternal fidelity, when they took leave of each other. But they hoped in the future, and looked forward to Duroc's return, and to the precious recompense that Bonaparte had significantly promised to his friend. That recompense was the hand of Hortense. Until then, they had to content themselves with that sole and sweetest solace of all parted lovers, the letters that they interchanged, and which Bourrienne, Bonaparte's secretary, faithfully and discreetly transmitted.

"Nearly every evening," relates Bourrienne, in his Mémoires, "I played a game of billiards with Mademoiselle Hortense, who was an adept at it. When I said, in a low tone to her, 'I have a letter,' the game would cease at once, and she would hasten to her room, whither I followed her, and took the letter to her. Her eyes would instantly fill with tears of emotion and delight, and it was only after a long lapse of time that she would go down to the saloon whither I had preceded her." *

Hortense, thus busied only with her young lover and her innocent dreams of the future, troubled herself but little concerning what was taking place around her, and did not perceive that others were ready to make her young heart the plaything of domestic and political intrigue.

Bonaparte's brothers, who were jealous of the sway

* Bourrienne, vol. iv., p. 319.

that the beautiful and fascinating Josephine still exerted over the first consul, as in the first days of their wedded life, were anxious, by separating Hortense from her mother, to deprive Josephine of one of the strongest supports of her influence, and thus, by isolating Josephine, bring themselves nearer to their brother. They well knew the affection which Bonaparte, who was particularly fond of children, entertained for those of his wife, and they also knew that Eugene and Hortense had, one day, not by their entreaties or their tears, but by their mere presence, prevented Josephine and Bonaparte from separating.

This was at the time when the whisperings of his brothers and of Junot had succeeded in making Bonaparte jealous on his return from Egypt.

At that time, Bonaparte had resolved to separate from a woman, against whom, however, his anger was thus fiercely aroused, simply because he was so strongly attached to her ; and when Bourrienne implored him, at least, to hear Josephine before condemning her, and to see whether she could not clear herself, or he could not forgive her, he had replied :

" I forgive her ? Never ! Were I not sure of myself this time, I would tear my heart out and throw it into the fire ! " And, as Bonaparte spoke, his voice trembling the while with rage, he clutched his breast with his hand as though he would indeed rend it to pieces. This scene occurred in the evening, but, when Bourrienne came into the office next morning, Bonaparte stepped forward to meet him with a smile on his face, and a little confused.

"Now, Bourrienne," said he, "you will be content— she is here! Don't suppose that I have forgiven her— no, not at all! No, I reproached her vehemently, and sent her away. But, what would you have?—when she left me, weeping, I went after her, and, as she descended the stairs with her head drooping, I saw Eugene and Hortense, who went with her, sobbing violently. I have not the heart to look unmoved on any one in tears. Eugene had accompanied me to Egypt, and I have accustomed myself to regard him as my adopted son; he is so gallant, so excellent a young man. Hortense is just coming out into the world of society, and every one who knows her speaks well of her. I confess, Bourrienne, that the sight of her moved me deeply, and the sobbing of those two poor children made me sad as well. I said to myself, 'Shall they be the victims of their mother's fault?' I called Eugene back. Hortense turned round and, along with Josephine, followed her brother. I saw the movement, and said nothing. What could I do? One cannot be a mortal man without having his hours of weakness!"

"Be assured, general," exclaimed Bourrienne, "that your adopted children will reward you for it!"

"They must do so, Bourrienne—they must do so; for it is a great sacrifice that I have made for them!" *

This sacrifice, however, had its recompense imme-

* Bourrienne, vol. iv., p. 119.

diately, for Josephine had been able to set herself right, and Bonaparte had joyfully become convinced that the accusations of his jealous brothers had been unjust.

Hence it was that Bonaparte's brothers wished to re move Hortense, since they knew that she was her mother's main stay; that she, with her gentle, amiable disposition, her tact and good sense, her penetrating and never-failing sagacity, stood like a wise young Mentor at the side of her beautiful, attractive, impulsive, somewhat vain, and very extravagant mother.

It would be easier to set Josephine aside were Hortense first removed; and Josephine they wanted to get out of the way because she interfered with the ambitious designs of Bonaparte's brothers. Since they could not become great and celebrated by their own merits, they desired to be so through their illustrious brother ; and, in order that they might become kings, Bonaparte must, above all things, wear a crown. Josephine was opposed to this project; she loved Bonaparte enough to fear the dangers that a usurpation of the crown must bring with it, and she had so little ambition as to prefer her present brilliant and peaceful lot to the proud but perilous exaltation to a throne.

For this reason, then, Josephine was to be removed, and Bonaparte must choose another wife—a wife in whose veins there should course legitimate royal blood, and who would, therefore, be content to see a crown upon the head of her consort.

CHAPTER II.

LOUIS BONAPARTE AND DUROC.

THE brothers of Bonaparte went diligently to work then, above all things, to get Hortense out of the way. They told Bonaparte of the burning love of the you.ng couple, of the letters which they sent to each other, and proposed to him that Duroc should be transferred to the Italian army with a higher command, and that Hortense should then be given to him. They persuaded the unsuspecting, magnanimous hero, who was easy to deceive in these minor matters and thus easy because he was occupied with grand designs and grand things; they persuaded him to keep the proposed union a secret for the present, and then on Duroc's early return to surprise the young couple and Josephine alike.

But Josephine had, this time, seen through the plans of her hostile brothers-in-law. She felt that her whole existence, her entire future, was imperilled, should she not succeed in making friends and allies in the family of Bonaparte itself. There was only one of Bonaparte's brothers who was not hostile to her, but loved her as the wife of his brother, to whom he was, at that time, still devoted with the most enthusiastic and submissive tenderness.

This one was Bonaparte's brother Louis, a young man of serious and sedate disposition, more of a scholar than a warrior, more a man of science than fit for the council-chamber and the drawing-room. His was a reserved, quiet, somewhat timid character, which, notwithstanding its apparent gentleness, developed an inflexible determination and energy at the right, decisive moment, and then could not be shaken by either threats or entreaties. His external appearance was little calculated to please, nay, was even somewhat sinister, and commanded the respect of others only in moments of excitement, through the fierce blaze of his large blue eyes, that seemed rather to look inward than outward.

Louis Bonaparte was one of those deep, self-contained, undemonstrative, and by no means showy natures which are too rarely understood, because, in the noisy bustle of life, we have not the time and do not take the pains to analyze them. Only a sister or a mother is in a position to comprehend and love men of this stamp, because the confidential home relations of long years have revealed to them the hidden bloom of these sensitive plants which shrink back and close their leaves at every rude contact of the world. But rarely, however, do they find a loving heart outside, for, since their own hearts are too timid to seek for love, no one gives himself the trouble to discover them.

The young brother of her husband, now scarcely twenty-four, was the one who seemed destined in Josephine's eyes to afford her a point of support in the Bonaparte family.

Madame Letitia loved him more tenderly than she did any of them, next to her Napoleon, since he was the petted darling of the whole family of brothers, who had no fear of him, because he was neither egotistical nor ambitious enough to cross their plans, but quietly allowed them to have their way, and only asked that they would also leave him undisturbed to follow out his own quiet and unobtrusive inclinations. He was the confidant of his young and beautiful sisters, who were always sure to find in him a discreet counsellor, and never a betrayer. Finally, he was the one of the whole circle of brothers toward whom Napoleon felt the sincerest and warmest inclination, because he could not help esteeming him for his noble qualities, and because he was never annoyed by him as he was by his other brothers; for the ambition and the avarice of Jerome, Joseph, and Lucien, were even then a source of displeasure and chagrin to Bonaparte.

"Were any one to hear with what persistency my brothers demand fresh sums of money from me, every day, he would really think that I had consumed from them the inheritance their father left," said Bonaparte, one day, to Bourrienne, after a violent scene between him and Jerome, which had ended, as they all did, in Jerome getting another draft on the private purse of the first consul.

Louis, however, never asked for money, but always appeared thankfully content with whatever Bonaparte chose to give him, unsolicited, and there never were any wranglings with tradesmen on his account, or any debts of his to pay.

This last circumstance was what filled Josephine with

a sort of respectful deference for her young step-brother. He understood how to manage his affairs so well as never to run up debts, and this was a quality that was so sorely lacking in Josephine, that she could never avoid incurring debt. How many bitter annoyances, how much care and anxiety had not her debts cost her already ; how often Bonaparte had scolded her about them ; how often she had promised to do differently, and make no more purchases until she should be in a condition to pay at once !

But this reform was to her thoughtless and magnanimous nature an impossibility ; and however greatly she may have feared the flashing eyes and thundering voice of her husband when he was angered, she could not escape his wrath in this one point, for in that point precisely was it that the penitent sinner continually fell into fresh transgression—and again ran into debt !

Louis, however, never had debts. He was as cautious and regular as her own Hortense, and therefore, thought Josephine, these two young, careful, thoughtful temperaments would be well adapted to each other, and would know how to manage their hearts as discreetly as they did their purses.

So she wished to make a step-son of Louis Bonaparte, in order to strengthen her own position thereby. Josephine already had a premonitory distrust of the future, and it may sometimes have happened that she took the mighty eagle that fluttered above her head for a bird of evil omen whose warning cry she frequently fancied that she heard in the stillness of the night.

The negress at Martinique had said to her, "You will be more than a queen." But now, Josephine had visited the new fortune-teller, Madame Villeneuve, in Paris, and she had said to her, "You will wear a crown, but only for a short time."

Only for a short time! Josephine was too young, too happy, and too healthful, to think of her own early death. It must, then, be something else that threatened her—a separation, perhaps. She had no children, yet Bonaparte so earnestly desired to have a son, and his brothers repeated to him daily that this was for him a political necessity.

Thus Josephine trembled for her future; she stretched out her hands for help, and in the selfishness of her trouble asked her daughter to give up her own dreams of happiness, in order to secure the real happiness of her mother.

Yet Hortense was in love; her young heart throbbed painfully at the thought of not only relinquishing her own love, but of marrying an unloved man, whom she had never even thought of, and had scarcely noticed. She deemed it impossible that she could be asked to sacrifice her own beautiful and blessed happiness, to a cold-blooded calculation, an artificial family intrigue; and so, with all the enthusiasm of a first love, she swore rather to perish than to forego her lover.

"But Duroc has no fortune and no future to offer you," said Josephine. "What he is, he is only through the friendship of Bonaparte. He has no estate, no importance, no celebrity. Were Bonaparte to abandon him, he would fall back into nothingness and obscurity again."

Hortense replied, smiling through her tears : " I love him, and have no other ambition than to be his wife."

" But he ? Do you think that he too has no other ambition than to become your husband ? Do you think that he loves you for your own sake alone ? "

" I know it," said the young girl, with beaming eyes ; " Duroc has told me that he loved me, and me only. He has sworn eternal fidelity and love to me. Both of us ask for nothing more than to belong to each other."

Josephine shrugged her shoulders almost compassion-ately.

" Suppose," she rejoined, " that I were to affirm that Duroc is willing to marry you, only because he is ambitious, and thinks that Bonaparte would then advance him the more rapidly ? "

" It is a slander—it is impossible ! " exclaimed Hortense, glowing with honest indignation ; " Duroc loves me, and his noble soul is far from all selfish calculation."

" And if I were to prove the contrary to you ? " asked Josephine, irritated by her daughter's resistance, and made cruel by her alarm for her own fortunes.

Hortense turned pale, and her face, which had been so animated, so beautiful, a moment before, blanched as though the icy chill of death had passed over it.

" If you can prove to me," she said, in a hollow tone, " that Duroc loves me only through ambitious motives, I am ready to give him up, and marry whom you will."

Josephine triumphed. "Duroc gets back to-day from his journey," she replied, "and in three days more I will give you the proof that he does not love you, but the family alliance which you present."

Hortense had heard only the first of her mother's words: "Duroc returns to-day." What cared she for all the. rest? She should see him again—she should read consolation and love's assurance in his handsome manly face; not that she needed this to confirm her confidence, for she believed in him, and not the shadow of a doubt obscured her blissful greeting.

Meanwhile, Josephine's pretty hands were busy drawing the meshes of this intrigue tighter every moment. She absolutely required a supporting ally in the family, *against* the family itself; and for this reason Louis must become the husband of Hortense.

Bonaparte himself was against this union, and was quite resolved to marry Duroc to his step-daughter. But Josephine managed to shake his resolve, by means of entreaties, representations, caresses, and little endearments, and even succeeded in such eloquent argument to show that Duroc did not cherish any love whatever for Hortense, but wanted to make an ambitious speculation out of her, that Bonaparte resolved, at least, to put his friend to the test, and, if Josephine turned out to be right, to marry Hortense to his own brother.

After this last interview with Josephine, Bonaparte went back into his office, where he found Bourrienne, as ever, at the writing-desk.

" Where is Duroc ? " he hastily asked.

" He has gone out—to the opera, I think."

" So soon as he returns tell him that I have promised him Hortense—that he shall marry her. But I want the wedding to take place in two days, at the farthest. I give Hortense five hundred thousand francs, and I appoint Duroc to the command of the eighth military division. On the day after his wedding he shall start with his wife for Toulon, and we shall live apart. I will not have a son-in-law in my house ; and, as I want to see these matters brought to an end, at last, let me know to-day whether Duroc accepts my propositions."

" I don't think that he will, general."

" Very good ! Then, in that case, Hortense shall marry my brother Louis."

" Will she consent ? "

" She will have to consent, Bourrienne."

Duroc came in at a late hour that evening, and Bourrienne told him, word for word, the ultimatum of the first consul.

Duroc listened to him attentively ; but, as Bourrienne went on with his communication, his countenance grew darker and darker.

" If such be the case," he exclaimed at last, when Bourrienne had got through, " if Bonaparte will do nothing more than that for his son-in-law, I must forego a marriage with Hortense, however painful it may be to do so : and then, instead of going to Toulon, I can remain in Paris." And, as he ceased to speak, Duroc took up his hat, without a trace of excitement or concern, and departed.

That same evening, Josephine received from her husband his full consent to the marriage of her daughter to Louis Bonaparte.

On that very evening, too, Josephine informed her daughter that Duroc had not withstood the test, and that he had now relinquished her, through ambition, as, through ambition, he had previously feigned to love her.

Hortense gazed at her mother with tearless eyes. She had not a word of complaint or reproach to utter; she was conscious merely that a thunder-bolt had just fallen, and had forever dashed to atoms her love, her hopes, her future, and her happiness.

But she no longer had the strength and the will to escape the evil that had flung its meshes around her; she submitted meekly to it. She had been betrayed by love itself; and what cared she now for her future, her embittered, bloomless, scentless life, when *he* had deceived her —*he*, the only one whom she had loved ?

The next morning Hortense stepped, self-possessed and smiling, into Josephine's private cabinet, and declared that she was ready to fulfil her mother's wishes and marry Louis Bonaparte.

Josephine clasped her in her arms, with exclamations of delight. She little knew what a night of anguish, of wailing, of tears, and of despair, Hortense had struggled through, or that her present smiling unconcern was nothing more than the dull hopelessness of a worn-out heart.

She did not see that Hortense smiled now only in order
that Duroc should not observe that she suffered.   Her
love for him was dead, but her maidenly pride had survived, and it dried her tears, and conjured up a smile to
her struggling lips ; it, too, enabled her to declare that
she was ready to accept the husband whom her mother
might present to her.

Thus, Josephine had accomplished her purpose ; she
had made one of Bonaparte's brothers her son.   Now
there remained the question whether she should attain
her other aim through that son, and whether she should
find in him a support against the intrigues of the other
brothers of the first consul.

CHAPTER III.

CONSUL AND KING.

THERE was only two days' interval between the be-
trothal of the young couple and their wedding; and on
the 7th of January, 1802, Hortense was married to Louis
Bonaparte, the youngest brother but one of the first consul.   Bonaparte, who contented himself with the civil
ceremony, and had never given his own union with Josephine the sanction of the Church, was less careless and
unconcerned with regard to this youthful alliance, which
had, indeed, great need of the blessing of Heaven, in order to prove a source of any good fortune to the young

couple. Perhaps he reasoned that the consciousness of the indissoluble character of their union would lead them to an honorable and upright effort for a mutual inclination; perhaps it was because he simply wished to render their separation impossible. Cardinal Caprara was called into the Tuileries, after the civil ceremony concluded, and had to bestow the blessing of God and of the Church upon the bride and bridegroom.

Yet, not one word or one glance had thus far been interchanged by the young couple. It was in silence that they stepped, after the ceremonies were over, into the carriage that bore them to their new home, in the same small residence in the Rue de la Victoire which her mother had occupied in the first happy weeks of her youthful union with Bonaparte.

Now, another young, newly-married pair were making their entry into this dwelling, but love did not enter with them; affection and happiness did not shine in their faces, as had been the case with Bonaparte and Josephine. The eyes of Hortense were dimmed with tears, and the countenance of her young husband was dark and gloomy. For, on his side, he, too, felt no love for this young woman; and, as she never forgave him for having accepted her hand, although he knew that she loved another, he, in like manner, could never forgive her having consented to be his wife, although he had not been the one to solicit it, and although he had never told her that he loved her. Both had bowed to the will of him who gave the law, not merely to all France, but also to his own family, and who had already become the lord and master of the republic. Both had married through obedience, not for love; and the consciousness of this compulsion rose like an impassable wall between these two otherwise tender and confiding young hearts. In the consciousness of this compulsion, too, they would not even try to love one another, or find in each other's society the happiness that they were forbidden to seek elsewhere.

Pale and mournful, in splendid attire, but with a heavy heart, did Hortense make her appearance at the *fêtes* which were given in honor of her marriage; and it was with a beclouded brow and averted face that Louis Bonaparte received the customary congratulations. While every one around them exhibited a cheerful and joyous bearing, while parties were given in their honor, and people danced and sang, the young couple only, of all present, were dull and sad. Louis avoided speaking to Hortense, and she turned her gaze away from him, possibly so that he might not read in it her deep and angry aversion.

But she had to accept her lot; and, since she was thus indissolubly bound up with another, she had to try to live with that other. Hortense, externally so gentle and yielding, so full of maiden coyness and delicacy, nevertheless possessed a strong and resolute soul, and, in the noble pride of her wounded heart, was unwilling to give any one the right to pity her. Her soul wept, but she restrained her tears and still tried to smile, were it only that Duroc might not perceive the traces of her grief upon her sunken cheeks. She had torn this love from her heart, and she rebuked herself that it had left a wound. She laid claim to happiness no more; but her youth, her proud self-respect, revolted at the idea of continuing to be the slave of misfortune henceforth, and so she formed her firm resolve, saying to herself, with a melancholy smile, "I must manage to be happy, without happiness. Let me try!"

And she did try. She once more arrayed herself in smiles, and again took part in the festivities which now were filling the halls of St. Cloud, Malmaison, and the Tuileries, and which, too, were but the dying lay of the swan of the republic, or, if you will, the cradle-song of reviving monarchy.

For things were daily sweeping nearer and nearer to that great turning-point, at which the French people would have to choose between a seeming republic and a real monarchy. France was already a republic but in name; the new, approaching monarchy was, indeed, but a new-born, naked infant as yet, but only a bold hand was wanting, that should possess the determined courage to clothe it with ermine and purple, in order to transform the helpless babe into a proud, triumphant man.

That courage Bonaparte possessed; but he had, also, the higher courage to advance carefully and slowly. He let the infant of monarchy, that lay there naked and helpless at his feet, shiver there a little longer; but, lest it should freeze altogether, he threw over it, for the time

being, the mantle of his "consulship for life." Beneath
it, the babe could slumber comfortably a few weeks
longer, while waiting for its purple robes.

Bonaparte was now, by the will of the French people,
consul for life. He stood close to the steps of a throne,
and it depended only upon himself whether he would
mount those steps, or whether, like General Monk, he
would recall the fugitive king, and restore to him the
sceptre of his forefathers. The brothers of Bonaparte
desired the first; Josephine implored Heaven for the latter alternative. She was too completely a loving woman
only, to long for the chilly joys of mere ambition; she
was too entirely occupied with her personal happiness,
not to fear every danger that menaced it. Should Bonaparte place a crown upon his head, he would also have to
think of becoming the founder of a dynasty; and in
order to strengthen and fortify his position, he would
have to place a legitimate heir by his side. Josephine
had borne her husband no children; and she knew that
his brothers had, more than once, proposed to him to dis-
solve his childless union, and replace it with the presence
of a young wife. Hence, Bonaparte's assumption of
royal dignity meant a separation from her; and Josephine still loved him too well, and too much with a
young wife's love, to take so great a sacrifice upon her.

Moreover, Josephine was at heart a royalist, and considered the Count de Lille, who, after so many agitations
and wanderings, had found an asylum at Hartwell, in
England, the legitimate King of France.

The letters which the Count de Lille (afterward King Louis XVIII.) had written to Bonaparte, had filled Josephine's heart with emotion, and, with a kind of apprehensive foreboding, she had conjured her husband to, at least, give the brother of the beheaded king a mild and considerate answer. Yes, she had even ventured to beseech Bonaparte to comply with the request that Louis had made, and give him back the throne of his ancestors. But Bonaparte had laughed at this suggestion, as he would at some childish joke; for it had never entered into his head that any one could seriously ask him to lay his laurels and his trophies at the foot of a throne, which not he, but a member of that Bourbon family whom France had banished forever, should ascend.

Louis had written to Bonaparte: "I cannot believe that the victor at Lodi, Castiglione, and Arcola—the conqueror of Italy and Egypt—would not prefer real glory to mere empty celebrity. Meanwhile, you are losing precious time. *We* can secure the glory of France; I say *we*, because I have need of Bonaparte in the work, and because he cannot complete it without me."

But Bonaparte already felt strong enough to say, not "we," but "I," and to complete his work alone. Therefore, he replied to the Count de Lille: " You cannot desire your return to France, for you would have to enter it over a hundred thousand corpses; sacrifice your personal interests to the tranquillity and happiness of France. History will pay you a grateful acknowledgment."

7

Louis had said in his letter to Bonaparte, "Choose your own position, and mark out what you want for your friends." And Bonaparte did choose his position; but, unfortunately for the Count de Lille, it was the very one which the latter had wished to reserve for himself.

Josephine would have been glad to vacate the king's place for him, could she but have retained her husband by so doing. She had no longings for a diadem which, by-the-way, her beautiful head did not require in order to command admiration.

"You cannot avoid being a queen or an empress, one of these days," said Bourrienne to her, on a certain occasion.

Josephine replied, with tears: "*Mon Dieu!* I am far from cherishing any such ambition. So long as I live, to be the wife of Bonaparte—of the first consul—is the sum total of my wishes! Tell him so; conjure him not to make himself king." *

But Josephine did not content herself with requesting Bourrienne to tell her husband this; she had the courage to say so to him herself.

One day she went into Napoleon's cabinet, and found him at breakfast, and unusually cheerful and good-humored. She had entered without having been announced, and crept up on tiptoe to her husband, who sat with his back turned toward her, and had not yet noticed her. Lightly throwing her arm around his neck, and letting herself sink upon his breast, and then stroking his

* Bourrienne, vol. v., p. 47.

pale cheeks and glossy brown hair, with an expression of unutterable love and tenderness, she said:

"I implore you, Bonaparte, do not mount the throne. Your wicked brother Lucien will urge you to it, but do not listen to him."

Bonaparte laughed. "You are a little goose, poor Josephine," he said. "It's the old dowagers of the Faubourg St. Germain, and your La Rochefoucauld, more than all the rest, who tell you these wonderful stories; but you worry me to death with them. Come, now, don't bother me about them any more!"

Bonaparte had put off Josephine with a laugh and a jesting word, but he nevertheless conversed earnestly and seriously with his most intimate personal friends on the subject of his assuming the crown. In the course of one of these interviews, Bourrienne said to him:

"As first consul, you are the leading and most famous man in all Europe; whereas, if you place the crown upon your head, you will be only the youngest in date of all the kings, and will have to yield precedence to them."

Bonaparte's eyes blazed up with fiercer fire, and, with that daring and imposing look which was peculiar to him in great and decisive moments, he responded:

"The youngest of the kings! Well, then, I will drive *all* the kings from their thrones, and found a new dynasty: then, they will have to recognize me as the oldest prince of all."

CHAPTER IV.

THE CALUMNY.

THE union of Hortense with Bonaparte's brother had not been followed by such good results for her as Josephine had anticipated. She had made a most unfortunate selection, for Louis Bonaparte was, of all the first consul's brothers, the one who concerned himself the least about politics, and was the least likely to engage in any intrigue. Besides, this alliance had materially diminished the affection which Louis had always previously manifested for Josephine. He blamed her, in the depths of his noble and upright heart, for having been so egotistic as to sacrifice the happiness of her daughter to her own personal welfare; he blamed her, too, for having forced him into a marriage which love had not concluded, and, although he never sided with her enemies, Josephine had, at least, lost a friend in him.

The wedded life of this young couple was something unusually strange. They had openly confessed the repulsion they felt for each other, and reciprocally made no secret of the fact that they had been driven into this union against their own wishes. In this singular interchange of confidence, they went so far as to commiserate each other, and to condole with one another as friends, over the wretchedness they endured in their married bondage.

They said frankly to each other that they could never

love; that they detested one another: but they so keenly felt a mutual compassion, that out of that very compassion—that very hatred itself—love might possibly spring into being.

Louis could already sit for hours together beside his wife, busied with the effort to divert her with amusing remarks, and to drive away the clouds that obscured her brow; already, too, Hortense had come to regard it as her holiest and sweetest duty to endeavor to compensate her husband, by her kindly deportment toward him, and the delicate and attentive respect that distinguished her bearing, for the unhappiness he felt beside her; already had both, in fine, begun to console each other with the reflection that the child which Hortense now bore beneath her heart would, one day, be to them a compensation for their ill-starred marriage and their lost freedom.

"When I present you with a son," said Hortense, smiling, "and when he calls you by the sweet name of 'father,' you will forgive me for being his mother."

"And when you press that son to your heart—when you feel that you love him with boundless affection," said Louis, "you will pardon me for being your husband, and you will cease to hate me, at least, for I will be the father of your darling child."

Had sufficient time been allotted to these young, pure, and innocent hearts, to comprehend one another, they would have overcome their unhappiness, and love would have sprung up at last from hatred. But the world was pitiless to them; it had no compassion for their youth and their sufferings; with cruel hands it dashed away this tender blossoming of nascent affection, which was beginning to expand in their hearts. Josephine had wedded Hortense to her brother-in-law in order to secure in him an ally in the family, and to keep her daughter by her side; and now that daughter was made the target of insidious attacks and malicious calumnies—now another plan was adopted in order to remove Hortense from the scene. The conspirators had not succeeded in their designs by means of a matrimonial alliance, so they would now try the effect of calumny.

They went about whispering from ear to ear that Bonaparte had married his step-daughter to his brother, simply because he was attached to her himself, and had been jealous of Duroc.

These slanders were carried so far as to hint that the child whose birth Hortense expected was more nearly related to Bonaparte than merely through the fact that his step-daughter was his brother's wife.

This was an infernal but skilfully-planned calumny; for those who devised it well knew how Bonaparte detested the merest suspicion of such immorality, how strict he was in his own principles, and how repulsive it therefore would be to him to find himself made the object of such infamous slanders.

The conspirators calculated that, in order to terminate these evil rumors, the first consul would send his brother and Hortense away to a distance, and that the fated Josephine, being thus isolated, could also be the more readily

removed. Thus Bonaparte, being separated from his guardian angel, would no longer hear her whispering :
"Bonaparte, do not ascend the throne! Be content with the glory of the greatest of mankind! Place no diadem upon thy brows; do not make thyself a king!"

In Paris, as I have said, these shameful calumnies were but very lightly whispered, but abroad they were only the more loudly heard. Bonaparte's enemies got hold of the scandalous story, and made a weapon of it with which to assail him as a hero.

One morning Bonaparte was reading an English newspaper which had always been hostile to him, and which, as he well knew, was the organ of Count d'Artois, then residing at Hartwell. As he continued to read, a dark shadow stole over his face, and he crumpled the paper in his clinched fist with a sudden and vehement motion. Then as suddenly again his countenance cleared, and a proud smile flitted across it. He had his master of ceremonies summoned to his presence, and bade him issue the necessary invitations for a court ball to be given, on the evening of the next day, at St. Cloud. He then went to Josephine to inform her in person of the projected *fête*, and to say that he wished her to tell Hortense, who had been ailing for some time, that he particularly desired her to be present.

Hortense had·been too long accustomed to obey her step-father's requests, to venture a refusal. She rose, therefore, from her couch on which she had been in the habit, for weeks past, of reclining, busied with her own dreams and musings, and bade her waiting women prepare her attire for the ball. Still she felt unwell, and seriously burdened by this festive attire, which harmonized so little with her feelings, and was so far from becoming to her figure, for she was only a few weeks from her confinement; but with her gentle and yielding disposition she did not venture, even in thought, to murmur at the compulsion imposed upon her by her step-father's command. She therefore repaired, at the appointed hour, to the ball at St. Cloud. Bonaparte stepped forward to meet her with a friendly smile, and, instead of thanking her for coming at all, earnestly urged her to dance.

Hortense gazed at him with amazement. She knew that hitherto Bonaparte had always sought to avoid the sight of a woman in her condition; he had frequently said that he thought there was nothing more indecent than for a female to join in the dance under such circumstances, and now it was he who asked her to do that very thing.

For this reason Hortense hesitated at first to comply, but Bonaparte grew only the more pressing and vehement in his request.

" You know how I like to see you dance, Hortense," he said, with his irresistible smile ; " so do this much for me, even if you take the floor only once, and that for but a single *contredance*."

And Hortense, although most reluctant, although blushing with shame at the idea of exposing herself in such unseemly shape to the gaze of all, obeyed and joined the dances.

This took place in the evening—how greatly surprised, then, was Hortense when next morning she found, in the paper that she usually read, a poem, extolling her performance in words of ravishing flattery, and referring to the fact that, notwithstanding her advanced state of pregnancy, she had consented to tread a measure in the *contredance*, as a peculiar trait of amiability !

Hortense, however, far from feeling flattered by this very emphatic piece of verse, took it as an affront, and hastened at once to the Tuileries, to complain to her mother, and to ask her how it was possible that, so early as the very next morning, there could be verses published in the newspapers concerning what had taken place at the ball on the preceding evening.

Bonaparte, who happened to be with Josephine when Hortense came in, and was the first to be questioned by her, gave her only an evasive and jocose reply, and withdrew. Hortense then turned to her mother, who was leaning over on the divan, her eyes reddened with weeping and her heart oppressed with grief. To her, Bonaparte had given no evasive answer, but had told the whole truth, and Josephine's heart was at that moment too full of wretchedness, too overladen with this fresh and bitter trouble, for her possibly to retain it within her own breast.

Hortense insisted upon an explanation, and her mother gave it. She told her that Bonaparte had got the poet

Esmenard to write the verses beforehand, and that it was for this reason that he had urged her to dance; that he had ordered the ball for no other purpose than to have her dance, and have the poem that complimented her and referred to her pregnancy published in the next day's paper.

Then, when Hortense, in terror, begged to be informed of the ground for all these proceedings, Josephine had the cruel courage to tell her of the slanders that had been circulated in reference to herself and Bonaparte, and to say that he had arranged the poem, the ball, and her participation in the dance, because, on the preceding day, he had read in an English journal the calumnious statement that Madame Louis Bonaparte had safely given birth to a vigorous and healthy child some weeks previously, and he wished in this manner to refute the malicious statement.

Hortense received this fresh wound with a cold smile of scorn. She had not a word of anger or indignation for this unheard-of injury, this shameless slander; she neither wept nor complained, but, as she rose to take leave of her mother, she swooned away, and it required hours of exertion to restore her to consciousness.

A few weeks later, Hortense was delivered of a dead male infant, and so passed away her last dream of happiness; for thus was destroyed the hope of a better understanding between her and her husband.

Hortense rose from her sick-bed with a firm, determined heart. In those long, lonely days that she had

passed during her confinement, she had the time and opportunity to meditate on many things, and keenly to estimate her whole present position and probable future.
She had now become a mother, without having a child;
yet the resolute energy of a mother remained to her. ,
The youthful, gentle, dreamy, enthusiastic girl had now
become transformed into a determined, active, energetic
woman, that would no longer bow submissively to the
blows of fortune, but would meet them with an open and
defiant brow. Since her fate could not be changed, she
accepted it, all the while resolved no longer to bend to its
yoke, but to subdue it, and try to be happy by force of
resolution; and, since a charming, peaceful, and harmo-
nious fireside at home was denied her, to at least make
her house a pleasant gathering-point for her friends—for
men of scientific and artistic attainments, for poets and
singers, for painters and sculptors, and for men of learn-
ing. Ere long, all Paris was talking about Madame Louis
Bonaparte's drawing-rooms, the agreeable and elegant
entertainments that were given there, and the concerts
there arranged, in which the first singers of the day executed pieces that Hortense had composed, and Talma recited, with his wonderful, sonorous voice, the poems that
she had written. Every one was anxious for admission
to these entertainments, in which the participants not
merely performed their parts, but greatly enjoyed themselves as well; where the guests indulged in no backbit-
ing or abuse, but found more worthy and elevated subjects of conversation; where, in fine, they could admire

the works of poets and artists, and enjoy the newly-
awakened intellectual spirit of the age.

Hortense had firmly made up her mind that, since she
had resigned herself to accept the burden of existence,
she would strive to render it as agreeable as possible, and
not to see any of its hateful and repulsive features, but to
turn away from them with a noble and disdainful pride.
She had never even referred to the frightful calumnies
which her mother had privately made known to her, nor
had she deemed any defence or proof of her innocence at
all necessary.   She felt that there were certain accusations against which to even undertake defence is to admit their possibility, and which, therefore, could only be
combated by silence.   The slanders that had been flung
at her lay in a plane so far beneath her, that they could
not rise high enough to reach her, but fell powerless at
her feet, whence she did not deem it even worth her while
to thrust them.

But Bonaparte continued to feel outraged and wounded by this vile story, and it annoyed him deeply to learn
that these rumors were still spread abroad, and that his
foes still bestirred themselves to keep him ever on the
alert, and, if possible, to dim the lustre of his gloriously-
won laurels by the shadow of an infamous crime.

"There are still rumors abroad of a *liaison* between
me and Hortense," said he one day to Bourrienne. "They
have even invented the most repulsive stories concerning
her first infant.   At the time, I thought that these calumnies were circulated among the public because the latter

so earnestly desired that I might have a child to inherit my name. But it is still spoken of, is it not?"

"Yes, general, it is still spoken of; and I confess that I did not believe this calumny would be so long continued."

"This is really abominable!" exclaimed Bonaparte, his eyes flashing with anger. "You, Bourrienne, you best know what truth there is in it. You have heard and seen all; not the smallest circumstance could escape you. You were her confidant in her love-affair with Duroc. I expect you to clear me of this infamous reproach if you should some day write my history. Posterity shall not associate my name with such infamy. I shall depend on you, Bourrienne, and you will at least admit that you have never believed in this abominable calumny?"

"No, never, general."

"I shall rely on you, Bourrienne, not only on my own account, but for the sake of poor Hortense. She is, without this, unhappy enough, as is my brother also. I am concerned about this, because I love them both, and because this very circumstance gives color to the reports which idle chatterboxes have circulated regarding my relations to her. Therefore, bear this in mind when you write of me hereafter."

"I shall do so, general; I shall tell the truth, but, unfortunately, I can not compel the world to believe the truth."

Bourrienne has, at all events, kept his word, and

spoken the truth. With deep indignation he spurns the
calumny with which it has been attempted to sully the
memory of Bonaparte and Hortense, even down to our
time ; and, in his anger, he even forgets the elegant and
considerate language of the courteous diplomat, which is
elsewhere always characteristic of his writings.

"He lies in his throat," says Bourrienne, "who asserts
that Bonaparte entertained other feelings for Hortense
than those a step-father should entertain for his step-
daughter ! Hortense entertained for the first consul a
feeling of reverential fear. She always spoke to him
tremblingly. She never ventured to approach him with
a petition. She was in the habit of coming to me, and I
then submitted her wishes ; and only when Bonaparte
received them unfavorably did I mention the name of
the petitioner. ' The silly thing ! ' said the first consul ;
' why does she not speak to me herself ? Is she afraid of
me ? ' Napoleon always entertained a fatherly affection
for her ; since his marriage, he loved her as a father
would have loved his child. I, who for years was a witness of her actions in the most private relations of life, I
declare that I have never seen or heard the slightest circumstance that would tend to convict her of a criminal intimacy. One must consider this calumny as belonging to
the category of those which malice so willingly circulates
about those persons whose career has been brilliant, and
which credulity and envy so willingly believe. I declare
candidly that, if I entertained the slightest doubt with regard to this horrible calumny, I would say so. But Bona-

parte is no more! Impartial history must not and shall not give countenance to this reproach; she should not make of a father and friend a libertine! Malicious and hostile authors have asserted, without, however, adducing any proof, that a criminal intimacy existed between Bonaparte and Hortense. A falsehood, an unworthy falsehood! And this report has been generally current, not only in France, but throughout all Europe. Alas! can it, then, be true that calumny exercises so mighty a charm that, when it has once taken possession of a man, he can never be freed from it again?"

CHAPTER V.

KING OR EMPEROR.

JOSEPHINE's entreaties had been fruitless, or Bonaparte had, at least, only yielded to them in their literal sense. She had said: "I entreat you, do not make yourself a king!" Bonaparte did not make himself king, he made himself emperor. He did not take up the crown that had fallen from the head of the Bourbons; he created a new one for himself—a crown which the French people and Senate had, however, offered him. The revolution still stood a threatening spectre behind the French people; its return was feared, and, since the discovery of the conspiracy of Georges, Moreau, and Pichegru, the people anxiously asked themselves what was to become

of France if the conspirators should succeed in murdering Bonaparte; and when the republic should again be
sent adrift, without a pilot, on the wild sea of revolution.
The people demanded that their institutions should be
securely established and maintained, and believed that
this could only be accomplished by a dynasty—by a mo-
narchical form of government. The consulate for life
must therefore be changed into an hereditary empire.
Had not Bonaparte himself said : " One can be emperor
of a republic, but not king of a republic ; these two terms
are incompatible ! " They desired to make Napoleon
emperor, because they flattered themselves that in so
doing they should still be able to preserve the republic.

On the 18th of May, of the year 1804, the plan that
had been so long and carefully prepared was carried into
execution. On the 18th of May, the Senate repaired to
St. Cloud, to entreat Bonaparte, in the name of the people and army, to accept the imperial dignity, and exchange the Roman chair of a consul for the French
throne of an emperor.

Cambacérès, the late second consul of the republic,
stood at the head of the Senate, and upon him devolved
the duty of imparting to Bonaparte the wishes of the
French people. Cambacérès—who, as a member of the
Convention, had voted for the condemnation of Louis
XVI., in order that royalty should be forever banished
from French soil—this same Cambacérès was now the
first to salute Bonaparte with " imperial majesty," and
with the little word, so full of significance, " sire." He

rewarded Cambacérès for this by writing to him on the same day, and appointing him high constable of the empire, as the first act of his imperial rule. In this letter, the first document in which Bonaparte signed himself merely Napoleon, the emperor retained the republican style of writing. He addressed Cambacérès as "citizen consul," and followed the revolutionary method of reckoning time, his letter being dated "the 20th Floréal, of the year 12."

The second act of the emperor, on the first day of his new dignity, was to invest the members of his family also with new dignities, and to confer upon them the rank of Princes of France, with the title "imperial highness." Moreover, he made his brother Joseph prince elector, and his brother Louis connétable. On the same day it devolved upon Louis, in his new dignity, to present the generals and staff officers to the emperor, and then to conduct them to the empress—the Empress Josephine.

The prophecy of the negress of Martinique was now fulfilled. Josephine was "more than a queen." But Josephine, in the midst of the splendor of her new dignity, could only think, with an anxious heart, of the prophecy of the clairvoyante of Paris, who had told her, "You will wear a crown, but only for a short time." She felt that this wondrous fortune could not last long—that the new emperor would have to do as the kings of old had done, and sacrifice his dearest possession to Fate, in order to appease the hungry demons of vengeance and envy; and that he would, therefore, sacrifice her,

8

in order to secure the perpetuity of his fortune and
dynasty.

It was this that weighed down the heart of the new
empress, and made her shrink in alarm from her new
grandeur. It was, therefore, with a feeling of deep anxiety that she took possession of the new titles and honors
that Fate had showered upon her, as from an inexhausti-
ble horn of plenty. With a degree of alarm, and almost
with shame, she heard herself addressed with the titles
with which she had addressed the Queen of France years
before, in these same halls, when she came to the Tuileries as Marquise de Beauharnais, to do homage to the
beautiful Marie Antoinette. She had died on the scaffold and now Josephine was the "majesty" that sat enthroned in the Tuileries, her brilliant court assembled
around her, while in a retired nook of England the
legitimate King of France was leading a lonely and
gloomy life.

Josephine, as we have said, was a good royalist; and,
as empress, she still mourned over the fate of the unfortunate Bourbons, and esteemed it her sacred duty to
assist and advise those who, true to their principles and
duties, had followed the royal family, or had emigrated,
in order that they might, at least, not be compelled to do
homage to the new system. Her purse was always at
the service of the emigrants; and, if Josephine continually made debts, in spite of her enormous monthly allowance, her extravagance was not alone the cause, but also
her kindly, generous heart; for she was in the habit of

setting apart the half of her monthly income for the relief of poor emigrants, and, no matter how great her own embarrassment, or how pressing her creditors, she never suffered the amount devoted to the relief of misfortune and the reward of fidelity to be applied to any other purpose.*

Now that Josephine was an empress, her daughter, the wife of the High Constable of France, took the second position at the brilliant court of the emperor. The daughter of the beheaded viscount was now a "Princess of France," an "imperial highness," who must be approached with reverence, who had her court and her maids of honor, and whose liberty and personal inclinations, as was also the case with her mother, were confined in the fetters of the strict etiquette which Napoleon required to be observed at the new imperial court.

But neither Josephine nor Hortense allowed herself to be blinded by this new splendor. A crown could confer upon Josephine no additional happiness; glittering titles could neither enhance Hortense's youth and beauty, nor alleviate her secret misery. She would have been contented to live in retirement, at the side of a beloved husband; her proud position could not indemnify her for her lost woman's happiness.

But Fate seemed to pity the noble, gentle being, who knew how to bear misery and grandeur with the same smiling dignity, and offered her a recompense for the

* Mémoires sur la reine Hortense, par le Baron van Schelten, vol. L, p. 145.

overthrow of her first mother's hope—a new hope—she promised to become a mother again.

Josephine received this intelligence with delight, for her daughter's hope was a hope for her too. If Hortense should give birth to a son, the gods might be reconciled, and misfortune be banished from the head of the empress. With this son, the dynasty of the new imperial family would be assured; this son could be the heir of the imperial crown, and Napoleon could well adopt as his own the child who was at the same time his nephew and his grandson.

Napoleon promised Josephine that he would do this; that he would rather content himself with an adopted son, in whom the blood of the emperor and of the empress was mixed, than be compelled to separate himself from her, from his Josephine. Napoleon still loved his wife; he still compared with all he thought good and beautiful, the woman who shed around his grandeur the lustre of her grace and loveliness.

When the people greeted their new emperor with loud cries of joy and thunders of applause, Napoleon, his countenance illumined with exultation, exclaimed: "How glorious a music is this! These acclamations and greetings sound as sweet and soft as the voice of Josephine! How proud and happy I am, to be loved by such a people!" *

But his proud ambition was not yet sated. As he had once said, upon entering the Tuileries as first consul,

* Bourrienne, vol. iv., p. 228.

" It is not enough to *be* in the Tuileries; one must also *remain* there "—he now said : " It is not enough to have been made emperor by the French people; one must also have received his consecration as emperor from the Pope of Rome."

And Napoleon was now mighty enough to give laws to the world ; not only to bend France, but also foreign sovereigns, to his will.

Napoleon desired for his crown the papal consecration; and the Pope left the holy city and repaired to Paris, to give the new emperor the blessing of the Church in the Cathedral of Notre-Dame. This was a new halo around Napoleon's head—a new, an unbounded triumph, which he celebrated over France, over the whole world and its prejudices, and over all the dynasties by the " grace of God." The Pope came to Paris to crown the emperor. The German emperors had been compelled to make a pilgrimage to Rome, to receive the papal benediction, and now the Pope made a pilgrimage to Paris to crown the French emperor, and acknowledge the son of the Revolution as the consecrated son of the Church. All France was intoxicated with delight at this intelligence ; all France adored the hero, who made of the wonders of fiction a reality, and converted even the holy chair at Rome into the footstool of his grandeur. Napoleon's journey with Josephine through France, undertaken while they awaited the Pope's coming, was, therefore, a single, continuous triumph. It was not only the people who received him with shouts of joy, but the

Church also sang to him, everywhere, her *sanctus, sanctus,* and the priests received him at the doors of their churches with loud benedictions, extolling him as the savior of France. Everywhere, the imperial couple was received with universal exultation, with the ringing of bells, with triumphal arches, and solemn addresses of welcome, the latter partaking sometimes of a transcendental nature.

"God created Bonaparte," said the Prefect of Arras, in his enthusiastic address to the emperor—"God created Bonaparte, and then He rested." And Count Louis of Narbonne, at that time not yet won over by the emperor, and not yet grand-marshal of the imperial court, whispered, quite audibly: "God would have done better had He rested a little sooner!"

Finally, the intelligence overran all France, that the wonder, in which they had not yet dared to believe, had become reality, and that Pope Pius VII. had crossed the boundaries of France, and was now approaching the capital. The Holy Father of the Church, that had now arisen victoriously from the ruins of the revolution, was everywhere received by the people and authorities with the greatest honor. The old royal palace at Fontainebleau had, by order of the emperor, been refurnished with imperial magnificence, and, as a peculiarly delicate attention, the Pope's bedchamber had been arranged in exact imitation of his bedchamber in the Quirinal at Rome. The emperor, empress, and their suite, now repaired to Fontainebleau, to receive Pope Pius VII. The whole ceremony had, however, been previously arranged, and understanding had with the Pope concerning the various questions of etiquette. In conformity with this prearranged ceremony, when the couriers announced the approach of the Pope, Napoleon rode out to the chase, to give himself the appearance of meeting the Pope accidentally on his way. The equipages and the imperial court had taken position in the forest of Nemours. Napoleon, however, attired in hunting-dress, rode, with his suite, to the summit of a little hill, which the Pope's carriage had just reached. The Pope at once ordered a halt, and the emperor also brought his suite to a stand with a gesture of his hand. A brief interval of profound silence followed. All felt that a great historical event was taking place, and the eyes of all were fastened in wondering expectation on the two chief figures of this scene—on the emperor, who sat there on his horse, in his simple huntsman's attire; and on the Pope, in his gold-embroidered robes, leaning back in his equipage, drawn by six horses.

As Napoleon dismounted, the Pope hastened to descend from his carriage, hesitating a moment, however, after he had already placed his foot on the carriage-step; but Napoleon's foot had already touched the earth. Pius could, therefore, no longer hesitate; he must make up his mind to step, in his white, gold-embroidered satin slippers, on the wet soil, softened by a shower of rain, that had fallen on the previous day. The emperor's hunting-boots were certainly much better adapted to this meeting in the mud than the Pope's white satin slippers.

Emperor and Pope approached and embraced each other tenderly; then, through the inattention of the coachmen, seemingly, the imperial equipage was set in motion, and, in its rapid advance, interrupted this tender embrace. It seemed to be the merest accident that the emperor stood on the right, and the Pope on the left side of the equipage, that had now been brought to a stand again. The two doors of the carriage were simultaneously thrown open by the lackeys; at the same time, the Pope entered the carriage on the left, and the emperor on the right side, both seating themselves side by side at the same time. This settled the question of etiquette. Neither had preceded the other, but the emperor occupied the seat of honor on the Pope's right.

The coronation of the imperial pair took place on the 2d of December, 1804, in the Cathedral of Notre-Dame. Not only all Paris, but all France, was in motion on this day. An immense concourse of people surged to and fro in the streets; the windows of all the houses were filled with richly-adorned and beautiful women, the bells were ringing in all the churches, and joyous music, intermixed with the shouts of the people, was heard in every direction. For a moment, however, these shouts were changed into laughter, and that was when the papal procession approached, headed by an ass led by the halter, in accordance with an ancient custom of Rome. While the Pope, with the high dignitaries of the Church, repaired to the cathedral to await there the coming of the imperial couple, Napoleon was putting on the imperial insignia in the Tuileries, enveloping himself in the green velvet mantle, bordered with ermine, and thickly studded with brilliants, and arraying himself in the whole glittering paraphernalia of his new dignity. When already on the point of leaving the Tuileries with his wife, who stood at his side in her imperial attire, Bonaparte suddenly gave the order that the notary Ragideau should be called to the palace, as he desired to see him at once.

A messenger was at once sent, in an imperial equipage, to bring him from his dwelling, and in a quarter of an hour the little notary Ragideau entered the cabinet of the empress, in which the imperial pair were alone, awaiting him in their glittering attire.

His eyes beaming, a triumphant smile on his lips, Napoleon stepped forward to meet the little notary. "Well, Master Ragideau," said he, gayly, "I have had you called, merely to ask you whether General Bonaparte really possesses nothing besides his hat and his sword, or whether you will now forgive Viscountess Beauharnais for having married me;" and, as Ragideau looked at him in astonishment, and Josephine asked the meaning of his strange words, Bonaparte related how, while standing in Ragideau's antechamber on a certain occasion, he had heard the notary advising Josephine not to marry poor little Bonaparte; not to become the wife of the general, who possessed nothing but his hat and his sword.

The notary's words had entered the ambitious young man's heart like a dagger, and had wounded him deeply. But he had uttered no complaint, and made no mention of it; but to-day, on the day of his supreme triumph, to-day the emperor remembered that moment of humiliation, and, arrayed with the full insignia of the highest earthly dignity, he accorded himself the triumph of reminding the little notary that he had once advised Josephine not to marry him, because of his poverty.

The poor General Bonaparte had now transformed himself into the mighty Emperor Napoleon. Then he possessed nothing but his hat and his sword, but now the Pope awaited him in the cathedral of Notre-Dame, to place the golden imperial crown on his head.

CHAPTER VI.

NAPOLEON'S HEIR.

HORTENSE had not been able to take any part in the festivities of the coronation; but another festivity had been prepared for her in the retirement of her apartments. She had given birth to a son; and in this child the happy mother found consolation and a new hope.

Josephine, who had assumed the imperial crown with a feeling of foreboding sadness, received the intelligence of the birth of her grandson with exultation. It seemed to her that the clouds that had been gathering over her

head were now dissipated, and that a day of unclouded
sunshine now smiled down upon her. Hortense had assured her mother's future; she had given birth to a son,
and had thus given a first support to the new imperial
dynasty. There was now no longer a reason why Napoleon should entertain the thoughts of a separation, for
there was a son to whom he could one day bequeath the
imperial throne of France.

The emperor also seemed to be disposed to favor Josephine's wishes, and to adopt his brother's son as his own.
Had he not requested the Pope to delay his departure
for a few days, in order to baptize the child? The Pope
performed this sacred rite at St. Cloud, the emperor holding the child, and Madame Letitia standing at his side as
second witness. Hortense now possessed an object upon
which she could lavish the whole wealth of love that had
until now lain concealed in her heart. The little Napoleon Charles was Hortense's first happy love; and she
gave way to this intoxicating feeling with the most intense delight.

Josephine's house was now her home in the fullest
sense of the word; she no longer shared her home with
her husband, and could now bestow her undivided love
and care upon her child. Louis Napoleon, the Grand-
Constable of France, had been appointed Governor of
Piedmont by Napoleon; and Hortense, owing to her
delicate health, had not been compelled to accompany
him, but had been permitted to remain in her little
house in Paris, which she could exchange when sum-

mer came for her husband's new estate, the castle of Saint-Leu.

But the tranquillity which Josephine enjoyed with her child in this charming country-resort was to be of short duration. The brother and sister-in-law of the emperor could not hope to be permitted to lead a life of retirement. They were rays of the sun that now dazzled the whole world ; they must fulfil their destiny, and contribute their light to the ruling sun.

An order of Napoleon recalled the constable, who had returned from Piedmont a short time before, and repaired to Saint-Leu to see his son, to Paris. Napoleon had appointed his brother to a brilliant destiny ; the Constable of France was to become a king. Delegates of the Republic of Batavia, the late Holland, had arrived in Paris, and requested their mighty neighbor, the Emperor Napoleon, to give them a king, who should unite them with the glittering empire, through the ties of blood. Napoleon intended to fulfil their wishes, and present them with a king, in the person of his brother Louis.

But Louis was rather appalled than dazzled by this offer, and refused to accept the proposed dignity. In this refusal he was also in perfect harmony with his wife, who did all in her power to strengthen his resolution. Both felt that the crown which it was proposed to place on their heads would be nothing more than a golden chain of dependence ; that the King of Holland could be nothing more than the vassal of France ; and

their personal relations to each other added another ob-
jection to this political consideration.

In Paris, husband and wife could forget the chain
that bound them together; there they were in the circle
of their friends, and could avoid each other. The great,
glittering imperial court served to separate and reconcile
the young couple, who had never forgiven themselves
for having fettered each other in this involuntary union.
In Paris they had amusements, friends, society; while in
Holland they would live in entire dependence on each
other, and hear continually the rattling of the chain with
which each had bound the other to the galley of a union
without love.

Both felt this, and both were, therefore, united in the
endeavor to ward off this new misfortune that was suspended over their heads, in the form of a kingly crown.

But how could they resist successfully the iron will of
Napoleon? Hortense had never had the courage to address Napoleon directly on the subject of her wishes and
petitions, and Josephine already felt that her wishes no
longer exercised the power of earlier days over the emperor. She therefore avoided interceding where she was
not sure of being successful.

At the outset, Louis had the courage to resist his
brother openly; but Napoleon's angry glance annihilated
his opposition, and his gentle, yielding nature was forced
to succumb. In the presence of the deputation of the
Batavian Republic, that so ardently longed for a sceptre
and crown, Napoleon appealed to his brother Louis to ac-

cept the crown which had been freely tendered him, and
to be to his country a king who would respect and protect its liberties, its laws, and its religion.

With emotion, Louis Bonaparte declared himself
ready to accept this crown, and to be a good and true
ruler to his new country.

And to keep this oath faithfully was from this time
the single and sacred endeavor to which he devoted his
every thought and energy. The people of Holland having chosen him to be their king, he was determined to do
honor to their choice ; having been compelled to give up
his own country and nationality, he determined to belong
to his new country with his whole heart and being—to
become a thorough Hollander, as he could no longer remain a Frenchman.

This heretofore so gentle and passive nature now developed an entirely new energy ; this dreamer, this pale,
silent brother of the emperor, was now suddenly transformed into a bold, self-reliant man of action, who had
fixed his gaze on a noble aim, and was ready to devote
all the powers of his being to its attainment. As King
of Holland, he desired, above all, to be beloved by his
subjects, and to be able to contribute to their welfare and
happiness. He studied their language with untiring diligence, and made himself acquainted with their manners
and customs, for the purpose of making them his own.
He investigated the sources of their wealth and of their
wants, and sought to develop the former and relieve the
latter. He was restless in his efforts to provide for his

country, and to merit the love and confidence which his subjects bestowed on him.

His wife also exerted herself to do justice to her new and glittering position, and to wear worthily the crown which she had so unwillingly accepted. In her drawing-rooms she brought together, at brilliant entertainments, the old aristocracy and the new nobility of Holland, and taught the stiff society of that country the fine, unconstrained tone, and the vivacious intellectual conversation of Parisian society. It was under Hortense's fostering hand that art and science first made their way into the aristocratic parlors of Holland, giving to their social reunions a higher and nobler importance.

And Hortense was not only the protectress of art and science, but also the mother of the poor, the ministering angel of the unhappy, whose tears she dried, and whose misery she alleviated—and this royal pair, though adored and blessed by their subjects, could not find within their palaces the least reflection of the happiness they so well knew how to confer upon others without its walls. Between these two beings, so gentle and yielding to others, a strange antipathy continued to exist, and not even the birth of a second, and of a third, son could fill up the chasm that separated them.

And this chasm was soon to be broadened by a new blow of destiny. Hortense's eldest, the adopted son of Napoleon, the presumptive heir to his throne, the child that Napoleon loved so dearly that he often played with him for hours on the terraces of St. Cloud, the child Josephine worshipped, because its existence seemed to assure her own happiness, the child that had awakened the first feeling of motherly bliss in Hortense's bosom, the child that had often even consoled Louis Bonaparte for the unenjoyable present with bright hopes for the future —the little Napoleon Charles died in the year 1807, of the measles.

This was a terrific blow that struck the parents, and the imperial pair of France with equal force. Napoleon's eyes filled with tears when this intelligence was brought him, and a cry of horror escaped Josephine's lips.

"Now I am lost!" she murmured in a low voice; "now my fate is decided. He will put me away."

But after this first egotistical outburst of her own pain, she hastened to the Hague to weep with her daughter, and bring her away from the place associated with her loss and her anguish. Hortense returned with the empress to St. Cloud; while her husband, who had almost succumbed to his grief, was compelled to seek renewed health in the baths of the Pyrenees. The royal palace at the Hague now stood desolate again; death had banished life and joy from its halls; and, though the royal pair were subsequently compelled to return to it, joy and happiness came back with them no more.

King Louis had returned from the Pyrenees in a more gloomy and ill-natured frame of mind than ever; a sickly distrust, a repulsive irritability, had taken possession of his whole being, and his young wife no longer had the good-will to bear with his caprices, and excuse his irritable disposition. They were totally different in their views, desires, inclinations, and aspirations; and their children, instead of being a means of reuniting, seemed to estrange them the more, for each insisted on considering them his or her exclusive property, and in having them educated according to his or her views and wishes.

But Hortense was soon to forget her own household troubles and cares, in the greater misery of her mother. A letter from Josephine, an agonized appeal to her daughter for consolation, recalled Hortense to her mother's side, and she left the Hague and hastened to Paris.

CHAPTER VII.

PREMONITIONS.

JOSEPHINE's fears, and the prophecies of the French clairvoyante, were now about to be fulfilled. The crown which Josephine had reluctantly and sorrowfully accepted, and which she had afterward worn with so much grace and amiability, with such natural majesty and dignity, was about to fall from her head. Napoleon had the cruel courage, now that the dreamed-of future had been realized, to put away from him the woman who had loved him and chosen him when he had nothing to offer her but his hopes for the future. Josephine, who,

9

with smiling courage and brave fidelity, had stood at his side in the times of want and humiliation, was now to be banished from his side into the isolation of a glittering widowhood. Napoleon had the courage to determine that this should be done, but he lacked the courage to break it to Josephine, and to pronounce the word of separation himself. He was determined to sacrifice to his ambition the woman he had so long called his "good angel;" and he, who had never trembled in battle, trembled at the thought of her tears, and avoided meeting her sad, entreating gaze.

But Josephine divined the whole terrible misfortune that hung threateningly over her head. She read it in the gloomy, averted countenance of the emperor, who, since his recent return from Vienna, had caused the door that connected his room with that of his wife to be locked; she read it in the faces of the courtiers, who dared to address her with less reverence, but with a touch of compassionate sympathy; she heard it in the low whispering that ceased when she approached a group of persons in her parlors; it was betrayed to her in the covert, mysterious insinuations of the public press, which attached a deep and comprehensive significance to the emperor's journey to Vienna.

She knew that her destiny must now be fulfilled, and that she was too weak to offer any resistance. But she was determined to act her part as wife and empress worthily to the end. Her tears should not flow outwardly, but inwardly to her grief-stricken heart; she suppressed her sighs with a smile, and concealed the pallor of her cheeks with rouge. But she longed for a heart to whom she could confide her anguish, and show her tears, and therefore called her daughter to her side.

How painful was this reunion of mother and daughter, how many tears were shed, how bitter were the lamentations Josephine whispered in her daughter's ear!

"If you knew," said she, "in what torments I have passed the last few weeks, in which I was no longer his wife, although compelled to appear before the world as such! What glances, Hortense, what glances courtiers fasten upon a discarded woman! In what uncertainty, what expectancy more cruel than death, have I lived and am I still living, awaiting the lightning stroke that has long glowed in Napoleon's eyes!" *

Hortense listened to her mother's lamentations with a heart full of bitterness. She thought of how she had been compelled to sacrifice her own happiness to that of her mother, of how she had been condemned to a union without love, in order that the happiness of her mother's union might be established on a firm basis. And now all had been in vain; the sacrifice had not sufficed to arrest the tide of misfortune now about to bear down her unhappy mother. Hortense could do nothing to avert it. She was a queen, and yet only a weak, pitiable woman, who envied the beggar on the street her freedom and her humble lot. Both mother and daughter stood on the summit of earthly magnificence, and yet this empress and

* Josephine's own words.—Bourrienne, vol. viii., p. 243.

this queen felt themselves so poor and miserable, that
they looked back with envy at the days of the revolution
—the days in which they had led in retirement a life of
poverty and want. Then, though struggling with want
and care, they had been rich in hopes, in wishes, in illusions ; now, they possessed all that could adorn life ; now
millions of men bowed down to them, and saluted them
with the proud word "majesty," and yet empress and
queen were now poor in hopes and wishes, poor in the
illusions that lay shattered at their feet, and rejoicing
only in the one happiness, that of being able to confide
their misery to each other. .

A few days after her arrival, the emperor caused Hor
tense to be called to his cabinet. He advanced toward
her with vivacity, but before the gaze of her large eyes
the glance of the man before whom the whole world now
bowed, almost quailed.

" Hortense," said he, " we are now called on to decide
an important matter, and it is our duty not to recoil.
The nation has done so much for me and my family,
that I owe them the sacrifice which they demand of me.
The tranquillity and welfare of France require that I
shall choose a wife who can give the country an heir to
the throne. Josephine has been living in suspense and
anguish for six months, and this must end. You, Hortense, are her dearest friend and her confidante ; she loves
you more than all else in the world. Will you undertake
to prepare your mother for this step ? You would thereby relieve my heart of a heavy burden."

Hortense had the strength to suppress her tears, and fasten her eyes on the emperor's countenance in a firm, determined gaze. His glance again quailed, as the lion recoils from the angry glance of a pure, innocent woman. Hortense had the courage to positively refuse the emperor's request.

"How, Hortense!" exclaimed Napoleon with emotion. "You then refuse my request?"

"Sire," said she, hardly able longer to restrain her tears, "sire, I have not the strength to stab my mother to the heart." *

And regardless of etiquette, Hortense turned away and left the emperor's cabinet, the tears pouring in streams from her eyes.

CHAPTER VIII.

THE DIVORCE.

Napoleon made one other attempt to impart to Josephine, through a third person, the distressing tidings of his determination with regard to herself. He begged Eugene, the Viceroy of Italy, to come to Paris, and on his arrival informed him of his intentions and of his wish. Eugene, like his sister, received this intelligence in silent submissiveness, but like his sister, he refused to impart to his mother, tidings that must destroy her happiness forever.

* Schelten, vol. ii,, p. 45.

The emperor had finally to make up his mind to impart the distressing tidings in person.

It was on the 30th of November, 1809.   The emperor and empress dined, as usual, at the same table. His gloomy aspect on entering the room made Josephine's heart quake ; she read in his countenance that the fatal hour had come.   But she repressed the tears which were rushing to her eyes, and looked entreatingly at her daughter, who sat on the opposite side of the table, a deathly pallor on her countenance.

Not a word was spoken during this gloomy, ominous dinner.   The sighs and half-suppressed moaning that escaped Josephine's heaving breast were quite audible. Without, the wind shrieked and howled dismally, and drove the rain violently against the window-panes ; within, an ominous, oppressive silence prevailed.   The commotion of Nature contrasted, and yet, at the same time, harmonized strangely with this human silence.   Napoleon broke this silence but once, and that was when, in a harsh voice, he asked the lackey, who stood behind him, what time it was.   Then all was still as before.

At last Napoleon gave the signal to rise from the table, and coffee was then taken standing.   Napoleon drank hastily, and then set the cup down with a trembling hand, making it ring out as it touched the table. With an angry gesture he dismissed the attendants.

"Sire, may Hortense remain ?" asked Josephine, almost inaudibly.

"No!" exclaimed the emperor, vehemently.   Hortense made a profound obeisance, and, taking leave of her mother with a look of tender compassion, left the room, followed by the rest.

The imperial pair were now alone. And how horrible was this being left alone under the circumstances; how sad the silence in which they sat opposite each other! How strange the glance which the emperor fastened on his wife!

She read in his excited, quivering features the struggle that moved his soul, but she also read in them that her hour was come!

As he now approached her, his outstretched hand trembled, and Josephine shudderingly recoiled.

Napoleon took her hand in his, and laid it on his heart, regarding her with a long and sorrowful farewell-glance.

"Josephine," said he, his voice trembling with emotion, "my good Josephine, you know that I have loved you! To you, and to you alone, do I owe the only moments of happiness I have enjoyed in this world. Josephine, my destiny is stronger than my will. My dearest desires must yield to the interests of France." *

"Speak no further," cried Josephine, withdrawing her hand angrily—"no, speak no further. I understand you, and I expected this, but the blow is not the less deadly."

She could speak no further, her voice failed. A feeling of despair came over her; the long-repressed storm

* The emperor's own words. See Bourrienne, vol. iii., p. 344.

of agony at last broke forth. ˙ She wept, she wrung her hands; groans escaped her heaving breast, and a loud cry of anguish burst from her lips. She at last fainted away, and was thus relieved from a consciousness of her sufferings.

When she awoke she found herself on her bed, and Hortense and her physician Corvisart at her side. Josephine stretched out her trembling arms toward her daughter, who threw herself on her mother's heart, sobbing bitterly. Corvisart silently withdrew, feeling that he could be of no further assistance. It had only been in his power to recall Josephine to a consciousness of her misery; but for her misery itself he had no medicine; he knew that her tears and her daughter's sympathy could alone give relief.

Josephine lay weeping in her daughter's arms, when Napoleon came in to inquire after her condition. As he seated himself at her bedside, she shrank back with a feeling of horror, her tears ceased to flow, and her usually so mild and joyous eyes now shot glances of anger and offended love at the emperor. But love soon conquered anger. She extended her tremulous hand to Napoleon; the sad, sweet smile, peculiar to woman, trembled on her lips, and, in a gentle, touching voice, she said: " Was I not right, my friend, when I shrank back in terror from the thought of becoming an empress?" *

Napoleon made no reply. He turned away and

* Josephine's own narrative. See Bourrienne, vol. iii., p. 342, *et seq.*

wept. But these farewell tears of his love could not change Josephine's fate; the emperor had already determined it irrevocably. His demand of the hand of the Archduchess Marie Louise had already been acceded to in Vienna. Nothing now remained to be done but to remove Josephine from the throne, and elevate a new, a legitimate empress, to the vacant place!

The emperor could not and would not retrace his steps. He assembled about him all his brothers, all the kings, dukes, and princes, created by his mighty will, and in the state-chambers of the Tuileries, in the presence of his court and the Senate, the emperor appeared; at his side the empress, arrayed for the last time in all the insignia of the dignity she was about to lay aside forever.

In a loud, firm voice the emperor declared to the assembly his determination to divorce himself from his wife; and Josephine, in a trembling voice, often interrupted by tears, repeated her husband's words. The arch-chancellor, Cambacérès, then caused the appropriate paragraph of the *Code Civile* to be read, applied it to the case under consideration, in a short, terse address, and pronounced the union of the emperor and empress dissolved.

This ended the ceremony, and satisfied the requirements of the law. Josephine had now only to take leave of her husband and of the court, and she did this with the gentle, angelic composure, in the graceful, sweet manner, which was hers in a degree possessed by few other women.

As she bowed profoundly to Napoleon, her pale face illumined by inward emotion, his lips murmured a few inaudible words, and his iron countenance quivered for an instant with pain. As she then walked through the chamber, her children, Hortense and Eugene, on either side, and greeted all with a last soft look, a last inclination of the head, nothing could be heard but weeping, and even those who rejoiced over her downfall, because they hoped much from the new empress and the new dynasty, were now moved to tears by this silent and yet so eloquent leave-taking.

The sacrifice was accomplished. Napoleon had sacrificed his dearest possession to ambition; he had divorced himself from Josephine.

On the same day she left the Tuileries to repair to Malmaison, her future home—to Malmaison, that had once been the paradise, and was now to be the widow's seat, of her love.

Josephine left the court, but the hearts of those who constituted this court did not leave her. During the next few weeks the crowds of the coming and going on the road from Paris to Malmaison presented the appearance of a procession; the equipages of all the kings and princes who were sojourning in Paris, and of all the nobles and dignitaries of the new France, were to be seen there. Even the Faubourg St.-Germain, that still preserved its sympathy for the Bourbons, repaired to the empress at Malmaison. And this pilgrimage was made by the poor and humble, as well as by the rich and great.

All wished to say to the empress that they still loved and honored her, and that she was still enthroned in their hearts, although her rule on the throne was at an end.

The whole people mourned with Josephine and her children. It was whispered about that Napoleon's star would now grow pale; that, with Josephine, his good angel had left him, and that the future would avenge her tears.

————

CHAPTER IX.

THE KING OF HOLLAND.

While Josephine was weeping over her divorce at Malmaison, Hortense was seeking one for herself. A divorce which her mother lamented as a misfortune, because she still loved her husband, would have conferred happiness upon Hortense, who never had loved her husband. Once again in harmony with her husband, Hortense entreated the emperor to permit them to be divorced, and the king united his entreaties with those of the queen.

But Napoleon was unrelenting. His family should not appear before the people as disregarding the sanctity of the marriage bond. For state reasons he had separated from his wife, and for state reasons he could not give his consent to the dissolution of the union of his brother and step-daughter. They must, therefore, continue to drag the chain that united them; and they did, but with angry hearts.

Louis returned to Holland in a more depressed state of mind than ever; while Hortense and her two children, in obedience to Napoleon's express command, remained in Paris for some time. They were to attend the festivities that were soon to take place at the imperial court in honor of the marriage of the emperor with the Archduchess Marie Louise of Austria. The daughter of the divorced empress, with the emperor's sisters, had been selected to carry the train of the new empress on the marriage-day. Napoleon wished to prove to France and to all Europe that there was no other law in his family than his will, and that the daughter of Josephine had never ceased to be his obedient daughter also. Napoleon wished, moreover, to retain near his young wife, in order that she might have at her side a gentle and tender mentor, the queen who had inherited Josephine's grace and loveliness, and who, in her noble womanhood, would set a good example to the ladies of his court. Hortense mutely obeyed the emperor's command; on the 1st of April, 1810, the day of the union of Marie Louise with the emperor, she, together with his sisters, bore the train of the new empress. She alone did this without making any resistance, while it was only after the most violent opposition to Napoleon's command that his sisters, Queen Caroline of Naples, the Duchess Pauline of Guastalla, and the Grand-duchess Elise of Tuscany, consented to undergo the humiliation of walking behind their new sovereign as humble subjects. And the emperor's sisters were not the only persons who regarded the imperial pair with displeasure on the day of the marriage celebration. Only a small number of the high dignitaries of the Church had responded to the invitation of the grand-master of ceremonies, and attended the marriage celebration in the chapel in the Tuileries.

The emperor, who did not wish to punish his sisters for their opposition, could at least punish the absence of the cardinals, and he did this on the following day. He exiled those cardinals who had not appeared in the chapel, forbade them to appear in their red robes thenceforth, and condemned them to the black penitent's dress.

The people of Paris also received the new empress with a languid enthusiasm. They regarded the new "Austrian" with gloomy forebodings; and when, on the occasion of the ball given by Prince Schwartzenberg in honor of the imperial marriage, a short time afterward, the fearful fire occurred that cost so many human lives and destroyed so much family happiness, the people remembered with terror that other misfortune that had occurred on the day of the entry of Marie Antoinette into Paris, and called this fire an earnest of the misfortunes which the "Austrian" would bring upon France and the emperor.

While Hortense was compelled to attend the festivities given in honor of the new empress in Paris, a dark storm-cloud was gathering over her husband's head, that was soon to threaten his life and his crown.

When Louis, at the emperor's command, accepted the crown of Holland, he had solemnly sworn to be a faithful ruler to his new people, and to devote his whole being to their welfare. He was too honest a man not to keep this oath sacredly. His sole endeavor was to make such arrangements, and provide such laws, as the welfare and prosperity of Holland seemed to require, without in the least considering whether these laws were conducive to the interests of France or not. He would not regard Holland as a province dependent upon France, of which he was the governor, but as an independent land that had chosen him to be its free and independent king. But Napoleon did not view the matter in the same light; in his eyes it was sacrilege for the kingdom of Holland to refuse to conform itself in every respect to the interests of its powerful neighbor, France.

When Napoleon invested his brother with the crown of Holland, he had charged him " to be a good king to his people, but at the same time to remain a good Frenchman, and protect the interests of France." Louis had, however, endeavored to become a good Hollander ; and when the interests of France and Holland came into conflict, the king took the side of his new country, and acted as a Hollander. He was of the opinion that the welfare of Holland depended on its commerce and industry only, and that it could only be great through its commercial importance ; he therefore reduced the army and navy, making merchantmen of the men-of-war, and peaceful sailors of their warlike seamen.

Napoleon, however, regarded this conversion with dismay, and angrily reproached the King of Holland for "disarming whole squadrons, discharging seamen, and disorganizing the army, until Holland was without power, both on land and water, as though warehouses and clerks were the material elements of power." Napoleon reproached the king still more bitterly, however, for having re-established commercial relations with England, for having raised the blockade for Holland which France had established against England, and for having permitted the American ships, that had been banished from the ports of France, to anchor quietly in those of Holland.

The emperor demanded of the King of Holland that he should conform himself to his will and to the interests, of France unconditionally ; that he should immediately break off all commercial relations between Holland and England ; that he should re-establish a fleet, of forty ships-of-the-line, seven frigates, and seven brigs, and an army of twenty-five thousand men, and that he should abolish all the privileges of the nobility that were contrary to the constitution.

King Louis had the courage to resist these demands, in the name of Holland, and to refuse to obey instructions, the execution of which must necessarily have affected the material interests of Holland most injuriously.

Napoleon responded to this refusal with a declaration of war. The ambassador of Holland received his passport, and a French army corps was sent to Holland, to punish the king's insolence.

But the misfortune that threatened Holland had called the king's whole energy into activity, and Napoleon's anger and threats were powerless to break his resolution. As the commander of the French troops, the Duke of Reggio, approached Amsterdam, to lay siege to that city and thereby compel the king to yield, Louis determined rather to descend from his throne than to submit to the unjust demands of France. He, therefore, issued a proclamation to his people, in which he told them that he, convinced that he could do nothing more to promote their welfare, and, on the contrary, believing that he was an obstacle in the way of the restoration of friendly relations between his brother and Holland, had determined to abdicate in favor of his two sons, Napoleon Louis and Charles Louis Napoleon. Until they should attain their majority the queen, in conformity with the constitution, was to be regent. He then took leave of his subjects, in a short and touching address. He now repaired, in disguise, and under the name of Count de St. Leu, through the states of his brother Jerome, King of Westphalia, and through Saxony to Töplitz.

Here he learned that Napoleon, far from respecting and fulfilling the conditions of his abdication, had united the kingdom of Holland with the empire. The king published a protest against this action of the emperor, in which, in the name of his son and heir, Napoleon Louis, he denounced this act of the emperor as a totally unjustifiable act of violence, and demanded that the kingdom of

Holland should be re-established, in all its integrity, declaring the annexation of Holland to France to be null and void, in the name of himself and his sons.

Napoleon responded to this protest by causing the king to be informed by the French ambassador in Vienna that unless he returned to France by the 1st of December, 1810, he should be regarded and treated as a rebel, who dared to resist the head of his family and violate the constitution of the empire.

Louis neither answered nor conformed to this threat. He repaired to Grätz, in Styria, and lived there as a private gentleman, beloved and admired, not only by those who came in contact with him there, but enjoying the esteem of all Europe, which he had won by the noble and truly magnanimous manner in which he had sacrificed his own grandeur to the welfare of his people. Even his and Napoleon's enemies could not withhold from the King of Holland the tribute of their respect, and even Louis XVIII. said of him : " By his abdication, Louis Bonaparte has become a true king; in renouncing his crown, he has shown himself worthy to wear it. He is the first monarch who has made so great a sacrifice out of pure love for his people ; others have also relinquished their thrones, but they did it when weary of power. But in this action of the King of Holland there is something truly sublime—something that was not duly appreciated at first, but which will be admired by posterity, if I mistake not, greatly." *

* Mémoires d'une Femme de Qualité, vol. v., p. 47.
10

In Grätz, Louis Bonaparte, Count de St. Leu, lived a few peaceful, tranquil years, perhaps the first years of happiness he had enjoyed in his short and hitherto stormy life. Occupied with work and study, he easily forgot his former grandeur and importance. As it had once been his ambition to become a good king, it was now his ambition to become a good writer. He published his romance Marie, and, encouraged by the success which it met with in his circle of friends, he also gave his poems to the public—poems whose tender and passionate language proved that this so often misunderstood, so often repulsed, and, therefore, so timid and distrustful heart, could warm with a tenderness of love that Marie Pascal, the beautiful artist of the harp, could hardly have had the cruelty to withstand.

But a day came when Louis Bonaparte closed his ear to all these sweet voices of happiness, of peace, and of love, to listen only to the voice of duty, that appealed to him to return to France, to his brother's side. While the sun of fortune shone over Napoleon, the king, who had voluntarily descended from a throne, remained in obscurity; but when the days of misfortune came upon the emperor, there could be but one place for his brave and faithful brother, and that was at Napoleon's side.

Madame de St. Elme, who was at Grätz at this time, and who witnessed the farewell scene between Louis Bonaparte and the inhabitants of Grätz, says: "On the day when Austria so unexpectedly sundered its alliance with France, King Louis felt the necessity of abandoning an

asylum, for which he would henceforth have been indebted to the enemies of France, and hastened to claim
of the great unjust man who had repulsed him, the only
place commensurate with the dignity of his character, the
place at his side.

" This was a subject of profound sorrow and regret
for the inhabitants of Grätz, and of all Styria, for there
was not a pious or useful institution, or a poor family in
Styria, that had not been the object of his beneficence,
and yet it was well known that the king who had descended from his throne so hastily, and with so little
preparation, had but small means, and denied himself
many of the enjoyments of life, in order that he might
lend a helping hand to others. He was entreated, conjured with tears, to remain, but he held firm to his resolution. And when the horses, that they had at first determined to withhold from him, were at last, at his earnest and repeated solicitation, provided, the people unhar-
nessed these horses from his carriage, in order that they
might take their places, and accompany him to the gates
of the city with this demonstration of their love. This
departure had the appearance of a triumphal procession;
and this banished king, without a country, was greeted
with as lively plaudits on leaving his place of exile as
when he mounted his throne." *

* Mémoires d'une contemporaine, vol. iv., p. 377.

CHAPTER X.

JUNOT, THE DUKE D'ABRANTES.

WHILE the faithful were rallying around Napoleon to render assistance to the hero in his hour of peril—while even his brother Louis, forgetting the mortifications and injuries he had sustained at the emperor's hands, hastened to his side, there was one of the most devoted kept away from him by fate—one upon whom the emperor could otherwise have depended in life and death.

This one was his friend and comrade-in-arms, Junot, who, descended from an humble family, had by his merit and heroism elevated himself to the rank of a Duke d'Abrantes. He alone failed to respond when the ominous roll of the war-drum recalled all Napoleon's generals to Paris. But it was not his will, but fate, that kept him away.

Junot—the hero of so many battles, the chevalier without fear and without reproach, the former governor of Madrid, the present governor of Istria and Illyria—Junot was suffering from a visitation of the most fearful of all diseases—his brain was affected! The scars that covered his head and forehead, and testified so eloquently to his gallantry, announced at the same time the source of his disease. His head, furrowed by sabre-strokes, was outwardly healed, but the wounds had affected his brain.

The hero of so many battles was transported into a

madman. And yet, this madman was still the all-powerful, despotic ruler of Istria and Illyria. Napoleon, in appointing him governor of these provinces, had invested him with truly royal authority. Knowing the noble disposition, fidelity, and devotion of his brother-in-arms, he had conferred upon him sovereign power to rule in his stead. There was, therefore, no one who could take the sceptre from his hand, and depose him from his high position. Napoleon had placed this sceptre in his hand, and he alone could demand it of him. Even the Viceroy of Italy—to whom the Chambers of Istria appealed for help in their anxiety—even Eugene, could afford them no relief. He could only say to them: "Send a courier to the emperor, and await his reply."

But at that time it was not so easy a matter to send couriers a distance of a thousand miles; then there were no railroads, no telegraphs. The Illyrians immediately sent a courier to the emperor, with an entreaty for their relief, but the Russian proverb, "Heaven is high, and the emperor distant," applied to them also! Weeks must elapse before the courier could return with the emperor's reply; until then, there was no relief; and until then, there was no authority to obey but the Duke d'Abrantes, the poor madman!

No other authority, no institution, had the right to place itself in his stead, or to assume his prerogatives for an instant even, without violating the seal of sovereignty that Napoleon had impressed on the brow of his governor!

Napoleon, whose crown was already trembling on his head, who was already so near his own fall, still possessed such gigantic power that its reflection sufficed to protect, at a distance of a thousand miles from the boundaries of France, the inviolability of a man who had lost his reason, and no longer had the power of reflection and volition.

How handsome, how amiable, how chivalrous, had Junot been in his earlier days! How well he had known how to charm beautiful women in the drawing-rooms, soldiers on the battle-field, and knights at the tourney! In all knightly accomplishments he was the master— always and everywhere the undisputed victor and hero. These accomplishments had won the heart of Mademoiselle de Premont. The daughter of the proud baroness of the Faubourg St. Germain had joyfully determined, in spite of her mother's dismay, to become the wife of the soldier of the republic, of Napoleon's comrade-in-arms. Although Junot had no possession but his pay, and no nobility but his sword and his renown, this nevertheless sufficed to win him the favor of the daughter of this aristocratic mother—of the daughter who was yet so proud of being the last descendant of the Comneni. Napoleon, who loved to see matrimonial alliances consummated between his generals and his nobility and the old legitimist nobility of France, rewarded the daughter of the Faubourg St. Germain richly for the sacrifice she had made for his comrade-in-arms, in giving up her illustrious name, and her coat-of-arms, to become the wife of a general without ancestors and without fortune. He made his friend a duke, and the Duchess d'Abrantes had no longer cause to be ashamed of her title; the descendant of the Comneni could content herself with the homage done her as the wife of the governor of Lisbon, contented with the laurels that adorned her husband's brow—laurels to which he added a new branch, but also new wounds, on every battle-field.

The consequences of these wounds had veiled the hero's laurels with mourning-crape, and destroyed the domestic happiness of the poor duchess forever. She had first discovered her husband's sad condition, but she had known how to keep it a secret from the rest of the world. She had, however, refused to accompany the duke to Illyria, and had remained in Paris, still hoping that the change of climate and associations might restore him to health.

But her hopes were not to be realized. The attacks of madness, that had hitherto occurred at long intervals only, now became more frequent, and were soon no longer a secret. All Illyria knew that its governor was a madman, and yet no one dared to oppose his will, or to refuse to obey his commands; all still bowed to his will, in humility and silent submissiveness, hopefully awaiting the return of the courier who had been dispatched to Napoleon at Paris.

"But heaven is high, and the emperor distant!" And much evil could happen, and did happen, before the courier returned to Trieste, where Junot resided.

The poor duke's condition grew worse daily; his attacks
of madness became more frequent and more dangerous,
and broke out on the slightest provocation.

On one occasion a nightingale, singing in the bushes
beneath his window, had disturbed his rest; on the following morning he caused the general alarm to be
sounded, and two battalions of Croats to be drawn up in
the park, to begin a campaign against the poor nightingale, who had dared to disturb his repose.

On another occasion, Junot fancied he had discovered a grand conspiracy of all the sheep of Illyria;
against this conspiracy he brought the vigilance of the
police, all the means of the administration, and the whole
severity of the law, into requisition for its suppression.

At another time, he suddenly became desperately
enamoured of a beautiful Greek girl, who belonged to
his household. Upon her refusal to meet his advances
favorably, a passionate desperation took possession of Junot, and he determined to set fire to his palace, and perish with his love in the flames. Fortunately, his purpose was discovered, and the fire he had kindled stifled
at once.

He would suddenly be overcome with a passionate
distaste for the grandeur and splendor that surrounded
him, and long to lay aside his brilliant position, and fly
to the retirement of an humble and obscure life.

It was his dearest wish to become a peasant, and be
able to live in a hut; and, as there was no one who had
the right to divest him of his high dignities and grant

his desire, he formed the resolution to divest himself of this oppressive grandeur, by the exercise of his own fulness of power, and to withdraw himself from the annoyances imposed upon him by his high position.

Under the pretence of visiting the provinces, he left Trieste, to lead for a few weeks an entirely new life—a life that seemed, for a brief period, to soothe his excited mind. He arrived, almost incognito, in the little city of Gorizia, and demanded to be conducted to the most unpretending establishment to which humble and honest laborers were in the habit of resorting for refreshment and relaxation. He was directed to an establishment called the Ice-house, a place to which poor daily laborers resorted, to repose after the labors of the day, and refresh themselves with a glass of beer or wine.

In this Ice-house the governor of Illyria now took up his abode. He seldom quitted it, either by day or night; and here, like Haroun-al-Raschid, he took part in the harmless merriment of happy and contented poverty. And here this poor man was to find a last delight, a last consolation; here he was to find a last friend.

This last friend of the Duke d'Abrantes—this Pylades of the poor Orestes—was—a madman!—a poor simpleton, of good family, who was so good-humored and harmless that he was allowed to go at large, and free scope given to his innocent freaks. He, however, possessed a kind of droll, pointed wit, which he sometimes brought to bear most effectively, sparing neither rank nor position. The half-biting, half-droll remarks of this

Diogenes of Istria was all that now afforded enjoyment to the broken-down old hero. It was with intense delight that he heard the social grandeur and distinctions that had cost him so dear made ridiculous by this half-witted fellow, whose peculiar forte it was to jeer at the pomp that surrounded the governor, and imitate French elegance in a highly-burlesque manner; and when he did this, his poor princely friend's delight knew no bounds.

On one occasion, after the poor fellow had been en-tertaining him in this manner, the Duke d'Abrantes threw himself, in his enthusiasm, in his friend's arms, and invested him with the insignia of the Legion of Honor, by hanging around his neck the grand-cross of this order hitherto worn by himself. The emperor had given Junot authority to distribute this order to the deserving throughout the provinces of Illyria and Istria, and the governor himself having invested this mad Diogenes with the decoration, there was no one who was competent to deprive him of it. For weeks this mad fool was to be seen in the streets of Gorizia, parading himself like a peacock, with the grand-cross of the honorable order of the Emperor Napoleon, and, at the same time, uttering the most pointed and biting *bon mots* at the expense of his own decoration. The duke often accompanied him in his wanderings through the town, sometimes laughing loudly at the fool's jests, sometimes listening with earnest attention, as though his utterances were oracles. Thus this strange couple passed the time, either lounging through the streets together, or seated side by side on a stone by the way, engaged in curious reflections on the passers-by, or philosophizing over the emptiness of all glory and grandeur, and over the littleness and malice of the world, realizing the heart-rending, impressive scenes between Lear and his fool, which Shakespeare's genius has depicted.

After weeks of anxious suspense, the imperial message, relieving Junot of his authority, and placing the Duke of Otranto in his place, at last arrived. The poor Duke d'Abrantes left Illyria, and returned to France, where, in the little town of Maitbart, after long and painful struggles, he ended, in sadness and solitude, a life of renown, heroism, and irreproachable integrity.

CHAPTER XI.

LOUIS NAPOLEON AS A VENDER OF VIOLETS.

GRADUALLY, the brilliancy of the sun that had so long dazzled the eyes of all Europe began to wax pale, and the luminous star of Napoleon to grow dim among the dark clouds that were gathering around him. Fortune had accorded him all that it could bestow upon a mortal. It had laid all the crowns of Europe at his feet, and made him master of all the monarchies and peoples. Napoleon's antechamber in Erfurt and in Dresden had been the rendezvous of the emperors, kings, and princes of Europe, and England alone had never disguised its

hostility beneath the mask of friendship, and bent the
knee to a hated and feared neighbor. Napoleon, the
master of Europe, whom emperors and kings gladly
called "brother," could now proudly remember his past;
he had now risen so high that he no longer had cause
to deny his humble origin; this very lowliness had now
become a new triumph of his grandeur.

On one occasion, during the congress at Erfurt, all
the emperors, kings, and princes, were assembled around
Napoleon's table. He occupied the seat between his enthusiastic friend the Emperor of Russia, and his father-
in-law, the Emperor of Austria. Opposite them sat the
King of Prussia, his ally, although Napoleon had deprived him of the Rhine provinces; and the Kings of
Bavaria and Würtemberg, to whom Napoleon had given
crowns, whose electorate and duchy he had converted
into kingdoms, and of whom the first had given his
daughter in marriage to Napoleon's adopted son, Eugene,
and the second his daughter to Napoleon's brother Jerome. There were, further, at the table, the King of
Saxony and the Grand-duke of Baden, to the latter of
whom Napoleon had given the hand of Josephine's
niece, Stephanie de Beauharnais. All these were princes,
" by the grace of God," of brilliant and haughty dynasties; and in their midst sat the son of the advocate of
Corsica—he, the Emperor of France—he, upon whom the
gaze of all these emperors and kings was fastened in admiration and respect. Napoleon's extraordinary memory
had just been the topic of conversation, and the emperor

was about to explain how he had brought it to such a
state of perfection.

"While I was still a sub-lieutenant," began Napoleon,
and instantly his hearers let fall their gaze, and looked
down in shame at their plates, while a cloud of displeasure passed over the brow of the emperor of Austria at
this mention of the low origin of his son-in-law. Napoleon observed this, and for an instant his eagle glance
rested on the embarrassed countenances that surrounded
him; he then paused for a moment. He began again,
speaking with sharp emphasis: "When I still had the
honor of being a sub-lieutenant," said he, and the Emperor Alexander of Russia, the only one of the princes
who had remained unembarrassed, laid his hand on the
emperor's shoulder, smiled approvingly, and listened with
interest and pleasure to the emperor's narrative of the
time when he "still had the honor of being a sub-lieutenant." *

Napoleon, as we have said, had already mounted so
high that for him there was no longer a summit to be
attained, and now his heart's last and dearest wish had
been granted by destiny. His wife, Marie Louise, had
given birth to a son on the 20th of May, 1811, and the
advent of the little King of Rome had fulfilled the
warmest desires of Napoleon and of France. The emperor now had an heir; Napoleon's dynasty was assured.

Festivities were therefore held in honor of this event,
in the Tuileries, at the courts of the Queen of Naples, of

* Bossuet, Mémoires, vol. v.

the Grand-duchess de Guastalla, of all the dukes of the empire, and of the Queen of Holland.

Hortense was ill and in pain ; a nervous headache, that she had been suffering from for some time, betrayed the secret of the pain and grief she had so long concealed from observation. Her cheeks had grown pale, and her eyes had lost their lustre. Her mother wept over her lost happiness in Malmaison, and, when Hortense had wept with and consoled her mother, she was compelled to dry her eyes and hasten to the Tuileries, and appear, with a smiling countenance, before her who was now her empress and her mother's happy rival.

But Hortense had accepted her destiny, and was determined to demean herself as became her own and her mother's dignity. She endeavored to be a true and sincere friend to the young empress, and fulfil the emperor's wishes, and to give brilliant entertainments in honor of the King of Rome, in spite of the pain it must cost her. "The emperor wills it, the emperor requires it ;" that was sufficient for all who were about him, and it was sufficient for her. Her mother had gone because it was his will, she had remained because it was his will, and she now gave these entertainments for the same reason. But there was an element of sadness and gloom even in these festivities of the carnival of 1813 ; the presence of so many cripples and invalids recalled the memory of the reverses of the past year. At the balls there was a great scarcity of young men who could dance ; incessant wars had made the youth of France old before their time, and had converted vigorous men into cripples.

Her heart filled with dark forebodings, Hortense silently prepared herself against the days of misfortune which she knew must inevitably come. When these days should come, she wished to be ready to meet them with a brave heart and a resolute soul, and she also endeavored to impress on the minds of her two beloved sons the inconstancy of fortune, in order that they might look misfortune boldly in the face. She had no compassion with the tender youth of these boys, who were now eight and six years old; no compassion, because she loved them too well not to strive to prepare them for adversity.

One day the Duchess of Bassano gave a ball in honor of the queen, and Hortense, although low-spirited and indisposed, summoned her resolution to her aid, and arrayed herself for the occasion. Her blond hair, that reached to her feet when unbound, was dressed in the ancient Greek style, and adorned with a wreath of flowers, not natural flowers, however, but consisting of Hortensias in diamonds. Her dress was of pink-crape embroidered with Hortensias in silver. The hem of her dress and its train was encircled with a garland of flowers composed of roses and violets. A bouquet of Hortensias in diamonds glittered on her bosom, and her necklace and bracelets consisted of little diamond Hortensias. In this rich and tasteful attire, a present sent her by the Empress Josephine the day before, Hortense

entered the parlor where the ladies and gentlemen of her
court awaited her, brilliantly arrayed for the occasion.

The parlor, filled with these ladies glittering with
diamonds, and with these cavaliers in their rich, gold-
embroidered uniforms, presented a brilliant spectacle.
The queen's two sons, who came running into the room
at this moment to bid their "bonne petite maman" adieu,
stood still for an instant, dazzled by this magnificence,
and then timidly approached the mother who seemed to
them a queen from the fairy-realm floating in rosy
clouds. The queen divined the thoughts of her boys,
whose countenances were for her an open book in which
she read every emotion.

She extended a hand to each of her children, and led
them to a sofa, on which she seated herself, taking the
youngest, Louis Napoleon, who was scarcely six years
old, in her lap, while his elder brother, Napoleon Louis,
stood at her side, his curly head resting on Hortense's
shoulder, gazing tenderly into the pale, expressive face
of his beautiful mother.

"I am very prettily dressed to-day, am I not, Napoleon?" said Hortense, laying her little hand, that sparkled
with diamonds, on the head of her eldest son. "Would
you like me less if I were poor, and wore no diamonds,
but merely a plain black dress? Would you love me less
then?"

"No, *maman!*" exclaimed the boy, almost angrily,
and little Louis Napoleon, who sat in his mother's lap,
repeated in his shrill little voice: "No, *maman!*"

The queen smiled. "Diamonds and dress do not constitute happiness, and we three would love each other just as much if we had no jewelry, and were poor. But tell me, Napoleon, if you had nothing, and were entirely alone in the world, what would you do for yourself?"

"I would become a soldier," cried Napoleon, with sparkling eyes, "and I would fight so bravely that I should soon be made an officer."

"And you, Louis, what would you do to earn your daily bread?"

The little fellow had listened earnestly to his brother's words, and seemed to be thinking over them still. Perhaps he felt that the knapsack and musket were too heavy for his little shoulders, and that he was, as yet, too weak to become a soldier.

"I," said he, after a pause, "I would sell bouquets of violets, like the little boy who stands at the gates of the Tuileries, and from whom we buy our flowers every day."

The ladies and cavaliers, who had listened to this curious conversation in silence, now laughed loudly at this naive reply of the little prince.

"Do not laugh, ladies," said the queen, earnestly, as she now arose; "it was no jest, but a lesson that I gave my children, who were so dazzled by jewelry. It is the misfortune of princes that they believe that everything is subject to them, that they are made of another stuff than other men, and have no duties to perform. They know nothing of human suffering and want, and do not believe that they can ever be affected by anything of the kind.

11

And this is why they are so astounded, and remain so helpless, when the hand of misfortune does strike them. I wish to preserve my sons from this." *

She then stooped and kissed her boys, who, while she and her brilliant suite were driving to the Tuileries, busied their little heads, considering whether it was easier to earn one's bread as a soldier, or by selling violets at the gates of the Tuileries, like the little beggar-boy.

———

CHAPTER XII.

THE DAYS OF MISFORTUNE.

THE round of festivities with which the people of France endeavored to banish the shadow of impending misfortune, was soon to be abruptly terminated. The thunder of the cannon on the battle-fields of Hanau and Leipsic silenced the dancing-music in the Tuileries; and in the drawing-rooms of Queen Hortense, hitherto devoted to music and literature, the ladies were now busily engaged in picking lint for the wounded who were daily arriving at the hospitals of Paris from the army. The declaration of war of Austria and Russia had aroused France from its haughty sense of invincibility. All felt that a crisis was at hand. All were preparing for the ominous events that were gathering like storm-clouds over France. Each of the faithful hastened to assume

* The queen's own words.

the position to which honor and duty called him. And it was in response to such an appeal that Louis Bonaparte now returned from Grätz to Paris; he had heard the ominous tones of the voice that threatened the emperor, and wished to be at his side in the hour of danger.

It was not as the wife, but in the spirit of a French-woman and a queen, that Hortense received the intelligence of her husband's return. "I am delighted to hear it," said she; "my husband is a good Frenchman, and he proves it by returning at the moment when all Europe has declared against France. He is a man of honor, and if our characters could not be made to harmonize, it was probably because we both had defects that were irreconcilable.

"I," added she, with a gentle smile, "I was too proud, I had been spoiled, and was probably too deeply impressed with a sense of my own worth; and this defect is not conducive to pleasant relations with one who is distrustful and low-spirited. But our interests were always the same, and his hastening to France, to enroll himself with all his brother Frenchmen, for the defence of his country, is worthy of the king's character. It is only by doing thus that we can testify our gratitude for the benefits the people have conferred upon our family." *

In the first days of January, 1814, the news that the enemy had crossed the boundaries of France, and that the Austrians, Russians, and Prussians, were marching on Paris, created a panic throughout the entire city. For

* Cochelet, Mémoires sur la reine Hortense, vol. i., p. 167.

the first time, after so many years of triumph, France
trembled for its proud army, and believed in the possibility of defeat.

In the Tuileries, also, gloom and dejection ruled the
hour for the first time; and while, when the army had
heretofore gone forth, the question had been, "When
shall we receive the first intelligence of victory?" there
were now only mute, inquiring glances bent on the emperor's clouded countenance.

On the 24th of January, Napoleon left Paris, in order to repair to the army. The empress, whom he had
made regent, giving her a council, consisting of his
brothers and the ministers, as a support—the empress
had taken leave of him in a flood of tears, and Queen
Hortense, who had alone been present on this occasion,
had been compelled to remain for some time with the
empress, in order to console and encourage her.

But Hortense was far from feeling the confidence
which she exhibited in the presence of the empress and
of her own court. She had never believed in the duration of these triumphs and of this fortune; she had
always awaited the coming evil in silent expectation,
and she was therefore now ready to face it bravely, and
to defend herself and her children against its attacks.
She therefore was calm and self-possessed, while the entire imperial family was terror-stricken, while all Paris
was in a panic, while the fearful intelligence, "The Cossacks are coming, the Cossacks are marching on Paris!"
was overrunning the city. "The Grand-duke Constan-

tine has promised his troops that they shall warm themselves at the burning ruins of Paris, and the Emperor Alexander has sworn that he will sleep in the Tuileries."

Nothing was now dreamed of but plundering, murder, and rapine; people trembled not only for their lives, but also for their property, and hastened to bury their treasures, their jewelry, their gold and silver, to secure it from the rapacious hands of the terrible Cossacks. Treasures were buried in cellars, or hid away in the walls of houses. The Duchess de Bassano caused all her valuable effects to be put in a hidden recess, and the entrance to the same to be walled up and covered with paper. There were among these valuable effects several large clocks, in golden cases, that were richly studded with precious stones, but it had unfortunately been forgotten to stop them, so that for the next week they continued to strike the hours regularly, and thereby betrayed to the neighbors the secret the duchess had so anxiously endeavored to conceal.

But the cry, "The Cossacks are coming!" was not the only alarm-cry of the Parisians. Another, and a long-silent cry, was now heard in Paris—a strange cry, that had no music for the ear of the imperialist, but one that, to the royalist, had a sweet and familiar sound. This cry was, "The Count de Lille!" or, as the royalists said, "King Louis XVIII." The royalists no longer whispered this name, but proclaimed it loudly and with enthusiasm, and even those of them who had attached themselves to the imperial court, and played a part at

the same, now dared to remove their masks a little, and
show their true countenance.

Madame Ducayla, one of the most zealous royalists,
although attached to the court society of the Tuileries,
had gone to Hartwell, to convey to him messages of love
and respect in the name of all the royalists of Paris, and
to tell him that they had now begun to smooth the way
for his return to France and the throne of his ancestors.
She had returned with authority to organize the conspiracy of the royalists, and to give them the king's sanction.   Talleyrand, the minister of Napoleon, the glittering weathercock in politics, had already experienced a
change in disposition, in consequence of the shifting political wind, and when Countess Ducayla, provided with
secret instructions for Talleyrand from Louis XVIII.,
entered his cabinet and said in a loud voice, " I come
from Hartwell, I have seen the king, and he has instructed me—" he interrupted her in loud and angry
tones, exclaiming : " Are you mad, madame ?   You dare
to confess such a crime to me ? "   He had, however,
then added in a low voice : " You have seen him, then ?
Well, I am his most devoted servant." *

The royalists held meetings and formed conspiracies
with but little attempt at concealment, and the minister
of police, Fouché, whose eyes and ears were always on
the alert, and who knew of everything that occurred in
Paris, also knew of these conspiracies of the royalists;
he did not prevent them, however, but advised caution,

* Mémoires d'une femme de qualité, vol. i., p. 133.

endeavoring to prove to them thereby the deep reverence which he himself experienced for the unfortunate royal family.

In the midst of all this confusion and anxiety, Queen Hortense alone preserved her composure and courage, and far from endeavoring, like others, to conceal and secure her treasures, jewelry, and other valuables, she determined to make no change or reduction whatever in her manner of living; she wished to show the Parisians that the confidence of the imperial family in the emperor and his invincibility was not to be shaken. She therefore continued to conduct her household in truly royal style, although she had received from the exhausted state treasury no payment of the appanage set apart for herself and children for a period of three months. But she thought little of this; her generous heart was occupied with entirely different interests than those of her own pecuniary affairs.

She wished to inspire Marie Louise, whom the emperor had constituted empress-regent on his departure for the army, with the courage which she herself possessed. She conjured her to show herself worthy of the confidence the emperor had reposed in her at this critical time, and to adopt firm and energetic measures. When, on the 28th of March, the terror-inspiring news was circulated that the hostile armies were only five leagues from Paris, and while the people were flying from the city in troops, Hortense hastened to the Tuileries to conjure the empress to be firm, and not to leave Paris. She entreated Marie Louise, in the name of the emperor, her husband, and the King of Rome, her son, not to heed the voice of the state council, who, after a long sitting, had unanimously declared that Paris could not be held, and that the empress, with her son and her council, should therefore leave the capital.

But Marie Louise had remained deaf to all these pressing and energetic representations, and the queen had not been able to inspire her young and weak sister-in-law with her own resolution.

"My sister," Hortense had said to her, "you will at least understand that by leaving Paris now you paralyze its defence, and thereby endanger your crown, but I see that you are resigned to this sacrifice."

"It is true," Marie Louise had sadly replied. "I well know that I should act differently, but it is too late. The state council has decided, and I can do nothing!"

In sadness and dejection Hortense had then returned to her dwelling, where Lavalette, Madame Ney, and the ladies of her court, awaited her.

"All is lost," said she, sadly. "Yes, all is lost. The empress has determined to leave Paris. She lightly abandons France and the emperor. She is about to depart."

"If she does that," exclaimed General Lavalette, in despair, "then all is really lost, and yet her firmness and courage might now save the emperor, who is advancing toward Paris by forced marches. After all this weighing and deliberating, they have elected to take the worst course they could choose! But, as this has finally been determined on, what course will your majesty now pursue ? "

" I remain in Paris," said the queen, resolutely ; " as I am permitted to be mistress of my own actions, I am resolved to remain here and share the fortunes of the Parisians, be they good or evil ! This is at least a better and worthier course than to incur the risk of being made a prisoner on the public highway."

Now that she had come to a decision, the queen exhibited a joyous determination, and her mind recovered from its depression. She hastened to dispatch a courier to Malmaison to the Empress Josephine, now forgotten and neglected by all, to conjure her to leave for Novara at once. She then retired to her bedchamber to seek the rest she so much needed after so many hours of excitement.

But at midnight she was aroused from her repose to a sad awakening. Her husband, with whom she had held no kind of intercourse since his return, had now, in the hour of danger, determined to assert his marital authority over his wife and children. He wrote the queen a letter, requiring her to leave Paris with her children, and follow the empress.

Hortense replied with a decided refusal. A second categoric message from her husband was the response. He declared that if she should not at once conform to his will, and follow the empress with her children, he would immediately take his children into his own custody, by virtue of his authority as husband and father.

At this threat, the queen sprang up like an enraged lioness from her lair. With glowing cheeks and sparkling eyes she commanded that her children should be at once brought to her, and then, pressing her two boys to her heart with passionate tenderness, she exclaimed : " Tell the king that I shall leave the city within the hour ! "

CHAPTER XIII.

THE ALLIES IN PARIS.

THE anxiety of motherly love had effected what neither the departure of the empress nor the news of the approach of the Cossacks could do. Hortense had taken her departure. She had quitted Paris, with her children and suite, which had already begun to grow sensibly smaller, and arrived, after a hurried flight, endangered by bands of marauding Cossacks, in Novara, where the Empress Josephine, with tears of sorrow and of joy alike, pressed her daughter to her heart. Although her own happiness and grandeur were gone, and although the misfortunes of the Emperor Napoleon—whom she still dearly loved—oppressed her heart, Josephine now had her daughter and dearest friend at her side, and that was a sweet consolation in the midst of all these misfortunes and cares.

At Novara, Hortense received the intelligence of the fall of the empire, of the capitulation of Paris, of the entrance of the allies, and of the abdication of Napoleon.

When the courier sent by the Duke of Bassano with this intelligence further informed the Empress Josephine that the island of Elba had been assigned Napoleon as a domicile, and that he was on the point of leaving France to go into exile, Josephine fell, amid tears of anguish, into her daughter's arms, crying : " Hortense, he is unhappy, and I am not with him ! He is banished to Elba ! Alas ! but for his wife, I would hasten to his side, to share his exile ! "

While the empress was weeping and lamenting, Hortense had silently withdrawn to her apartments. She saw and fully appreciated the consequences that must ensue to the emperor's entire family, from his fall ; she already felt the mortifications and insults to which the Bonapartes would now be exposed from all quarters, and she wished to withdraw herself and children from their influence. She formed a quick resolve, and determined to carry it out at once. She caused Mademoiselle de Cochelet, one of the few ladies of her court who had remained faithful, to be called, in order that she might impart to her her resolution.

" Louise," said she, " I intend to emigrate. I am alone and defenceless, and ever threatened by a misfortune that would be more cruel than the loss of crown and grandeur—the misfortune of seeing my children torn from me by my husband. My mother can remain in France—her divorce has made her free and independent;

but I bear a name that will no longer be gladly heard in France, now that the Bourbons are returning. I have no other fortune than my diamonds. These I shall sell, and then go, with my children, to my mother's estate in Martinique. I lived there when a child, and have retained a pleasant remembrance of the place. It is undoubtedly hard to be compelled to give up country, mother, and friends; but one must face these great strokes of destiny courageously. I will give my children a good education, and that shall be my consolation."

Mademoiselle de Cochelet burst into tears, kissed the queen's extended hand, and begged so earnestly that she might be permitted to accompany her, that Hortense at last gave a reluctant consent. It was arranged between them that Louise should hasten to Paris, in order to make the necessary preparations for the queen's long journey; and she departed on this mission, under the protection of the courier, on the following morning.

How changed and terrible was the aspect Paris presented on her arrival! At the gate through which they entered Cossacks stood on guard; the streets were filled with Russian, Austrian, and Prussian soldiery, at whose side the proud ladies of the Faubourg St. Germain were to be seen walking, in joyous triumph, bestowing upon the vanquishers of France as great a devotion as they could have lavished upon the beloved Bourbons themselves, whose return was expected in a few days.

A Swedish regiment was quartered in the queen's dwelling; her servants had fled; her glittering drawing-rooms now sheltered the conquerors of France; and in the Tuileries preparations were already being made for the reception of the Bourbons.

No one dared to pronounce the name of Napoleon. Those who were formerly his most zealous flatterers were now the most ready to condemn him. Those upon whom he had conferred the greatest benefits were now the first to deny him, hoping thereby to wipe out the remembrance of the benefits they had received. The most zealous Napoleonists now became the most ardent royalists, and placed the largest white cockades in their hats, in order that they might the sooner attract the attention of the new rulers.

But there was still one man who pronounced the name of Napoleon loudly, and with affectionate admiration, and publicly accorded him the tribute of his respect.

This one was the Emperor Alexander of Russia. He had loved Napoleon so dearly, that even the position of hostility which policy compelled him to assume could not banish from his heart friendship for the hero who had so long ruled Europe.

Napoleon's fate was decided; and it was attributable to the zealous efforts of the czar that the allies had consented to the emperor's demands, and appointed him sovereign of the island of Elba. Now that Alexander could do nothing more for Napoleon, he desired to make himself useful to his family, at least, and thereby testify the admiration which he still felt for the fallen Titan.

The Empress Marie Louise and the little King of

Rome had no need of his assistance. The empress had not availed herself of the permission of the allies to accompany her husband to Elba, but had placed herself and son under the protection of her father, the Emperor of Austria.

The Emperor Alexander therefore bestowed his whole sympathy upon Napoleon's divorced wife and her children, the Viceroy of Italy and the Queen of Holland. He took so great an interest in the queen, that he declared his intention, in case Hortense should not come to Paris, of going to Novara to see her, in order to learn from her own lips in what manner he could serve her, and how she desired that her future should be shaped.

Count Nesselrode, the emperor's minister, was also zealous in his endeavors to serve the queen. The count had long been the intimate friend of Louise de Cochelet; and, desirous of giving her a further proof of his friendship, he knew of no better way of doing so than by rendering a service to Queen Hortense and her children. Louise informed the count of the queen's intended departure for Martinique. Count Nesselrode smiled sadly over this desperate resolve of a brave mother's heart, and instructed Louise to beg the queen to impart to him, through her confidante, all her wishes and demands, in order that he might lay them before the emperor.

The queen's fate was the subject of great sympathy in all quarters. When, in one of the sessions of the ministers of the allies, in which the fate of France, of the Bourbons, and of the Bonapartes, was to be the subject of deliberation, the question of making some provision for the emperor's family came up for consideration, the Prince of Benevento exclaimed : "I plead for Queen Hortense alone ; for she is the only one for whom I have any esteem." Count Nesselrode added : " Who would not be proud to claim her as a countrywoman ? She is the pearl of her France ! " And Metternich united with the rest in her praise.*

But it was in vain that Louise de Cochelet imparted this intelligence to the queen ; the entreaties and representations of her friends were powerless to persuade Hortense to leave her retirement and come to Paris.

The following letter of the queen, written to Louise, concerning her affairs, will testify to her beautiful and womanly sentiments. This letter is as follows :

" MY DEAR LOUISE,—You and all my friends write me the same questions : ' What do you want ? What do you demand ?' I reply to all of you : I want nothing whatever ! What should I desire ? Is not my fate already determined ? When one has the strength to form a great resolution, and when one can firmly and calmly contemplate the idea of making a journey to India or America, it is unnecessary to demand any thing of any one. I entreat you to take no steps that I should be compelled to disavow ; I know that you love me, and this might induce you to do so. I am really not to be pitied ; it was in the midst of grandeur and splendor that I have suffered ! I

* Cochelet, vol. i., p 270.

shall now, perhaps, learn the happiness of retirement, and prefer it to all the magnificence that once surrounded me. I do not believe I can remain in France ; the lively interest now shown in my behalf might eventually occasion mistrust. This idea is annihilating ; I feel it, but I shall not willingly occasion sorrow to any one. My brother will be happy ; my mother can remain in her country, and retain her estates. I, with my children, shall go to a foreign land, and, as the happiness of those I love is assured, I shall be able to bear the misfortune that strikes only at my material interests, but not at my heart. I am still deeply moved and confounded by the fate that has overtaken the Emperor Napoleon and his family. Is it true ? Has all been finally determined ? Write me on this subject. I hope that my children will not be taken from me ; in that case I should lose all courage. I will so educate them that they shall be happy in any station of life. I shall teach them to bear fortune and misfortune with equal dignity, and to seek true happiness in contentment with themselves. This is worth more than crowns. Fortunately, they are healthy. Thank Count Nesselrode for his sympathy. I assure you there are days that are properly called days of misfortune, and that are yet not without a charm ; such are those that enable us to discern the true sentiments people hold toward us. I rejoice over the affection which you show me, and it will always afford me gratification to tell you that I return it.   HORTENSE." *

* Cochelet, vol. i., pp. 275–277.

CHAPTER XIV.

CORRESPONDENCE BETWEEN THE QUEEN AND LOUISE DE COCHELET.

In the meanwhile, Hortense was still living with her mother in Novara, firmly resolved to remain in her retirement, sorrowing over the fate of the imperial house, but quite indifferent as to her own fate.

But her friends—and even in misfortune Hortense still had friends—and above all her truest friend, Louise de Cochelet, busied themselves all the more about her future, endeavoring to rescue out of the general wreck of the imperial house at least a few fragments for the queen.

Louise de Cochelet was still sojourning in Paris, and the letters which she daily wrote to the queen at Novara, and in which she informed her of all that was taking place in the city, are so true a picture of that strange and confused era, that we cannot refrain from here inserting some of them.

In one of her first letters Louise de Cochelet relates a conversation which she had had with Count Nesselrode, in relation to the queen's future.

"The Bourbons," she writes, "have now been finally accepted. I asked Count Nesselrode, whom I have just left : 'Do you believe that the queen will be permitted to remain in France? Will the new rulers consider this proper?' 'Certainly,' he replied, 'I am sure of it, for

12

we will make it a condition with them, and without us they would never have come to the throne at all! It is not the Bourbons, but it is we, it is all Europe, that arranges and regulates these matters. I therefore trust that they will never violate the agreement. Rest assured that the Emperor Alexander will always support the right.'

" All of these strangers here speak of you, madame, with great enthusiasm. Metternich, who doubtlessly recollects your great kindness to his wife and children, inquired after you with lively interest. Prince Leopold is devotedly attached to yourself and the Empress Josephine, and ardently desires to be able to serve you both. Count Nesselrode thinks it would be well for you to write to the Emperor Alexander, as he takes so warm an interest in your affairs.

" The old nobility is already much discontented; it considers itself debased, because it sees itself mixed with so many new elements."

" Come to Malmaison with the empress," she writes a few days later, " the Emperor Alexander will then go there at once to meet you; he is anxious to make your acquaintance, and you already owe him some thanks, as he devotes himself to your interests as though they were his own. The Duke of Vicenza, who demeans himself so worthily with regard to the Emperor Napoleon, requests me to inform you that the future of your children depends on your coming to Malmaison.

" The Emperor Napoleon has signed an agreement,

that secures the future of all the members of his family ;
you can remain in France, and retain your titles.   You
are to have for yourself and children an income of four
hundred thousand francs.

" It is said here that the Faubourg St. Germain is
furious over the brilliant positions provided for the imperial family and the empress.   This is their gratitude
for all her goodness to them.

" You wish to make Switzerland your home.   Count
Nesselrode thinks you may be right, that it is a good retreat; but you should not give up the one you have
here, and should in any event retain the right to return
to France.

" Fancy, madame, Count Nesselrode insists on my
seeing his emperor !   I have not yet consented, because
I do not like to do any thing without your assent; but I
confess I long to make his acquaintance.   I am made
quite happy by hearing you so well spoken of here.

" Count Nesselrode said to me yesterday : ' Tell the
queen that I shall be happy to fulfil all her wishes, and
that I can do so, that I have the power.'   For great security he wishes to have a future assured you that shall
be independent of the treaty.   I do not know what to
say to him.   Write to me, and demand something, I conjure you ! "

The queen's only response to this appeal was a letter
addressed to the Emperor Napoleon, and sent to Count
Nesselrode, with the request that it should be forwarded
to its destination.

"It is strange," wrote Louise de Cochelet in relation to this matter—"strange that all my efforts to serve you here have had no other result than your sending a commission to Count Nesselrode to forward to Fontainebleau a letter addressed to the Emperor Napoleon. He at first thought I was bringing him the letter he had solicited for his emperor; but he well knows how to appreciate all that is noble and great, and as he possesses the most admirable tact, he thinks the letter cannot well reach the emperor through him, and will therefore send it to the Duke of Vicenza, at Fontainebleau, to be delivered by him to the Emperor Napoleon."

Another letter of Louise de Cochelet is as follows: "I have just seen Count Nesselrode again; he makes many inquiries concerning you; the Emperor of Russia now resides on the Elysée Bourbon. The count tells me a story that is in circulation here, and has reference to the Empress Marie Louise and the kings her brothers-in-law. They were about to force her to enter a carriage, in which they were to continue their journey with her; when she refused to enter, it is said the King of Westphalia became so violent that he gave her a little beating. She cried for help, and General Caffarelli,* who commanded the guards, came to her rescue. On the following day she and her son were made prisoners, and all

* According to Napoleon's instructions, his brothers were to prevent the empress and the King of Rome from falling into the hands of the enemy. De Baussue narrates this scene in his memoirs, and it is self-evident that it was not so stormy as the gossip of Paris portrayed it.

the crown diamonds in her possession seized by the authorities; but it seems as though capture was precisely
what she wished.

"The Queen of Westphalia has just arrived in Paris;
the Emperor Alexander, her cousin, called on her immediately. It is supposed that she will return to her father.

"Your brother's future is not yet determined on, but
it will certainly be a desirable and worthy one. There
are many intrigues going on in connection with it, as
Count Nesselrode informs me. As for the kingdom of
Naples, it is no longer spoken of. By the details of the
last war with us, narrated to me by the count, I see that
he despises many of our ministers and marshals, and that
these must be very culpable; and yet he tells me that
they considered the result uncertain a week before our
overthrow; as late as the 10th of March they believed
that peace had been made with Prussia at least.

"Do not grieve over the fate of the emperor on the
island of Elba. The emperor selected it himself; the
allies would have preferred any other place.

"All the mails arriving at Paris have been seized by
the allies. Among the letters there was one from the
Empress Marie Louise to her husband. She writes that
her son is well, but that on awakening from a good
night's rest he had cried and told her he had dreamed
of his father; notwithstanding all her coaxing and promises of playthings, he had, however, refused to tell what
he had dreamed of his father, and that this circumstance
had made her uneasy in spite of her will.

"Prince Leopold resides in the same house with
Countess Tascher; he is incessantly busied with yours
and your mother's affairs; he at least is not oblivious of
the kindness you have both shown him. I know that it
is his intention to speak to the Emperor of Russia, and
then write to you.

" All your friends say that you must consider the interest of your children, and accept the future offered
you. M. de Lavalette and the Duke of Vicenza are also
of this opinion. You lose enough without this, and you
may well permit the victors to return a small portion of
that which they have taken from you, and which is right-
fully yours.

" In short, all your friends demand that you shall repair to Malmaison as soon as the Emperor Napoleon
shall have departed from Fontainebleau. I am assured
that the Emperor Alexander intends to hunt you up in
Novara if you should not come to Malmaison. It will
therefore be impossible to avoid him. Consider that the
fate of your children lies in his hands! In the treaty
of Fontainebleau you and your children were provided
for together; this is a great point for you, and proves
how highly you are thought of.

" It is to the Emperor of Russia alone that you owe
this; and when the Duke of Vicenza submitted this article of the treaty to the Emperor Napoleon for his signature, it met with his entire approval. Your sole and
undivided authority over your children is thereby acknowledged. You should, therefore, not reject the good

offered you for your children.   I do not think it would
require much persuasion to induce others to accept that
which is tendered you.

"Madame Tascher, who has proved herself to be
your true friend and relative, has just had her first interview with the Duke of Dalberg, the member of the provisional government.   She spoke of you, and I will here
give you his response, word for word: 'She is considered as being altogether foreign to the Bonaparte family,
because she has separated herself from her husband.   She
will be the refuge of her children, who are left to her.
She is so dearly beloved and highly esteemed, that she
can be very happy.   She can remain in France, and do
whatever she pleases; but she must now return to Paris.'
Countess Tascher came to me immediately after leaving the duke, in order to acquaint me with what he
had said.

"Friends and foes alike say this about you: 'Those
who are not delighted with what is being done for the
queen are bad people!   And as for her, what has she to
regret in all this?   Only the good she has done!   Now,
the world will dare to love her, and to express their love;
she has so few wishes, she is so perfect!'

"In short, it would seem almost that the people are
pleased with the misfortune that places you in the right
light, and they say, 'She is far more worthy in herself
than when surrounded by a glittering court!'

"Yesterday I saw the new arrivals from Fontainebleau, M. de Lascour and M. de Lavoestine.   They came

to me to learn where you were to be found, and intend visiting you at once, either at Novara or at Malmaison, as the case may be. These two gentlemen are true knights. 'No matter what she is to become,' said they; 'we can now show our devotion, without incurring the risk of being considered flatterers.'

"The last two weeks at Fontainebleau have been a period of the greatest interest. All these young men, together with M. de Labédoyère and M. de Montesquieu, wished to accompany the emperor; but he forbade their doing so, and, in taking leave of them, appealed to them to remain, and to continue to serve their country zealously.

"Lascour and Lavoestine, together with many other officers of the army, are much displeased with the generals who left Fontainebleau without taking leave of the emperor.

"Upon taking leave of the Empress Josephine, the emperor is reported to have said: 'She was right; my separation from her has brought misfortune upon my head.'

"It is said that the Duchess of Montebello will leave the Empress Marie Louise."

But all these entreaties and flatteries, and these appeals to a mother's heart, were, as yet, powerless to break the queen's pride. She still considered it more worthy and becoming to remain away from the city in which the ladies of the Faubourg St. Germain were celebrating the orgies of their victorious royalism with the soldiers of the allied armies. Instead of yielding to Louise de Cochelet's entreaties, the queen wrote her the following letter:

"MY DEAR LOUISE,—My resolution gives you pain! You all accuse me of childish waywardness. You are unjust! My mother can follow the Duke de Vicenza's counsel; she will go to Malmaison, but *I remain here*, and I have good reasons for doing so. I cannot separate my interests from those of my children. It is they, it is their nearest relatives, who are being sacrificed by all that is taking place, and I am, therefore, determined not to approach those who are working our ruin. I must be saddened by our great misfortune, and I will appear so, and abstain from approaching those who would still consider me a supplicant, even though I should demand nothing of them.

"I can readily believe that the Emperor Alexander is kindly disposed toward me; I have heard much good of him, even from the Emperor Napoleon. Although I was once anxious to make his acquaintance, I at this moment have no desire to see him. Is he not our vanquisher? In their hearts, your friends must all approve of my determination, whatever they may say. I find retirement congenial. When you have seen enough of your friends, you will return to me. I am suffering in my breast, and shall perhaps go to some watering-place. I do not know whether it is due to the air of Novara, but since I have been here I cannot breathe. My friends maintain that it is due to the mental shocks resulting from the great events that have transpired; but they are in error; death has spared us all, and the loss of a glittering position is not the greatest loss one can sustain. What personal happiness do I lose? My brother will, I trust, be well and suitably provided for, and he will be no longer exposed to danger. He must be very uneasy on our account, and yet I dare not write to him, as my letters would probably never reach him; if an opportunity should present itself, please let him know that we are no longer surrounded by dangers. Adieu. I entreat you once more to undertake nothing in my behalf. I fear your impetuosity and friendship, and yet I love to be able to count on you. My children are well. My mother opposes all my plans; she asserts that she has need of me; but I shall, nevertheless, go to her who must now be more unhappy than all of us.   HORTENSE."

She of whom Hortense thought that she must be more unhappy than all of them, was the wife of Napoleon, Marie Louise, who had now left Blois, to which place she had gone as empress-regent, and repaired to Rambouillet, to await the decision of the allies with regard to the future of herself and son. It was certainly one of the most peculiar features of this period, so rich in extraordinary occurrences, to see the sovereigns of Europe, the overthrown rulers of France, and those who were about to grasp the sceptre once more, thrown confusedly together in Paris, and within a circuit of some fifty miles around that city : a Bourbon in the Tuileries, Bonaparte at Fontainebleau, his wife and his son at Rambouillet, the divorced empress at Novara, the Emperors of Russia and Austria, and the King of Prussia, at Paris; moreover, a whole train of little German potentates and princes, and the Napoleonic kings and princes, who were all sojourning in Paris or its vicinity.

The Queen of Holland considered it her duty, in these days of misfortune and danger, to stand at the side of her whom Napoleon had commanded them to consider the head of the family, and to serve faithfully in life and death. Hortense therefore determined to go to the Empress Marie Louise at Rambouillet, in accordance with the emperor's commands.

This determination filled the hearts of the queen's friends with sorrow; and Louise had no sooner received the letter in which the queen announced her impending departure, than she hastened to reply, imploring her to abandon this intention. M. de Marmold, the queen's equerry, departed with all speed to bring this letter to the queen at Louis, where she was to pass the night, and to add his entreaties to those of Louise.

" M. de Marmold, the bearer of this letter, will deliver it to you at Louis, if he arrives there in good time," wrote Louise de Cochelet. " If you go to Rambouillet, you will destroy your own position, and also that of your children; this is the conviction of all your friends. I was so happy, for Prince Leopold had written you, in the name of the Emperor Alexander, and begged you to come to Malmaison. You could not have avoided seeing him, as he would even have gone to Novara. Instead, however, of returning with the Empress Josephine, you are on the point of uniting yourself with a family that has never loved you. With them you will experience nothing but distress, and they will not be thankful for the sacrifice you are about to make. You will regret this step when it is too late. I conjure you, do not go to Rambouillet!

"Your course will touch those to whom you are going but little, and will displease the allies, who take so much interest in you.

"The empress is a thorough Austrian at heart, and the visits of members of her husband's family are regarded with disfavor. I tell you this at the request of Prince Leopold and Madame de Caulaincourt. The latter, if you do not come here soon, will go to you, in spite of her great age. She conjures you not to go to Rambouillet, as your lady of honor, and the friend of your mother; she even forbids your doing so.

"When I informed Prince Leopold of your intention to go to the Empress Marie Louise at Rambouillet, his eyes filled with tears. 'It is beautiful to be proud,' said he, 'but she can no longer retreat; she is already under obligations to the Emperor of Russia, who effected the treaty of the 11th of April. I await her reply, to deliver it to the emperor: she owes him a reply.'

"I passed an hour with our good friend Lavalette this morning. This excellent man knew nothing of the measures we have been taking to persuade you to return, and said to me : 'How fortunate it would be for her and her children, if the emperor should desire to see her!' Do come, do come; show your friends this favor; we shall all be in despair if you go to Rambouillet!

"Prince Leopold will write you a few lines. He could not be more devoted to yourself and the Empress Josephine if you were his mother and his sister. Count Tschernitscheff has been to see me. The Emperor of Austria arrives here to-morrow, and the new French princes and the king will soon follow. What a change!

"You must see the Emperor of Russia, because he so much desires it. I conjure you, on my knees, to do me this favor! The emperor conducts himself so handsomely that every one is constrained to respect him; one forgets that he is the conqueror, and can only remember him as the protector. He seems to be the refuge of all those who have lost all, and are in distress. His conduct is admirable; he receives none but business calls, and such others as are absolutely necessary. The fair ladies of the Faubourg St. Germain cannot boast of his attention to them, and this does him all the more credit, he being, as it is said, very susceptible to the fair sex. He told Prince Leopold that he intended going to Novara, adding : 'You know that I love and esteem this family ; Prince Eugene is the prince of knights; I esteem the Empress Josephine, Queen Hortense, and Prince Eugene, all the more from the fact that her demeanor toward the Emperor Napoleon has been so much more noble than that of so many others, who should have shown him

more devotion.' How could it be possible not to respect
a man of such nobility of character? I trust you will
soon have an opportunity of judging of this yourself.
For God's sake, return!   LOUISE."

But these entreaties were all in vain. M. de Marmold arrived at Louis in time to see the queen; he delivered the letters of her friends, and did all that lay in
his power to persuade her not to go to Rambouillet.

But Hortense held firmly to her intention. "You
are right," said she. "All this is true; but I shall, nevertheless, go to the Empress Marie Louise, for it is my
duty to do so. If unpleasant consequences should result
from this step for me, I shall pay no attention to them,
but merely continue to do my duty. Of all of us, the
Empress Marie Louise must be the most unhappy, and
must stand most in need of consolation; it is, therefore,
at her side that I can be of most use, and nothing can
alter my determination."

CHAPTER XV.

QUEEN HORTENSE AND THE EMPEROR ALEXANDER.

QUEEN HORTENSE had gone to Rambouillet, in spite
of the entreaties and exhortations of her friends. The
Empress Marie Louise had, however, received her with
an air of embarrassment. She had told the queen that
she was expecting her father, the Emperor of Austria,

and that she feared the queen's presence might make him feel ill at ease. Moreover, the young empress, although dejected and grave, was by no means so sorrowful and miserable as Hortense expected. The fate of her husband had not wounded the heart of Marie Louise as deeply as that of the Empress Josephine.

Hortense felt that she was not needed there; that the presence of the Emperor of Austria would suffice to console the Empress of France for her husband's overthrow. She thought of Josephine, who was so deeply saddened by Napoleon's fate; and finding that, instead of consoling, she only embarrassed the Empress Marie Louise, she hastened to relieve her of her presence.

And now, at last, Hortense bowed her proud, pure heart beneath the yoke of necessity; now, at last, she listened to the prayers and representations of her mother, who had returned to Malmaison, and of her friends, and went to Paris. It had been too often urged upon her that she owed it to her sons to secure their fortune and future, not to overcome her personal repugnance, and conform herself to this new command of duty.

She had, therefore, returned to Paris for a few days, and taken up her abode in her dwelling, whose present dreariness recalled, with sorrowful eloquence, the grandeur of the past.

These drawing-rooms, once the rendezvous of so many kings and princes, were now desolate, and bore on their soiled floors the footprints of the hostile soldiers who had recently been quartered there. At the czar's solicitation, they had now been removed; but the queen's household servants had also left it. Faithless and ungrateful, they had turned their backs on the setting sun, and fled from the storm that had burst over the head of their mistress.

The Emperor Alexander hastened to the queen's dwelling as soon as her arrival in Paris was announced, the queen advancing to meet him as far as the outermost antechamber.

"Sire," said she, with a soft smile, "I have no means of receiving you with due ceremony; my antechambers are deserted."

The appearance of this solitary woman, this queen without a crown, without fortune, and without protection and support, who nevertheless stood before him in all the charms of beauty and womanhood, a soft smile on her lips, made a deep impression on the emperor, and his eyes filled with tears.

The queen observed this, and hastened to say, "But what of that? I do not think that antechambers filled with gold-embroidered liveries would make those who come to see me happier, and I esteem myself happy in being able to do you the honors of my house alone. I have, therefore, only won."

The emperor took her hand, and, while conducting the queen to her room, conversed with her, with that soft, sad expression peculiar to him, lamenting with bitter self-reproaches almost that he was himself, in part, to blame for the misfortunes that had overtaken the emperor and his family. He then conjured her to abandon her intention of leaving France, and to preserve herself for her mother and friends. He told her that, in abandoning her country, her friends, and her rights, she would be guilty of a crime against her own children, against her two sons, who were entitled to demand a country and a fortune at her hands.

The queen, overcome at last by these earnest and eloquent representations, declared her readiness to remain in France, if the welfare of her sons should require it.

"Until now," said she, "I had formed all my resolutions with reference to misfortune. I was entirely resigned, and I never thought of the possibility of any thing fortunate happening for me; and even yet, I do not know what I can desire and demand. I am, however, determined to accept nothing for myself and children that would be unworthy of us, and I do not know what that could be."

With an assuring smile, the emperor extended his hand to the queen. "Leave that to me," said he. "It is, then, understood, you are to remain in France?"

"Sire, you have convinced me that the future of my sons requires it. I shall therefore remain."

CHAPTER XVI.

THE NEW UNCLES.

MALMAISON, to which place Hortense had returned after a short stay in Paris, and where the Empress Josephine was also sojourning, was a kind of focus for social amusement and relaxation for the sovereigns assembled in Paris. Each of these kings and princes wished to pay his homage to the Empress Josephine and her daughter, and thereby, in a measure, show the last honors to the dethroned emperor.

On one occasion, when the King of Prussia, with his two sons, Prince Frederick William (the late king) and William, had come to Malmaison, and announced their desire to call on the empress, she sent them an invitation to a family dinner, at which she also invited the Emperor of Russia and his two brothers to attend.

The emperor accepted this invitation, and on entering, with the young archdukes, the parlor in which the Duchess de St. Leu was sitting, he took his two brothers by the hand and conducted them to Hortense.

"Madame," said he, "I confide my brothers to your keeping. They are now making their *début* in society. My mother fears their heads may be turned by the beauties of France; and in bringing them to Malmaison, where so many charming persons are assembled, I am certainly fulfilling my promise to preserve them from such a fate but poorly."

"Reassure yourself, sire," replied the queen, gravely; "I will be their mentor, and I promise you a motherly surveillance."

The emperor laughed, and, pointing to Hortense's two sons, who had just been brought in, he said: "Ah, madame, it would be much less dangerous for my brothers if they were of the age of these boys."

He approached the two boys with extended hands, and while conversing with them in a kindly and affectionate manner, addressed them with the titles "monseigneur" and "imperial highness."

The children regarded him wonderingly, for the Russian emperor was the first to address the little Napoleon and his younger brother, Louis Napoleon, with these imposing titles. The queen had never allowed them to be called by any but their own names. She wished to preserve them from vain pride, and teach them to depend on their own intrinsic merit.

Shortly afterward the King of Prussia and his sons were announced, and the emperor and his brothers left the young princes, and advanced to meet the king.

While the emperor and the king were exchanging salutations, Hortense's two sons inquired of their governess the names of the gentlemen who had just entered.

"It is the King of Prussia," whispered the governess; "and the gentleman who has just spoken with you is the Emperor of Russia."

The little Louis Napoleon regarded the tall figures of these princes thoughtfully for a moment, by no means impressed by their imposing titles. He was so accustomed to see his mother surrounded by kings, and these kings had always been his uncles.

"Mademoiselle," said the little Louis Napoleon, after a short pause, "are these two new gentlemen, the emperor and the king, also our uncles, like all the others, and must we call them so?"

"No, Louis, you must simply call them 'sire.'"

"But," said the boy, after a moment's reflection, "why is it that they are not our uncles?"

The governess withdrew with the two children to the back of the parlor, and explained to them, in a low voice, that the emperors and kings then in Paris, far from being their uncles, were their vanquishers.

"Then," exclaimed the elder boy, Napoleon Louis, his face flushing with anger, "then they are the enemies of my uncle, the emperor! Why did this Emperor of Russia embrace us?"

"Because he is a noble and generous enemy, who is endeavoring to serve you and your mother in your present misfortune. Without him you would possess nothing more in the world, and the fate of your uncle, the emperor, would be much sadder than it already is."

"Then we ought to love this emperor very dearly?" said the little Louis Napoleon.

"Certainly; for you owe him many thanks."

The young prince regarded the emperor, who was conversing with the empress Josephine, long and thoughtfully.

When the emperor returned to Malmaison on the following day, and while he was sitting at his mother's side in the garden-house, little Louis Napoleon, walking on tiptoe, noiselessly approached the emperor from behind, laid a small glittering object in his hand, and ran away.

The queen called him back, and demanded with earnest severity to know what he had done.

The little prince returned reluctantly, hanging his head with embarrassment, and said, blushing deeply: "Ah, *maman*, it is the ring Uncle Eugene gave me. I wished to give it to the emperor, because he is so good to my *maman!*"

Deeply touched, the emperor took the boy in his arms, seated him on his knees, and kissed him tenderly.

Then, in order to give the little prince an immediate reward, he attached the ring to his watch-chain, and swore that he would wear the token as long as he lived.*

CHAPTER XVII.

DEATH OF THE EMPRESS JOSEPHINE.

SINCE Napoleon's star had grown pale, and himself compelled to leave France as an exile, life seemed to Josephine also to be enveloped in a gloomy mourning-veil; she felt that her sun had set, and night come upon her.

* Cochelet, vol. i., p. 355.

But she kept this feeling a profound secret, and never allowed a complaint or sigh to betray her grief to her tenderly-beloved daughter. Her complaints were for the emperor, her sighs for the fate of her children and grandchildren. She seemed to have forgotten herself; her wishes were all for others. With the pleasing address and grace of which age could not deprive her, she did the honors of her house to the foreign sovereigns in Malmaison, and assumed a forced composure, in which her soul had no share. She would have preferred to withdraw with her grief to the retirement of her chambers, but she thought it her duty to make this sacrifice for the welfare of her daughter and grandchildren; and she, the loving mother, could do what Hortense's pride would not permit—she could entreat the Emperor Alexander to take pity on her daughter's fate.

When, therefore, the czar had finally succeeded in establishing her future, and had received the letters-patent which secured to the queen the duchy of St. Leu, Alexander hastened to Malmaison, to communicate this good news to the Empress Josephine.

She did not reward him with words, but with gushing tears, as she extended to the emperor both hands. She then begged him, with touching earnestness, to accept from her a remembrance of this hour.

The emperor pointed to a cup, on which a portrait of Josephine was painted, and begged her to give him that.

"No, sire," said she; "such a cup can be bought anywhere. But I wish to give you something that cannot be had anywhere else in the world, and that will sometimes remind you of me.   It is a present that I received from Pope Pius VII., on the day of my coronation.   I present you with this token in commemoration of the day on which you bring my daughter the ducal crown, in order that it may remind you of mother and daughter alike—of the dethroned empress and of the dethroned queen."

This present, which she now extended to the emperor with a charming smile, was an antique cameo, of immense size, and so wondrously-well executed that the empress could well say its equal was nowhere to be found in the world.   On this cameo the heads of Alexander the Great and of his father, Philip of Macedonia, were portrayed, side by side; and the beauty of the workmanship, as well as the size of the stone, made this cameo a gem of inestimable value.   And for this reason the emperor at first refused to accept this truly imperial present, and he yielded only when he perceived that his refusal would offend the empress, who seemed to be more pale and irritable than usual.

Josephine was, in reality, sadder than usual, for the royal family of the Bourbons had on this day caused her heart to bleed anew.   Josephine had read an article in the journals, in which, in the most contemptuous and cruel terms, attention was called to the fact that the eldest son of the Queen of Holland had been interred in the Cathedral of Notre-Dame, and that the Minister Blacas had now issued an order to have the coffin removed from its resting-place, and buried in an ordinary grave-yard.

Hortense, who had read this article, had hastened to Paris, in order that she might herself superintend the removal of the body of her beloved child from Notre-Dame, and its reinterment in the Church of St. Leu.

While she informed the emperor of this new insult, Josephine's whole figure trembled, and a deathly pallor overspread her countenance. Josephine lacked the strength to conceal her sufferings to-day, for the first time; Hortense was not present, and she might therefore, for once, allow herself the sad consolation of showing, bereft of its smile and its paint, the pale countenance, which death had already lightly touched.

"Your majesty is ill!" exclaimed the emperor, in dismay.

With a smile, which brought tears to Alexander's eyes, Josephine pointed to her breast, and whispered: "Sire, I have received the death-wound here!"

Yes, she was right; she had received a fatal wound, and her heart was bleeding to death.

Terrified by Josephine's condition, the emperor hurried to Paris, and sent his own physician to inquire after her condition. When the latter returned, he informed the emperor that Josephine was dangerously ill, and that he did not believe her recovery possible.

He was right, and Alexander saw the empress no more! Hortense and Eugene, her two children, held a sad watch at their mother's bedside throughout the night.

The best physicians were called in, but these only confirmed what the Russian physician had said—the condition of the empress was hopeless.   Her heart was broken !   With strong hands, she had held it together as long as her children's welfare seemed to require.   Now that Hortense's future was also assured—now that she knew that her grandchildren would, at least, not be compelled to wander about the world as exiled beggars—now Josephine withdrew her hands from her heart, and suffered it to bleed to death.

On the 29th of May, 1814, the Empress Josephine died, of an illness which had apparently lasted but two days.   Hortense had not heard her mother's death-sigh ; when she re-entered the room with Eugene, after her mother had received the sacrament from Abbé Bertrand —when she saw her mother, with outstretched arms, vainly endeavoring to speak to them—Hortense fainted away at her mother's bedside, and the empress breathed her last sigh in Eugene's arms.

The intelligence of the death of the empress affected Paris profoundly.   It seemed as though all the city had forgotten for a day that Napoleon was no longer the ruler of France, and that the Bourbons had reascended the throne of their fathers.   All Paris mourned ; for the hearts of the French people had not forgotten this woman, who had so long been their benefactress, and of whom each could relate the most touching traits of goodness, of generosity, and of gentleness.

Josephine, now that she was dead, was once more enthroned as empress in the hearts of the French people, and thousands poured into Malmaison, to pay their last homage to their deceased empress. Even the Faubourg St. Germain mourned with the Parisians; these haughty and insolent royalists, who had returned with the Bourbons, may, perhaps, for a moment, have recalled the benefits which the empress had shown them, when, as the mighty Empress of France, she employed the half of her allowance for the relief of the emigrants. They had returned without thinking of the thanks they owed their forgotten benefactress; now that she was dead, they no longer withheld the tribute of their admiration.

"Alas!" exclaimed Madame Ducayla, the king's friend; "alas! how interesting a lady was this Josephine! What tact, what goodness! How well she knew how to do everything! And she shows her tact and good taste to the last, in dying just at this moment!"

Immediately after the death of the empress, Eugene had conducted the queen from the death-chamber, almost violently, and had taken her and her children to St. Leu. The body of the empress was interred in Malmaison, and followed to the grave by her two grandchildren only. Grief had made both of her children severely ill, and the little princes were followed, not by her relatives, but by the Russian General Von Sacken, who represented the emperor, and by the equipages of all those kings and princes who had helped to hurl the Bonapartes from their thrones and restore the Bourbons.

The emperor passed his last night in France, before

leaving for England, at St. Leu; and, on taking leave of
Eugene and Hortense, who, at the earnest solicitation of
her brother, had left her room for the first time since her
mother's death, for the purpose of seeing the emperor, he
assured them of his unchangeable friendship and attachment.   As he knew that, among those whom he strongly
suspected, Pozzo di Borgo,* the ambassador he left behind him in Paris, was an irreconcilable enemy of Napoleon and his family, he had assigned to duty at the em-
bassy as *attaché*, a gentleman selected for this purpose
by Louise de Cochelet—M. de Boutiakin—and it was
through him that the emperor directed that the letters
and wishes of the queen and of her faithful young lady
friend should be received and answered.

A few days later Eugene also left St. Leu and his
sister Hortense, to return, with the King of Bavaria, to
his new home in Germany.   It was not until his departure that Hortense felt to its full extent the gloomy loneliness and dreary solitude by which she was surrounded.
She had not wept over the downfall of all the grandeur
and magnificence by which she had formerly been surrounded; she had not complained when the whirlwind
of fate hurled to the ground the crowns of all her relations, but had bowed her head to the storm with resignation, and smiled at the loss of her royal titles; but now,
as she stood in her parlor at St. Leu and saw none about

* Upon receiving the intelligence of the death of the emperor at
St. Helena, Pozzo di Borgo said : "I did not kill him, but I threw the
last handful of earth on his coffin, in order that he might never rise
again."

her but her two little boys and the few ladies who still remained faithful—now, Hortense wept.

"Alas!" she cried, bursting into tears, as she extended her hand to Louise de Cochelet, "alas! my courage is at an end! My mother is dead, my brother has left me, the Emperor Alexander will soon forget his promised protection, and I alone must contend, with my two children, against all the annoyances and enmities to which the name I bear will subject me! I fear I shall live to regret that I allowed myself to be persuaded to abandon my former plan. Will the love I bear my country recompense me for the torments which are in store for me?"

The queen's dark forebodings were to be only too fully realized. In the great and solemn hour of misfortune, Fate lifts to mortal vision the veil that conceals the future, and, like the Trojan prophetess, we see the impending evil, powerless to avert it.

BOOK III.

THE RESTORATION.

CHAPTER I.

THE RETURN OF THE BOURBONS.

On the 12th of April, Count d'Artois, whom Louis XVIII. had sent in advance, and invested with the dignity of a lieutenant-general of France, made his triumphal entry into Paris. At the gates of the city, he was received by the newly-formed provisional government, Talleyrand at its head ; and here it was that Count d'Artois replied to the address of that gentleman in the following words : "Nothing is changed in France, except that from to-day there will be one Frenchman more in the land." The people received him with cold curiosity, and the allied troops formed a double line for his passage to the Tuileries, at which the ladies of the Faubourg St. Germain, adorned with white lilies and white cockades, received him with glowing enthusiasm. Countess Ducayla, afterward the well-known friend of Louis XVIII., had been one of the most active instruments of the restoration, and she it was who had first unfolded again in France the banner of the Bourbons—the white flag. A few days before the entrance of the prince, she had gone, with a number of her royalist friends, into the streets, in order to excite the people to some enthusiasm for the legitimate dynasty. But the people and the army had still preserved their old love for the emperor, and the proclamation of Prince Schwartzenberg, read by Bauvineux in the streets, was listened to in silence. True, the royalists cried, "*Vive le roi !*" at the end of this reading, but the people remained indifferent and mute.

This sombre silence alarmed Countess Ducayla; it seemed to indicate a secret discontent with the new order of things. She felt that this sullen people must be inflamed, and made to speak with energy and distinctness. To awaken enthusiasm by means of words and proclamations had been attempted in vain ; now the countess determined to attempt to arouse them by another means —to astonish them by the display of a striking symbol— to show them the white flag of the Bourbons !

She gave her companion, Count de Montmorency, her handkerchief, that he might wave it aloft, fastening it to the end of his cane, in order that it should be more conspicuous. This handkerchief of Countess Ducayla, fastened to the cane of a Montmorency, was the first royalist banner that fluttered over Paris, after a banishment of twenty years. The Parisians looked at this banner with a kind of reverence and shuddering wonder ; they did not greet it with applause ; they still remained silent, but they nevertheless followed the procession of royalists, who marched to the boulevards, shouting, " *Vive le roi!* " They took no part in their joyful demonstration, but neither did they attempt to prevent it.

This demonstration of the royalists, and particularly of the royalist ladies, transcended the bounds of propriety, and of their own dignity. In their fanaticism for the legitimate dynasty, they gave the allies a reception, which almost assumed the character of a declaration of love, on the part of the fair ladies of the Faubourg St. Germain, for all the soldiers and officers of the allied army. In a strange confusion of ideas, these warriors, who had certainly entered France as enemies, seemed to these fair ones to be a part of the beloved Bourbons; and they loved them with almost the same love they lavished upon the royal family itself. During several days they were, in their hearts, the daughters of all countries except their own!

Louis XVIII. was himself much displeased with this enthusiasm of the ladies of the Faubourg St. Germain, and openly avowed to Countess Ducayla his dissatisfaction with the ridiculous and contemptible behavior of these ladies at that time. He was even of the opinion that it was calculated to injure his cause, as the nation had then not yet pronounced in his favor.

"They should," said he, "have received the allies with a dignified reserve, without frivolous demonstrations, and without this inconsiderate devotion. Such a demeanor would have inspired them with respect for the nation, whereas they now leave Paris with the conviction that

we are still—as we were fifty years ago—the most giddy
and frivolous people of Europe. You particularly, ladies
—you have compromised yourselves in an incomprehensible manner. The allies seemed to you so lovable *en
masse*, that you gave yourselves the appearance of also
loving them *en détail;* and this has occasioned reports
concerning you which do little honor to French ladies!"

"But, *mon Dieu!*" replied Countess Ducayla to her
royal friend, "we wished to show them a well-earned
gratitude for the benefit they conferred in restoring to us
your majesty; we wished to offer them freely what we,
tired of resistance, were at last compelled to accord to
the tyrants of the republic and the sabre-heroes of the
empire! None of us can regret what we have done for
our good friends the allies!"

Nevertheless, that which the ladies "had done for
their good friends the allies" was the occasion of many
annoying family scenes, and the husbands who did not
fully participate in the enthusiasm of their wives were
of the opinion that they had good cause to complain of
their inordinate zeal.

Count G——, among others, had married a young
and beautiful lady a few days before the restoration.
She, in her youthful innocence, was entirely indifferent
to political matters; but her step-father, her step-mother,
and her husband, Count G——, were royalists of the first
water.

On the day of the entrance of the allies into Paris,
step-father, step-mother, and husband, in common with

all good legitimists, hurried forward to welcome " their good friends," and each of them returned to their dwelling with a stranger—the husband with an Englishman, the step-mother with a Prussian, and the step-father with an Austrian.   The three endeavored to outdo each other in the attentions which they showered upon the guests they had the good fortune to possess.   The little countess alone remained indifferent, in the midst of the joy of her family.   They reproached her with having too little attachment for the good cause, and exhorted her to do everything in her power to entertain the gallant men who had restored to France her king.

The husband requested the Englishman to instruct the young countess in riding; the marquise begged the Prussian to escort her daughter to the ball, and teach her the German waltz; and, finally, the marquis, who had discovered a fine taste for paintings in the Austrian, appealed to this gentleman to conduct the young wife through the picture-galleries.

In short, every opportunity was given the young countess to commit a folly, or rather three follies, for she did not like to give the preference to any one of the three strangers.   She was young, and inexperienced in matters of this kind.   Her triple intrigue was, therefore, soon discovered, and betrayed to her family; and now husband, step-father, and step-mother, were exasperated. This exceeded even the demands of their royalism; and they showered reproaches on the head of the young wife.

"It is not my fault!" cried she, sobbing.   "I only
14

did what you commanded. You ordered me to do everything in my power to entertain these gentlemen, and I
could therefore refuse them nothing."

But there were also cases in which the advances of
the enthusiastic ladies of the Faubourg St. Germain were
repelled. Even the high-born and haughty Marquise
M—— was to experience this mortification. She stepped
before the sullen, sombre veterans of the Old Guard of
the empire, who had just allowed Count d'Artois to pass
before their ranks in dead silence. She ardently appealed to their love for the dynasty of their fathers, and,
in her enthusiasm for royalism, went so far as to offer herself as a reward to him who should first cry " *Vive le
roi!* " But the faithful soldiers of the emperor stood
unmoved by this generous offer, and the silence remained
unbroken by the lowest cry!

The princes who stood at the head of the allied
armies were, of course, the objects of the most ardent
enthusiasm of the royalist ladies; but it was, above all,
with them that they found the least encouragement.
The Emperor of Austria was too much occupied with
the future of his daughter and grandson, and the King
of Prussia was too grave and severe, to find any pleasure in the coquetries of women. The young Emperor
Alexander of Russia, therefore, became the chief object
of their enthusiasm and love. But their enthusiasm also
met with a poor recompense in this quarter. Almost
distrustfully, the czar held himself aloof from the ladies
of the Faubourg St. Germain; and yet it was they who

had decided the fate of France with him, and induced him to give his vote for the Bourbons; for until then it had remained undetermined whom the allies should call to the throne of France.

In his inmost heart, the Emperor of Russia desired to see the universally-beloved Viceroy of Italy, Eugene Beauharnais, elevated to the vacant throne. The letter with which Eugene replied to the proposition of the allies, tendering him the ducal crown of Genoa, had won for Josephine's son the love and esteem of the czar for all time. Alexander had himself written to Eugene, and proffered him, in the name of the allies, a duchy of Genoa, if he would desert Napoleon, and take sides with the allies. Eugene Beauharnais had replied to him in the following letter:

"SIRE,—I have received your majesty's propositions. They are undoubtedly very favorable, but they are powerless to change my resolution. I must have known how to express my thoughts but poorly when I had the honor of seeing you, if your majesty can believe that I could sully my honor for any, even the highest, reward. Neither the prospect of possessing the crown of the duchy of Genoa, nor that of the kingdom of Italy, can induce me to become a traitor. The example of the King of Naples cannot mislead me; I will rather be a plain soldier than a traitorous prince.

"The emperor, you say, has done me injustice; I have forgotten it; I only remember his benefits. I owe

all to him—my rank, my titles, and my fortune, and I
owe to him that which I prefer to all else—that which
your indulgence calls my renown.   I shall, therefore,
serve him as long as I live; my person is his, as is my
heart.   May my sword break in my hands, if it could
ever turn against the emperor, or against France!   I
trust that my well-grounded refusal will at least secure
to me the respect of your imperial majesty.   I am, etc."

The Emperor of Austria, on the other hand, ardently
desired to secure the throne of France to his grandson,
the King of Rome, under the regency of the Empress
Marie Louise; but he did not venture to make this demand openly and without reservation of his allies, whose
action he had promised to approve and ratify.   The
appeals of the Duke of Cadore, who had been sent to
her father by Marie Louise from Blois, urging the emperor to look after her interests, and to demand of the
allies that they should assure the crown to herself and
son, were, therefore, fruitless.

The emperor assured his daughter's ambassador that
he had reason to hope for the best for her, but that he
was powerless to insist on any action in her behalf.

"I love my daughter," said the good emperor, "and
I love my son-in-law, and I am ready to shed my heart's
blood for them."

"Majesty," said the duke, interrupting him, "no such
sacrifice is required at your hands."

"I am ready to shed my blood for them," continued

the emperor, " to sacrifice my life for them, and I repeat it, I have promised the allies to do nothing except in conjunction with them, and to consent to all they determine. Moreover, my minister, Count Metternich, is at this moment with them, and I shall ratify everything which he has signed." *

But the emperor still hoped that that which Metternich should sign for him, would be the declaration that the little King of Rome was to be the King of France.

But the zeal of the royalists was destined to annihilate this hope.

The Emperor of Russia had now taken up his residence in Talleyrand's house. He had yielded to the entreaties of the shrewd French diplomat, who well knew how much easier it would be to bend the will of the Agamemnon of the holy alliance † to his wishes, when he should have him in hand, as it were, day and night. In offering the emperor his hospitality, it was Talleyrand's intention to make him his prisoner, body and soul, and to use him to his own advantage.

It was therefore to Talleyrand that Countess Ducayla hastened to concert measures with the Bonapartist of yesterday, who had transformed himself into the zealous legitimist of to-day.

Talleyrand undertook to secure the countess an audience with the Russian emperor, and he succeeded.

While conducting the beautiful countess to the czar's cabinet, Talleyrand whispered in her ear : "Imitate

* Bourrienne, vol. x., p. 129.   † Mémoires d'une Femme de Qualité,

Madame de Lemallé—endeavor to make a great stroke.
The emperor is gallant, and what he denies to diplomacy,
he may, perhaps, accord to the ladies."

He left her at the door, and the countess entered the
emperor's cabinet alone. She no sooner saw him, than
she sank on her knees, and stretched out her arms.

With a knightly courtesy, the emperor immediately
hastened forward to assist her to rise.

"What are you doing?" asked he, almost in alarm.
"A noble lady never has occasion to bend the knee to a
cavalier."

"Sire," exclaimed the countess, "I kneel before you,
because it is my purpose to implore of your majesty the
happiness which you alone can restore to us; it will be
a double pleasure to possess Louis XVIII. once more,
when Alexander I. shall have given him to us!"

"Is it then true that the French people are still devoted to the Bourbon family?"

"Yes, sire, they are our only hope; on them we bestow our whole love!"

"Ah, that is excellent," cried Alexander; "are all
French ladies filled with the same enthusiasm as yourself, madame?"

"Well, if this is the case, it will be France that recalls Louis XVIII., and it will not be necessary for us to
conduct him back. Let the legislative bodies declare
their will, and it shall be done." *

And of all women, Countess Ducayla was the one to

* Mémoires d'une Femme de Qualité, vol. i., p. 179.

bring the legislative bodies to the desired declaration. She hastened to communicate the hopes with which the emperor had inspired her to all Paris; on the evening after her interview with the emperor, she gave a grand *soirée*, to which she invited the most beautiful ladies of her party, and a number of senators.

"I desired by this means," says she in her memoirs, "to entrap the gentlemen into making a vow. How simple-minded I was! Did I not know that the majority of them had already made and broken a dozen vows?"

On the following day the senate assembled, and elected a provisional government, consisting of Talleyrand, the Duke of Dalberg, the Marquis of Jancourt, Count Bournonville, and the Abbé Montesquieu. The senate and the new provisional government thereupon declared Napoleon deposed from the throne, and recalled Louis XVIII. But while the senate thus publicly and solemnly proclaimed its legitimist sentiments in the name of the French people, it at the same time testified to its own unworthiness and selfishness. In the treaty made by the senate with its recalled king, it was provided in a separate clause, "that the salary which they had hitherto received, should be continued to them for life." While recalling Louis XVIII., these senators took care to pay themselves for their trouble, and to secure their own future.

CHAPTER II.

THE BOURBONS AND THE BONAPARTES.

THE allies hastened to consider the declaration of the senate and provisional government as the declaration of the people, and recalled to the throne of his fathers Louis XVIII., who, as Count de Lille, had so long languished in exile at Hartwell.

The Emperor of Austria kept his word; he made no resistance to the decrees of his allies, and allowed his grandson, the King of Rome, to be robbed of his inheritance, and the imperial crown to fall from his daughter's brow. The Emperor Francis was, however, as much astonished at this result as Marie Louise, for, until their entrance into Paris, the allies had flattered the Austrian emperor with the hope that the crown of France would be secured to his daughter and grandson. The emperor's astonishment at this turn of affairs was made the subject of a caricature, which, on the day of the entrance of Louis XVIII., was affixed to the same walls on which Chateaubriand's enthusiastic *brochure* concerning the Bourbons was posted. In this caricature, of which thousands of copies were sown broadcast throughout Paris, the Emperor of Austria was to be seen sitting in an elegant open carriage; the Emperor Alexander sat on the coachman's box, the Regent of England as postilion on the lead-horse, and the King of Prussia stood up behind as a lackey. Napoleon ran along on foot at the side of the carriage, holding fast to it, and crying out to the Emperor of Austria, "Father-in-law, they have thrown me out"—"And *taken me in*," was the reply of Francis I.

The exultation of the ladies of the Faubourg St. Germain was great, now that their king was at last restored to them, and they eagerly embraced every means of showing their gratitude to the Emperor of Russia. But Alexander remained entirely unsusceptible to their homage; he even went so far as to avoid attending the entertainments given by the new king at the Tuileries, and society was shocked at seeing the emperor openly displaying his sympathy for the family of the Emperor Napoleon, and repairing to Malmaison, instead of appearing at the Tuileries.

Count Nesselrode at last conjured his friend Louise de Cochelet to inform the czar of the feeling of dismay that pervaded the Faubourg St. Germain, when he should come to Queen Hortense's maid-of-honor, as he was in the habit of doing from time to time, for the purpose of discussing the queen's interests with her.

"Sire," said she to the czar, "the Faubourg St. Germain regards your majesty's zeal in the queen's behalf with great jealousy. It has even caused Count Nesselrode much concern. 'Our emperor,' said he to me, recently, 'goes to Malmaison much too often; the high circles of society, and the diplomatic body, are already in dismay about it; it is feared that he is there subjected to influences to which policy requires he should not be exposed.' "

" This is characteristic of my Nesselrode," replied the emperor, laughing, " he is so easily disquieted. What do I care for the Faubourg St. Germain? It speaks ill enough for these ladies that they have not made a conquest of me! I prefer the noble qualities of the soul to all outward appearances; and I find united in the Empress Josephine, in the Queen of Holland, and in Prince Eugene, all that is admirable and lovable. I am better pleased to be here with you in quiet, confidential intercourse, than with those who really demean themselves as though they were crazed, and who, instead of enjoying the triumph we have prepared for them, are only intent on destroying their enemies, and have commenced with those who formerly accorded them such generous protection; they really weary one with their extravagances.

" Frenchwomen are coquettish," said the emperor in the course of the conversation; " I came here in great fear of them, for I knew how far their amiability could extend; but their heart is undoubtedly no longer their own. I am therefore on my guard against being deceived by it, and I fancy these ladies love to please so well, that they are even angry with those who respond to the attentions which are so lavishly showered on them, with conventional politeness only."

Louise de Cochelet undertook to defend the French ladies against the emperor's attacks. She told him he should not judge of them by the manner in which they had conducted themselves toward him, as it was but natural that the ladies should be inspired with enthusiasm for a young emperor who appeared to them in so favorable a light, and that they must necessarily, even without being coquettish, ardently desire to be noticed by him.

"But," said the emperor, with his soft, sad smile, "have these ladies only been waiting for me in order to feel their heart palpitate? I seek mind and entertainment, but I fly from all those who display a desire to exercise a control over my heart; in this I see nothing but self-love, and I hold myself aloof from such contact."

While the royalists and the ladies of the Faubourg St. Germain were lavishing attentions upon the allies, and assuring the returned king of the boundless delight of his people, this people was already beginning to grumble. The allies had now completed their task, they had restored to France its legitimate king, and they now put the finishing-touch to their work by providing in the treaty, that France should be narrowed down to the boundaries it had had before the revolution.

France was compelled to conform to the will of its vanquishers. From the weakness of the legitimists they now snatched that which they had been compelled to accord to the strength of the empire.

All of those fortified places, that had been bought with so much French blood, and that were still held by Frenchmen, were to be given up, and the great, extended France was to shrink back into the France it had been thirty years before! It was this that made the people

murmur. The Frenchmen who had left Napoleon because they had grown weary of endless wars, were, nevertheless, proud of the conquests they had made under their
emperor. The surrender of these conquests wounded the
national pride, and they were angry with their king for
being so ready to put this shame upon France—for holding the crown of France in higher estimation than the
honor of France !

It must be conceded, however, that Louis XVIII. had
most bitterly felt the disgrace that attached to him in this
re-establishment of France within its ancient boundaries,
and he had endeavored to protest in every way against .
this demand of the allies. But his representative had
been made to understand that if Louis XVIII. could not
content himself with the France the allies were prepared
to give him, he was at liberty to relinquish it to Marie
Louise. The king was, therefore, compelled to yield to
necessity ; but he did so with bitter mortification, and
while his courtiers were giving free rein to their enthusiasm for the allies, he was heard to whisper, "*Nos chers
amis les ennemis !* " *

Thus embittered against the allies, it was only with
great reluctance, and after a long and bitter struggle, that
Louis XVIII. consented to the demands made by the
allies in behalf of the family of Napoleon. But the Emperor Alexander kept his word ; he defended the rights
of the Queen of Holland and her children against the ill-
will of the Bourbons, the dislike of the royalists, and the

* " Our dear friends the enemies ! "

disinclination of the allies, alike.   The family of the emperor owed it to him and to his firmness alone that the article of the treaty of the 11th of April, in which Louis XVIII. agreed " that the titles and dignities of all the members of the family of the Emperor Napoleon should be recognized, and that they should not be deprived of them," remained something more than a mere phrase.

It was only after repeated efforts that the emperor at last succeeded in obtaining for Hortense, from Louis XVIII., an estate and a title, that secured her position. King Louis finally yielded to his urgent solicitations, and conferred upon Hortense the title of Duchess of St. Leu, and made her estate, St. Leu, a duchy.

But this was done with the greatest reluctance, and only under the pressure of the king's obligations to the allies, who had given him his throne; and these obligations the Bourbons would have forgotten as willingly as the whole period of the revolution and of the empire.

For the Bourbons seemed but to have awakened from a long sleep, and were not a little surprised to find that the world had progressed in the meanwhile.

According to their ideas, every thing must have remained standing at the point where they had left it twenty years before; and they were at least determined to ignore all that had happened in the interval.   King Louis therefore signed his first act as in " the nineteenth " year of his reign, and endeavored in all things to keep up a semblance of the continuation of his reign since the year 1789.   Hence, the letters-patent in which King

Louis appointed Hortense Duchess of St. Leu were drawn up in a manner offensive to the queen, for they contained the following: " The king appoints Mademoiselle Hortense de Beauharnais Duchess of St. Leu."

The queen refused to accept this title, under the circumstances, and rejected the letters-patent. It was not until the czar had angrily demanded it, that M. de Blacas, the king's premier, consented to draw up the letters-patent in a different style. They read: " The king appoints Hortense Eugénie, included in the treaty of the 11th of April, Duchess of St. Leu." This was, to be sure, merely a negative and disguised recognition of the former rank of the queen ; but it was, at least no longer a degradation to accept it.

The Viceroy of Italy, the noble Eugene—who was universally beloved, and who had come to Paris, at the express wish of the czar, to secure his future—occasioned the Bourbons quite as much annoyance and perplexity.

The king could not refuse to recognize the brave hero of the empire and the son-in-law of the King of Bavaria, who was one of the allies ; and, as Eugene desired an audience of the king, it was accorded him at once.

But how was he to be received? With what title was Napoleon's step-son, the Viceroy of Italy, to be addressed? It would have been altogether too ridiculous to repeat the absurdity contained in Hortense's letters-patent, and call Eugene " Viscount de Beauharnais ; " but to accord him the royal title would have compromised the

dignity of the legitimate dynasty. A brilliant solution
of this difficult question suggested itself to King Louis.
When the Duke d'Aumont conducted Prince Eugene to
the royal presence, the king advanced, with a cordial
smile, and saluted him with the words, "M. Marshal of
France, I am happy to see you."

Eugene, who was on the point of making his saluta-
tion, remained silent, and looked over his shoulder to see
whom the king was speaking with. Louis XVIII. smiled,
and continued: "You, my dear sir, are a marshal of
France. I appoint you to this dignity."

"Sire," said Eugene, bowing profoundly, "I am
much obliged to your majesty for your kind intentions,
but the misfortune of the rank to which destiny has called
me will not allow me to accept the high title with which
you honor me. I thank you very much, but I must de-
cline it." *

The king's stratagem had thus come to grief, and
Eugene left the royal presence with flying colors. He
was not under the necessity of accepting benefits from
the King of France, for his step-father, the King of Bavaria, made Eugene a prince of the royal house of Bavaria, and created for him the duchy of Leuchtenberg.
Hither Eugene retired, and lived there, surrounded by
his wife and children, in peace and tranquillity, until
death tore him from the arms of his sorrowing family, in
the year 1824.

* Mémoires d'une Femme de Qualité, vol. i., p. 267.

CHAPTER III.

MADAME DE STAËL.

THE restoration, that had overthrown so many of the
great, and that was destined to restore to the light so
many names that had lain buried in obscurity, now
brought back to Paris a person who had been banished
by Napoleon, and who had been adding new lustre and
renown to her name in a foreign land. This personage
was Madame de Staël, the daughter of Necker, the renowned poetess of " Corinne " and " Delphine."

It had been a long and bitter struggle between
Madame de Staël and the mighty Emperor of the
French; and Madame de Staël, with her genius and her
impassioned eloquence, and adorned with the laurel-
wreath of her exile, had perhaps done Napoleon more
harm than a whole army of his enemies. Intense hatred
existed on both sides, and yet it had depended on Napoleon alone to transform this hatred into love. For
Madame de Staël had been disposed to lavish the whole
impassioned enthusiasm ·of her heart upon the young
hero of Marengo and Arcola—quite disposed to become
the Egeria of this Numa Pompilius. In the warm impulse of her stormy imagination, Madame de Staël, in
reference to Bonaparte, had even, in a slight measure,
been regardless of her position as a lady, and had only
remembered that she was a poetess, and that, as such, it
became her well to celebrate the hero, and to bestow on

the luminous constellation that was rising over France the glowing dithyrambic of her greetings.

Madame de Staël had, therefore, not waited for Napoleon to seek her, but had made the first advances, and sought him.

To the returning victor of Italy she wrote letters filled with impassioned enthusiasm; but these letters afforded the youthful general but little pleasure. In the midst of the din of battle and the grand schemes with which he was continually engaged, Bonaparte found but little time to occupy himself with the poetical works of Madame de Staël. He knew of her nothing more than that she was the daughter of the minister Necker, and that was no recommendation in Napoleon's eyes, for he felt little respect for Necker's genius, and even went so far as to call him the instigator of the great revolution. It was, therefore, with astonishment that the young general received the enthusiastic letter of the poetess; and, while showing it to some of his intimate friends, he said, with a shrug of his shoulders, "Do you understand these extravagances? This woman is foolish!"

But Madame de Staël did not allow herself to be dismayed by Bonaparte's coldness and silence—she continued to write new and more glowing letters.

In one of these letters she went so far in her inconsiderate enthusiasm as to say, that it was a great error in human institutions that the gentle and quiet Josephine had united her faith with his; that she, Madame de Staël, and Bonaparte, were born for each other, and
15

that Nature seemed to have created a soul of fire like
hers, in order that it might worship a hero such as he
was.

Bonaparte crushed the letter in his hands, and exclaimed, as he threw it in the fire: "That a blue-stock-
ing, a manufactress of sentiment, should dare to compare
herself to Josephine! I shall not answer these letters!"

He did not answer them, but Madame de Staël did
not, or rather would not, understand his silence. Little
disposed to give up a resolution once formed, and to see
her plans miscarry, Madame de Staël was now also determined to have her way, and to approach Bonaparte
despite his resistance.

And she did have her way; she succeeded in over-
coming all obstacles, and the interview, so long wished
for by her, and so long avoided by him, at last took
place. Madame de Staël was introduced at the Tuileries,
and received by Bonaparte and his wife. The personal
appearance of this intellectual woman was, however, but
little calculated to overcome Bonaparte's prejudice. The
costume of Madame de Staël was on this occasion, as it
always was, fantastic, and utterly devoid of taste, and
Napoleon loved to see women simply but elegantly and
tastefully attired. In this interview with Napoleon,
Madame de Staël gave free scope to her wit; but instead
of dazzling him, as she had hoped to do, she only succeeded in depressing him.

It was while in this frame of mind, and when Madame de Staël, in her ardor, had endeavored almost to

force him to pay her a compliment, that Napoleon responded to her at least somewhat indiscreet question: "Who is in your eyes the greatest woman?" with the sarcastic reply, "She who bears the most children to the state."

Madame de Staël had come with a heart full of enthusiasm; in her address to Napoleon, she had called him a "god descended to earth;" she had come an enthusiastic poetess; she departed an offended woman. Her wounded vanity never forgave the answer which seemed to make her ridiculous. She avenged herself, in her drawing-room, by the biting *bon mots* which she hurled at Napoleon and his family, and which were of course faithfully repeated to the first consul.

But the weapons which this intellectual woman now wielded against the hero who had scorned her, wounded him more severely than weapons of steel or iron. In the use of these weapons, Madame de Staël was his superior, and the consciousness of this embittered Bonaparte all the more against the lady, who dared prick the heel of Achilles with the needle of her wit, and strike at the very point where he was most sensitive.

A long and severe conflict now began between these two greatest geniuses of that period, a struggle that was carried on by both with equal bitterness. But Napoleon had outward power on his side, and could punish the enmity of his witty opponent, as a ruler.

He banished Madame de Staël from Paris, and soon afterward even from France. She who in Paris had

been so ready to sing the praises of her "god descended
from heaven," now went into exile his enemy and a royalist, to engage, with all her eloquence and genius, in
making proselytes for the exiled Bourbons, and to raise
in the minds of men an invisible but none the less formi-
dable army against her enemy the great Napoleon.

Madame de Staël soon gave still greater weight to
the flaming eruptions of her hatred of Napoleon, by her
own increasing renown and greatness; and the poetess
of Corinne and Delphine soon became as redoubtable an
opponent of Napoleon as England, Russia, or Austria,
could be.

But in the midst of the triumphs she was celebrating
in her exile, Madame de Staël soon began to long
ardently to return to France, which she loved all the
more for having been compelled to leave it. She therefore used all the influence she possessed in Paris, to obtain from Napoleon permission to return to her home,
but the emperor remained inexorable, even after having
read Delphine.

"I love," said he, "women who make men of themselves just as little as I love effeminate men. There is
an appropriate *rôle* for every one in the world. Of
what use is this vagabondizing of fantasy? What does
it accomplish? Nothing! All this is nothing but de-
rangement of mind and feeling. I dislike women who
throw themselves in my arms, and for this reason, if for
no other, I dislike this woman, who is certainly one of
that number."

Madame de Staël's petitions to be permitted to return to Paris were therefore rejected, but she was as little disposed to abandon her purpose now as she was at the time she sought to gain Bonaparte's good-will. She continued to make attempts to achieve her aim, for it was not only her country that she wished to reconquer, but also a million francs which she wished to have paid to her out of the French treasury.

Her father, Minister Necker, had loaned his suffering country a million francs, at a time of financial distress and famine, to buy bread for the starving people, and Louis XVI. had guaranteed, in writing, that this "national debt of France" should be returned.

But the revolution that shattered the throne of the unfortunate king, also buried beneath the ruins of the olden time the promises and oaths that had been written on parchment and paper.

Madame de Staël now demanded that the emperor should fulfil the promises of the overthrown king, and that the heir of the throne of the Bourbons should assume the obligations into which a Bourbon had entered with her father.

She had once called Napoleon a god descended from heaven; and she even now wished that he might still prove a god for her, namely, the god Pluto, who should pour out a million upon her from his horn of plenty.

As she could not go to France herself, she sent her son to plead with the emperor, for herself and her children.

Well knowing, however, how difficult it would be, even for her son to secure an audience of the emperor, she addressed herself to Queen Hortense in eloquent letters imploring her to exert her influence in her son's behalf.

Hortense, ever full of pity for misfortune, felt the warmest sympathy and admiration for the genius of the great poetess, and interceded for Madame de Staël with great courage and eloquence. She alone ventured, regardless of Napoleon's frowns and displeasure, to plead the cause of the poor exile again and again, and to solicit her recall to France, as a simple act of justice; she even went so far in her generosity as to extend the hospitalities of her drawing-rooms to the poetess's son, who was avoided and fled from by every one else.

Hortense's soft entreaties and representations were at last successful in soothing the emperor's anger. He allowed Madame de Staël to return to France, on the condition that she should never come to Paris or its vicinity; he then also accorded Madame de Staël's son the long-sought favor of an audience.

This interview of Napoleon with Madame de Staël's son is as remarkable as it is original. On this occasion, Napoleon openly expressed his dislike and even his hatred as well of Madame de Staël as of her father, although he listened with generous composure to the warm defence of the son and grandson.

Young Staël told the emperor of his mother's longing to return to her home, and touchingly portrayed the sadness and unhappiness of her exile.

"Ah, bah!" exclaimed the emperor, "your mother is in a state of exaltation. I do not say that she is a bad woman. She has wit, and much intellect, perhaps too much, but hers is an inconsiderate, an insubordinate spirit. She has grown up in the chaos of a falling monarchy, and of a revolution, and she has amalgamized the two in her mind. This is all a source of danger; she would make proselytes, she must be watched; she does not love me. The interests of those whom she might compromise, require that I should not permit her to return to Paris. If I should allow her to do so, she would place me under the necessity of sending her to Bicêtre, or of imprisoning her in the Temple, before six months elapsed; that would be extremely disagreeable, for it would cause a sensation, and injure me in the public opinion. Inform your mother that my resolution is irrevocable. While I live, she shall not return to Paris."

It was in vain that young Staël assured him in his mother's name, that she would avoid giving him the least occasion for displeasure, and that she would live in complete retirement if permitted to return to Paris.

"Ah, yes! I know the value of fine promises!" exclaimed the emperor. "I know what the result would be, and I repeat it, it cannot be! She would be the rallying-point of the whole Faubourg St. Germain. She live in retirement! Visits would be made her, and she would return them; she would commit a thousand indiscretions, and say a thousand humorous things, to which she attaches no importance, but which annoy me. My government is no jest, I take every thing seriously ; I wish this to be understood, and you may proclaim it to the whole world ! "

Young Staël had, however, the courage to continue his entreaties ; he even went so far as to inquire in all humility for the grounds of the emperor's ill-will against his mother. He said he had been assured that Necker's last work was more particularly the cause of the emperor's displeasure, and that he believed Madame de Staël had assisted in writing it. This was, however, not so, and he could solemnly assure the emperor that his mother had taken no part in it whatever. Besides, Necker had also done full justice to the emperor in this work.

" Justice, indeed !   He calls me the ' necessary man.' The necessary man ! and yet, according to his book, the first step necessary to be taken, was to take off this necessary man's head !   Yes, I was necessary to repair all that your grandfather had destroyed !   It is he who overthrew the monarchy, and brought Louis XVI. to the scaffold ! "

" Sire ! " exclaimed the young man, deeply agitated, " you are then not aware that my grandfather's estates were confiscated because he defended the king ! "

" A fine defence, indeed !   If I give a man poison, and then, when he lies in the death-struggle, give him an antidote, can you then maintain that I wished to save this man ?   It was in this manner that M. Necker defended Louis XVI.   The confiscations of which you speak prove nothing. Robespierre's property was also confiscated. Not even Robespierre, Marat, and Danton, have brought such misery upon France as Necker; he it is who made the revolution. You did not see it, but I was present in those days of horror and public distress; but I give you my word that they shall return no more while I live! Your schemers write out their utopias, the simple-minded read these dreams, they are printed and believed in; the common welfare is in everybody's mouth, and soon there is no more bread for the people; it revolts, and that is the usual result of all these fine theories! Your grandfather is to blame for the orgies that brought France to desperation."

Then lowering his voice, from the excited, almost angry tone in which he had been speaking, to a milder one, the emperor approached the young man, who stood before him, pale, and visibly agitated. With that charming air of friendly intimacy that no one knew so well how to assume as Napoleon, he gently pinched the tip of the young man's ear, the emperor's usual way of making peace with any one to whom he wished well, after a little difficulty.

" You are still young," said he ; " if you possessed my age and experience, you would judge of these matters differently. Your candor has not offended, but pleased me ; I like to see a son defend his mother's cause! Your mother has intrusted you with a very difficult commission, and you have executed it with much spirit. It gives me pleasure to have conversed with you, for I love the young when they are straightforward and not too 'argumentative.' But I can nevertheless give you no false hopes! You will accomplish nothing! If your mother were in prison, I should not hesitate to grant you her release. But she is in exile, and nothing can induce me to recall her."

"But, sire, is one not quite as unhappy far from home and friends, as in prison?"

"Ah, bah! those are romantic notions! You have heard that said about your mother. She is truly greatly to be pitied. With the exception of Paris, she has the whole of Europe for her prison!"

"But, sire, all her friends are in Paris!"

"With her intellect, she will be able to acquire new ones everywhere. Moreover, I cannot understand why she should desire to be in Paris. Why does she so long to place herself in the immediate reach of tyranny? You see I pronounce the decisive word! I am really unable to comprehend it. Can she not go to Rome, Berlin, Vienna, Milan, or London? Yes, London would be the right place! There she can perpetrate libels whenever she pleases. At all of these places I will leave her undisturbed with the greatest pleasure; but Paris is my residence, and there I will tolerate those only who love me! On this the world can depend. I know what would happen, if I should permit your mother to return to Paris. She would commit new follies; she would corrupt those who surround me; she would corrupt Garat, as she once corrupted the tribunal; of course, she would promise all things, but she would, nevertheless, not avoid engaging in politics."

"Sire," I can assure you that my mother does not occupy herself with politics at all; she devotes herself exclusively to the society of her friends, and to literature."

"That is the right word, and I fully understand it. One talks politics while talking of literature, of morals, of the fine arts, and of every conceivable thing! If your mother were in Paris, her latest *bon mots* and phrases would be recited to me daily; perhaps they would be only invented; but I tell you I will have nothing of the kind in the city in which I reside! It would be best for her to go to London; advise her to do so. As far as your grandfather is concerned, I have certainly not said too much; M. Necker had no administrative ability. Once more, inform your mother that I shall never permit her to return to Paris."

"But if sacred interests should require her presence here for a few days, your majesty would at least—"

"What? Sacred interests? What does that mean?"

"Sire," the presence of my mother will be necessary, in order to procure from your majesty's government the return of a sacred debt."

"Ah, bah! sacred! Are not all the debts of the state sacred?"

"Without doubt, sire; but ours is accompanied by peculiar circumstances."

"Peculiar circumstances!" exclaimed the emperor,

rising to terminate the long interview, that began to
weary him. "What creditor of the state does not say
the same of his debt? Moreover, I know too little of
your relations toward my government. This matter
does not concern me, and I will not be mixed up in it.
If the laws are for you, all will go well without my inter-
ference; but if it requires influence, I shall have nothing
to do with it, for I should be rather against than for
you!"

"Sire," said young Staël, venturing to speak once
more, as the emperor was on the point of leaving, "sire,
my brother and I were anxious to settle in France; but
how could we live in a land in which our mother would
not be allowed to live with us everywhere?"

Already standing on the threshold of the door, the
emperor turned to him hastily. "I have no desire whatever to have you settle here," said he; "on the contrary,
I advise you not to do so. Go to England. There they
have a *penchant* for Genevese, parlor-politicians, etc.;
therefore, go to England; for I must say, I should be
rather ill than well disposed toward you!" *

* Bourrienne, vol. viii., p. 355.

CHAPTER IV.

MADAME DE STAËL'S RETURN TO PARIS.

MADAME DE STAËL returned to her cherished France with the restoration. She came back thirsting for new honor and renown, and determined, above all, to have her work republished in Germany, its publication having been once suppressed by the imperial police. She entertained the pleasing hope that the new court would forget that she was Necker's daughter, receive her with open arms, and accord her the influence to which her active mind and genius entitled her.

But she was laboring under an error, by which she was not destined to be long deceived. She was received at court with the cold politeness which is more terrible than insult. The king, while speaking of her with his friends, called Madame de Staël "a Chateaubriand in petticoats." The Duchess d'Angoulême seemed never to see the celebrated poetess, and never addressed a word to her; the rest of the court met Madame de Staël armed to the teeth with all the hatred and prejudices of the olden time.

It was also in vain that Madame de Staël endeavored to act an important part at the new court; they refused to regard her as an authority or power, but treated her as a mere authoress; her counsel was ridiculed, and they dared even to question the renown of M. Necker.

"I am unfortunate," said Madame de Staël to Countess

Ducayla; "Napoleon hated me because he believed me to possess intellect; these people repel me because I at least possess ordinary human understanding! I can certainly get on very well without them; but, as my presence displeases them, I shall, at least, endeavor to get my money from them."

The "sacred debt" had not been paid under the empire, and it was now Madame de Staël's intention to obtain from the king what the emperor had refused.

She was well aware of the influence which Countess Ducayla exercised over Louis XVIII., and she now hastened to call on the beautiful countess—whose acquaintance she had made under peculiar circumstances, in a romantic love intrigue—in order to renew the friendship they had then vowed to each other.

The countess had not forgotten this friendship, and she was now grateful for the service Madame de Staël had then shown her. She helped to secure the liquidation of the sacred debt, and, upon the order of King Louis, the million was paid over to Madame de Staël. "But," says the countess, in her memoirs, "I believe the recovery of this million cost Madame de Staël four hundred thousand francs, besides a set of jewelry that was worth at least one hundred thousand."

The countess's purse and the jewelry case, however, doubtlessly bore evidence that she might as well have said "I know" as "I believe."

Besides the four hundred thousand francs and the jewelry, Madame de Staël also gave the countess a piece of advice. "Make the most of the favor you now enjoy," said she to her; "but do so quickly, for, as matters are now conducted, I fear that the restoration will soon have to be restored."

"What do you mean by that?" asked the countess, smiling.

"I mean that, with the exception of the king, who perhaps does not say all he thinks, the others are still doing precisely as they always have done, and Heaven knows to what extremities their folly is destined to bring them! They mock at the old soldiers and assist the young priests, and this is the best means of ruining France."

Countess Ducayla considered this prediction of her intellectual friend as a mere cloud with which discontent and disappointed ambition had obscured the otherwise clear vision of Madame de Staël, and ridiculed the idea, little dreaming how soon her words were to be fulfilled.

Madame de Staël consoled herself for her cold reception at court, by receiving the best society of Paris in her parlors, and entertaining them with biting *bon mots* and witty *persiflage*, at the expense of the grand notabilities, who had suddenly arisen with their imposing genealogical trees out of the ruins and oblivion of the past.

Madame de Staël now also remembered the kindness Queen Hortense had shown her during her exile; and not to her only, but also to her friend, Madame Récamier, who had also been exiled by Napoleon, not, however, as his enemies said, "because she was Madame de

Staël's friend," but simply because she patronized and belonged to the so-called "little church." The "little church" was an organization born of the spirit of opposition of the Faubourg St. Germain, and a portion of the Catholic clergy, and was one of those things appertaining to the internal relations of France that were most annoying and disagreeable to the emperor.

Queen Hortense had espoused the cause of Madame de Staël and of Madame Récamier with generous warmth. She had eloquently interceded for the recall of both from their exile; and, now that the course of events had restored them to their home, both ladies came to the queen to thank her for her kindness and generosity.

Louise de Cochelet has described this visit of Madame de Staël so wittily, with so much *naïveté*, and with such peculiar local coloring, that we cannot refrain from laying a literal translation of the same before the reader.

———

CHAPTER V.

MADAME DE STAËL'S VISIT TO QUEEN HORTENSE.

LOUISE DE COCHELET relates as follows: "Madame de Staël and Madame Récamier had begged permission of the queen to visit her, for the purpose of tendering their thanks. The queen invited them to visit her at St. Leu, on the following day.

"She asked my advice as to which of the members of her social circle were best qualified to cope with Madame de Staël.

"'I, for my part,' said the queen, 'have not the courage to take the lead in the conversation; one cannot be very intellectual when sad at heart, and I fear my dullness will infect the others.'

"We let quite a number of amiable persons pass before us in review, and I amused myself at the mention of each new name, by saying, 'He is too dull for Madame de Staël.'

"The queen laughed, and the list of those who were to be invited was at last agreed upon. We all awaited the arrival of the two ladies in great suspense. The obligation imposed on us by the queen, of being intellectual at all hazards, had the effect of conjuring up a somewhat embarrassed and stupid expression to our faces. We presented the appearance of actors on the stage looking at each other, while awaiting the rise of the curtain. Jests and *bon mots* followed each other in rapid succession until the arrival of the carriage recalled to our faces an expression of official earnestness.

"Madame Récamier, still young, and very handsome, and with an expression of *naïveté* in her charming countenance, made the impression on me of being a young lady in love, carefully watched over by too severe a *duenna*, her timid, gentle manner contrasted so strongly with the somewhat too masculine self-consciousness of her companion. Madame de Staël is, however, generally ad-

16

mitted to have been good and kind, particularly to this friend, and I only speak of the impression she made on one to whom she was a stranger, at first sight.

"Madame de Staël's extremely dark complexion, her original toilet, her perfectly bare shoulders, of which either might have been very beautiful, but which harmonized very poorly with each other; her whole *ensemble* was far from approximating to the standard of the ideal I had formed of the authoress of Delphine and Corinne. I had almost hoped to find in her one of the heroines she had so beautifully portrayed, and I was therefore struck dumb with astonishment. But, after the first shock, I was at least compelled to acknowledge that she possessed very beautiful and expressive eyes; and yet it seemed impossible for me to find anything in her countenance on which love could fasten, although I have been told that she has often inspired that sentiment.

"When I afterward expressed my astonishment to the queen, she replied: 'It is, perhaps, because she is capable of such great love herself, that she succeeds in inspiring others with love; moreover, it flatters a man's self-love to be noticed by such a woman, and, in the end, one can dispense with beauty, when one has Madame de Staël's intellect.'

"The queen inquired after Madame de Staël's daughter, who had not come with her, and who was said to be truly charming. I believe the young gentlemen of our party could have confronted the beautiful eyes of the daughter with still greater amiability than those of the mother, but an attack of toothache had prevented her coming.

"After the first compliments and salutations, the queen proposed to the ladies to take a look at her park. They seated themselves on the cushions of the queen's large *char à banc*, which has become historic on account of the many high and celebrated personages who have been driven in it at different times. The Emperor Napoleon was, however, not one of this number, as he never visited St. Leu ; but, with this exception, there are few of the great and celebrated who have not been seated in it at one time or another.

"As they drove through the park and the forest of Montmorency, in a walk only, the conversation was kept up as in the parlor, and the consumption of intellectuality was continued. The beautiful neighborhood, that reminded one of Switzerland, as it was remarked, was duly admired. Then Italy was spoken of. The queen, who had been somewhat *distraite*, and had good cause to be somewhat sad, and disposed to commune with herself, addressed Madame de Staël with the question, ' You have been in Italy, then ? '

"Madame de Staël was, as it were, transfixed with dismay, and the gentlemen exclaimed with one accord : ' And Corinne ? and Corinne ? '

"' Ah, that is true,' said the queen, in embarrassment, awakening, as it were, from her dreams.

"' Is it possible,' asked M. de Canonville, ' your majesty has not read Corinne ? '

" ' Yes—no,' said the queen, visibly confused, ' I shall read it again,' and, in order to conceal an emotion that I alone could understand, she abruptly changed the topic of conversation.

" She might have said the truth, and simply informed them that the book had appeared just at the time her eldest son had died in Holland. The king, disquieted at seeing her so profoundly given up to her grief, believed, in accordance with Corvisart's advice, that it was necessary to arouse her from this state of mental dejection at all hazards. It was determined that I should read ' Corinne ' to her. She was not in a condition to pay much attention to it, but she had involuntarily retained some remembrance of this romance. Since then, I had several times asked permission of the queen to read Corinne to her, but she had always refused. ' No, no,' said she, ' not yet; this romance has identified itself with my sorrow. Its name alone recalls the most fearful period of my whole life. I have not yet the courage to renew these painful impressions.'

" I, alone, had therefore been able to divine what had embarrassed and moved the queen so much when she replied to the question addressed to her concerning Corinne. But the authoress could, of course, only interpret it as indicating indifference for her master-work, and I told the queen on the following day that it would have been better to have confessed the cause of her confusion to Madame de Staël.

" ' Madame de Staël would not have understood me,'

said she; 'now, I am lost to her good opinion, she will consider me a simpleton, but it was not the time to speak of myself, and of my painful reminiscences.'

" The large *char à banc* was always preferred to the handsomest carriages (although it was very plain, and consisted of two wooden benches covered with cushions, placed opposite each other), because it was more favorable for conversation. But it afforded no security against inclement weather, and this we were soon to experience. The rain poured in streams, and we all returned to the castle thoroughly wet. A room was there prepared and offered the ladies, in which they might repair the disarrangement of their toilet caused by the storm. I remained with them long, kept there by the questions of Madame de Staël concerning the queen and her son, which questions were fairly showered upon me. There was now no longer a question of intellectuality, but merely of washing, hair-dressing, and reposing, with an entire abandonment of the display of mind, the copiousness of which I had been compelled to admire but a moment before. I said to myself: 'There they are, face to face, like the rest of the world, with material life, these two celebrated women, who are everywhere sought after, and received with such marked consideration. There they are, as wet as myself, and as little poetic.' We were really behind the curtain, but it was shortly to rise again.

" Voices were heard under the window; among other voices, a German accent was audible, and both ladies im-

mediately exclaimed: 'Ah, that is Prince Augustus of
Prussia!'

"No one expected the prince, and this meeting with
the two ladies had therefore the appearance of being acci-
dental. He had come merely to pay the queen a visit,
and it was so near dinner-time, that politeness required
that he should be invited to remain. And this was doubt-
less what he wished.

"The prince had the queen on his right, and Madame
de Staël on his left. The servant of the latter had laid a
little green twig on her napkin, which she twisted between her fingers while speaking, as was her habit. The
conversation was animated, and it was amusing to observe
Madame de Staël gesticulating with the little twig in her
fingers. One might have supposed that some fairy had
given her this talisman, and that her genius was dependent upon this little twig.

"Constantinople, with which city several of the gentlemen were well acquainted, was now the topic of conversation. Madame de Staël thought it would be a
delightful task for an intellectual woman, to turn the
sultan's head, and then to compel him to give his Turks
a constitution. After dinner, freedom of the press was
also a topic of conversation.

"Madame de Staël astonished me, not only by the
brilliancy of her genius, but also by the deep earnestness
with which she treated questions of that kind, for until
then custom had not allowed women to discuss such matters. At entertainments, philosophy, morals, sentiment,

MADAME DE STAËL'S VISIT TO QUEEN HORTENSE. 239

heroism, and the like, had been the subjects of conversation, but the emperor monopolized politics. His era was that of actions, and, we may say it with pride, of great actions, while the era that followed was essentially that of great words, and of political and literary controversies.

"Madame de Staël spoke to the queen of her motto: 'Do that which is right, happen what may.'

"'In my exile, which you so kindly endeavored to terminate,' said she, 'I often repeated this motto, and thought of you while doing so.'

"While speaking thus, her countenance was illumined by the reflection of inward emotion, and I found her beautiful. She was no longer the woman of mind only, but also the woman of heart and feeling, and I comprehended at this moment how charming she could be.

"Afterward, she had a long conversation with the queen touching the emperor. 'Why was he so angry with me?' asked she. 'He could not have known how much I admired him! I will see him—I shall go to Elba! Do you think he would receive me well? I was born to worship this man, and he has repelled me.'

"'Ah, madame,' replied the queen, 'I have often heard the emperor say that he had a great mission to fulfil, and that he could compare his labors with the exertions of a man who, having the summit of a steep mountain ever before his eyes, strains every nerve to attain it, ever toiling painfully upward, and allowing his progress to be arrested by no obstacle whatever. "All the worse for

those," said he, "who meet me on my course—I can show
them no consideration."'

"'You met him on his course, madame; perhaps he
would have extended you a helping hand, after having
reached the summit of his mountain.'

"'I must speak with him,' said Madame de Staël; 'I
have been injured in his opinion.'

"'I think so too,' replied the queen, 'but you would
judge him ill, if you considered him capable of hating
any one. He believed you to be his enemy, and he
feared you, which was something very unusual for him,'
added she, with a smile. 'Now that he is unfortunate,
you will show yourself his friend, and prove yourself to
be such, and I am satisfied that he will receive you
well.'

"Madame de Staël also occupied herself a great deal
with the young princes, but she met with worse success
with them than with us. It was perhaps in order to
judge of their mental capacity, that she showered unsuit-
able questions upon them.

"'Do you love your uncle?'

"'Very much, madame!'

"'And will you also be as fond of war as he is?'

"'Yes, if it did not cause so much misery.'

"'Is it true that he often made you repeat a fable
commencing with the words, "The strongest is always in
the right?"'

"'Madame, he often made us repeat fables, but this
one not oftener than any other.'

"Young Prince Napoleon, a boy of astounding mental capacity and precocious judgment, answered all these questions with the greatest composure, and, at the conclusion of this examination, turned to me and said quite audibly: 'This lady asks a great many questions. Is that what you call being intellectual?'

"After the departure of our distinguished visitors, we all indulged in an expression of opinion concerning them, and young Prince Napoleon was the one upon whom the ladies had made the least flattering impression, but he only ventured to intimate as much in a low voice.

"I for my part had been more dazzled than gladdened by this visit. One could not avoid admiring this genius in spite of its inconsiderateness, and its wanderings, but there was nothing pleasing, nothing graceful and womanly, in Madame de Staël's manner." *

CHAPTER VI.

THE OLD AND THE NEW ERA.

THE restoration was accomplished. The allies had at last withdrawn from the kingdom, and Louis XVIII. was now the independent ruler of France. In him, in the returned members of his family, and in the emigrants who were pouring into the country from all quarters, was

* Cochelet, Mémoires sur la Reine Hortense, vol. i., pp. 429–440.

represented the old era of France, the era of despotic
royal power, of brilliant manners, of intrigues, of aristocratic ideas, of ease and luxury. Opposed to them stood
the France of the new era, the generation formed by
Napoleon and the revolution, the new aristocracy, who
possessed no other ancestors than merit and valorous
deeds, an aristocracy that had nothing to relate of the
œil de bœuf and the *petites maisons,* but an aristocracy
that could tell of the battle-field and of the hospitals in
which their wounds had been healed.

These two parties stood opposed to each other.

Old and young France now carried on an hourly, continuous warfare at the court of Louis XVIII., with this
difference, however, that young France, hitherto ever
victorious, now experienced a continuous series of reverses and humiliations. Old France was now victorious.
Not victorious through its gallantry and merit, but
through its past, which it endeavored to connect with
the present, without considering the chasm which lay
between.

True, King Louis had agreed, in the treaty of the
11th of April, that none of his subjects should be deprived of their titles and dignities; and the new dukes,
princes, marshals, counts, and barons, could therefore appear at court, but they played but a sad and humiliating
rôle, and they were made to feel that they were only
tolerated, and not welcome.

The gentlemen who, before the revolution, had been
entitled to seats in the royal equipages, still retained this

privilege, but the doors of these equipages were never opened to the gentlemen of the new Napoleonic nobility. "The ladies of the old era still retained their *tabouret*, as well as their grand and little *entrée* to the Tuileries and the Louvre, and it would have been considered very arrogant if the duchesses of the new era had made claim to similar honors."

It was the Duchess d'Angoulême who took the lead and set the Faubourg St. Germain an example of intolerance and arrogant pretensions in ignoring the empire. She was the most unrelenting enemy of the new era, born of the revolution, and of its representatives; it is true, however, that she, who was the daughter of the beheaded royal pair, and who had herself so long languished in the Temple, had been familiar with the horrors of the revolution in their saddest and most painful features. She now determined, as she could no longer punish, to at least forget this era, and to seem to be entirely oblivious of its existence.

At one of the first dinners given by the king to the allies, the Duchess d'Angoulême, who sat next to the King of Bavaria, pointed to the Grand-duke of Baden, and asked: "Is not this the prince who married a princess of Bonaparte's making? What weakness to ally one's self in such a manner with that general!"

The duchess did not or would not remember that the King of Bavaria, as well as the Emperor of Austria, who sat on her other side, and could well hear her words, had also allied themselves with General Bonaparte.

After she had again installed herself in the rooms she had formerly occupied in the Tuileries, the duchess asked old Dubois, who had formerly tuned her piano, and had retained this office under the empire, and who now showed her the new and elegant instruments provided by Josephine—she asked him : " What has become of my piano ? "

This "piano " had been an old and worn-out concern, and the duchess was surprised at not finding it, as though almost thirty years had not passed since she had seen it last; as though the 10th of August, 1792, the day on which the populace demolished the Tuileries, had never been !

But the period from 1795 to 1814 was ignored on principle, and the Bourbons seemed really to have quite forgotten that more than one night lay between the last levee of King Louis XVI. and the levee of to-day of King Louis XVIII. They seemed astonished that persons they had known as children had grown up since they last saw them, and insisted on treating every one as they had done in 1789.

After the Empress Josephine's death, Count d'Artois paid a visit to Malmaison, a place that had hardly existed before the revolution, and which owed its creation to Josephine's love and taste for art.

The empress, who had a great fondness for botany, had caused magnificent greenhouses to be erected at Malmaison ; in these all the plants and flowers of the world had been collected. Knowing her taste, all the princes of Europe had sent her, in the days of her grandeur, in order to afford her a moment's gratification, the rarest exotics.   The Prince Regent of England had even found means, during the war with France, to send her a number of rare West-Indian plants.   In this manner her collection had become the richest and most complete in all Europe.

Count d'Artois, as above said, had come to Malmaison to view this celebrated place of sojourn of Josephine, and, while being conducted through the greenhouses, he exclaimed, as though he recognized his old flowers of 1789 : "Ah, here are our plants of Trianon!"

And, like their masters the Bourbons, the emigrants had also returned to France with the same ideas with which they had fled the country.   They endeavored, in all their manners, habits, and pretensions, to begin again precisely where they had left off in 1789.   They had so lively an appreciation of their own merit, that they took no notice whatever of other people's, and yet their greatest merit consisted in having emigrated.

For this merit they now demanded a reward.

All of these returned emigrants demanded rewards, positions, and pensions, and considered it incomprehensible that those who were already in possession were not at once deprived of them.   Intrigues were the order of the day, and in general the representatives of the old era succeeded in supplanting those of the new era in offices and pensions as well as in court honors.   All the high positions in the army were filled by the marquises, dukes, and counts, of the old era, who had served tapestry and picked silk in Coblentz, while the France of the new era was fighting on the battle-field, and they now began to teach the soldiers of the empire the old drill of 1780.

The etiquette of the olden time was restored, and the same luxurious and lascivious disposition prevailed among these cavaliers of the former century which had been approved in the *œil de bœuf* and in the *petites maisons* of the old era.

These old cavaliers felt contempt for the young Frenchmen of the new era on account of their pedantic morality ; they scornfully regarded men who perhaps had not more than one mistress, and to whom the wife of a friend was so sacred, that they never dared to approach her with a disrespectful thought even.

These legitimist gentlemen entertained themselves chiefly with reflections over the past, and their own grandeur. In the midst of the many new things by which they were surrounded, some of which they unfortunately found it impossible to ignore, it was their sweetest relaxation to give themselves up entirely to the remembrance of the old *régime*, and when they spoke of this era, they forgot their age and debility, and were once more the young *roués* of the *œil de bœuf*.

Once in the antechamber of King Louis XVIII., while the Marquis de Chimène and the Duke de Lauraguais, two old heroes of the frivolous era, in which the boudoir and the *petites maisons* were the battle-field, and the myrtle instead of the laurel the reward of victory,

while these gentlemen were conversing of some occurrence under the old government, the Duke de Lauraguais, in order to more nearly fix the date of the occurrence of which they were speaking, remarked to the marquis, " It was in the year in which I had my *liaison* with
your wife."

" Ah, yes," replied the marquis, with perfect composure, " that was in the year 1776."

Neither of the gentlemen found anything strange in
this allusion to the past. The *liaison* in question had
been a perfectly commonplace matter, and it would have
been as ridiculous in the duke to deny it as for the marquis to have shown any indignation.

The wisest and most enlightened of all these gentlemen was their head, King Louis XVIII. himself.

He was well aware of the errors of those who surrounded him, and placed but little confidence in the representatives of the old court. But he was nevertheless
powerless to withdraw himself from their influence, and
after he had accorded the people the charter, in opposition to the will and opinion of the whole royal family,
of his whole court and of his ministers, and had sworn
to support it in spite of the opposition of " Monsieur "
and the Prince de Condé, who was in the habit of call-
ing the charter " *Mademoiselle la Constitution de 1791*,"
Louis withdrew to the retirement of his apartments in
the Tuileries, and left his minister Blacas to attend to
the little details of government, the king deeming the
great ones only worthy of his attention.

CHAPTER VII.

KING LOUIS XVIII. was, however, in the retirement
of his palace, still the most enlightened and unprejudiced
of the representatives of the old era; he clearly saw many
things to which his advisers purposely closed their eyes.
To his astonishment, he observed that the men who had
risen to greatness under Bonaparte, and who had fallen
to the king along with the rest of his inheritance, were
not so ridiculous, awkward, and foolish, as they had been
represented to be.

"I had been made to suppose," said Louis XVIII.,
"that these generals of Bonaparte were peasants and ruf-
fians, but such is not the case.   He schooled these men
well.   They are polite, and quite as shrewd as the representatives of the old court.   We must conduct ourselves
very cautiously toward them."

This kind of recognition of the past which sometimes
escaped Louis XVIII., was a subject of bitter displeasure
to the gentlemen of the old era, and they let the king perceive it.

King Louis felt this, and, in order to conciliate his
court, he often saw himself compelled to humiliate "the
parvenus" who had forced themselves among the former.

Incessant quarrelling and intriguing within the Tuileries was the consequence, and Louis was often dejected,

uneasy, and angry, in the midst of the splendor that surrounded him.

"I am angry with myself and the others," said he on
one occasion to an intimate friend. "An invisible and
secret power is ever working in opposition to my will,
frustrating my plans, and paralyzing my authority."

"And yet you are king!"

"Undoubtedly I am king!" exclaimed Louis, angrily; "but am I also master? The king is he who all his
life long receives ambassadors, gives tiresome audiences,
listens to annihilating discourses, goes in state to Notre-
Dame, dines in public once a year, and is pompously
buried in St. Denis when he dies. The master is he who
commands and can enforce obedience, who puts an end
to intriguing, and can silence old women as well as
priests. Bonaparte was king and master at the same
time! His ministers were his clerks, the kings his
brothers merely his agents, and his courtiers nothing
more than his servants. His ministers vied with his senate in servility, and his *Corps Législatif* sought to outdo his senate and the church in subserviency. He was
an extraordinary and an enviable man, for he had not
only devoted servants and faithful friends, but also an
accommodating church." *

King Louis XVIII., weary of the incessant intrigues ·
with which his courtiers occupied themselves, withdrew
himself more and more into the retirement of his palace,
and left the affairs of state to the care of M. de Blacas,

* Mémoires d'une Femme de Qualité, vol. v., p. 35.
17

who, with all his arrogance and egotism, knew very little about governing.

The king preferred to entertain himself with his friends, to read them portions of his memoirs, to afford them an opportunity of admiring his verses, and to regale them with his witty and not always chaste anecdotes; he preferred all these things to tedious and useless disputes with his ministers. He had given his people the charter, and his ministers might now govern in accordance with this instrument.

"The people demand liberty," said the king. "I give them enough of it to protect them against despotism, without according them unbridled license. Formerly, the taxes appointed by my mere will would have made me odious; now the people tax themselves. Hereafter, I have nothing to do but to confer benefits and show mercy, for the responsibility for all the evil that is done will rest entirely with my ministers." *

While his ministers were thus governing according to the charter, and "doing evil," the king, who now had nothing but "good" to do, was busying himself in settling the weighty questions of the old etiquette.

One of the most important features of this etiquette was the question of the fashions that should now be introduced at court; for it was, of course, absurd to think of adopting the fashions of the empire, and thereby recognize at court that there had really been a change since 1789.

* Mémoires d'une Femme de Qualité, vol. i., p. 410.

They desired to effect a counter-revolution, not only in politics, but also in fashions; and this important matter occupied the attention of the grand dignitaries of the court for weeks before the first grand levee that the king was to hold in the Tuileries. But, as nothing was accomplished by their united wisdom, the king finally held a private consultation with his most intimate gentleman and lady friends on this important matter, that had, unfortunately, not been determined by the charter.

The grand-master of ceremonies, M. de Bregé, declared to the king that it was altogether improper to continue the fashions of the empire at the court of the legitimate King of France.

"We are, therefore, to have powder, coats-of-mail, etc.," observed the king.

M. de Bregé replied, with all gravity, that he had given this subject his earnest consideration day and night, but that he had not yet arrived at a conclusion worthy of the grand-master of ceremonies of the legitimate king.

"Sire," said the Duke de Chartres, smiling, "I, for my part, demand knee-breeches, shoe-buckles, and the cue."

"But I," exclaimed the Prince de Poir, who had remained in France during the empire, "I demand damages, if we are to be compelled to return to the old fashions and clothing before the new ones are worn out!"

The grand-master of ceremonies replied to this jest at his expense with a profound sigh only; and the king at last put an end to this great question, by deciding that every one should be permitted to follow the old or new fashions, according to his individual taste and inclination.

The grand-master of ceremonies was compelled to submit to this royal decision; but in doing so he observed, with profound sadness: "Your majesty is pleased to smile, but dress makes half the man; uniformity of attire confounds the distinctions of rank, and leads directly to an agrarian law."

"Yes, marquis," exclaimed the king, "you think precisely as Figaro. Many a man laughs at a judge in a short dress, who trembles before a procurator in a long gown." *

But while the king suppressed the counter-revolution in fashions, he allowed the grand-master of ceremonies to reintroduce the entire etiquette of the old era. In conformity with this etiquette, the king could not rise from his couch in the morning until the doors had been opened to all those who had the *grande entrée*—that is to say, to the officers of his household, the marshals of France, several favored ladies; further, to his *cafetier*, his tailor, the bearer of his slippers, his barber, with two assistants, his watchmaker, and his apothecaries.

The king was dressed in the presence of all these favored individuals, etiquette permitting him only to adjust his necktie himself, but requiring him, however, to empty his pockets of their contents of the previous day.

* Mémoires d'une Femme de Qualité, vol. i., p. 384.

The usage of the old era, "the public dinner of the royal family," was also reintroduced; and the grand-master of ceremonies not only found it necessary to make preparations for this dinner weeks beforehand, but the king was also compelled to occupy himself with this matter, and to appoint for this great ceremony the necessary "officers of provisions"—that is to say, the wine-taster, the cup-bearers, the grand doorkeepers, and the cook-in-chief.

At this first grand public dinner, the celebrated and indispensable "ship" of the royal board stood again immediately in front of the king's seat. This old "ship" of the royal board, an antique work of art which the city of Paris had once presented to a King of France, had also been lost in the grand shipwreck of 1792, and the grand-master of ceremonies had been compelled to have a new one made by the court jeweller for the occasion. This "ship" was a work in gilded silver, in form of a vessel deprived of its masts and rigging; and in the same, between two golden plates, were contained the perfumed napkins of the king. In accordance with the old etiquette, no one, not even the princes and princesses, could pass the "ship" without making a profound obeisance, which they were also compelled to make on passing the royal couch.

The king restored yet another fashion of the old era —the fashion of the "royal lady-friends."

Like his brother the Count d'Artois, Louis XVIII. also had his lady-friends; and among these the beautiful

and witty Countess Ducayla occupied the first position.
It was her office to amuse the king, and dissipate the
dark clouds that were only too often to be seen on the
brow of King Louis, who was chained to his arm-chair
by ill-health, weakness, and excessive corpulency. She
narrated to him the *chronique scandaleuse* of the imperial court; she reminded him of the old affairs of his
youth, which the king knew how to relate with so
much wit and humor, and which he so loved to relate;
it devolved upon her to examine the letters of the
"black cabinet," and to read the more interesting ones
to the king.

King Louis was not ungrateful to his royal friend,
and he rewarded her in a truly royal manner for sometimes banishing *ennui* from his apartments. Finding
that the countess had no intimate acquaintance with the
contents of the Bible, he gave her the splendid Bible of
Royaumont, ornamented with one hundred and fifty
magnificent engravings, after paintings of Raphael. Instead of tissue-paper, a thousand-franc note covered each
of these engravings.*

On another occasion, the king gave her a copy of the
"Charter;" and in this each leaf was also covered with
a thousand-franc note, as in the Bible.

For so many proofs of the royal generosity, the beautiful countess, perhaps willingly, submitted to be called
"the royal snuff-box," which appellation had its origin in

---

* Amours et Galanteries des Rois de France, par St. Edme, vol. ii.,
p. 383. Mémoires d'une Femme de Qualité, vol. i., p. 409.

the habit which the king fondly indulged in of strewing snuff on the countess's lovely shoulder, and then snuffing it up with his nose.

CHAPTER VIII.

THE DRAWING-ROOM OF THE DUCHESS OF ST. LEU.

WHILE the etiquette and frivolity of the old era were being introduced anew at the Tuileries, and while M. de Blacas was governing in complacent recklessness, time was progressing, notwithstanding his endeavors to turn it backward in his flight.

While, out of the incessant conflict between the old and the new France, a discontented France was being born, Napoleon, the Emperor of Elba, was forming great plans of conquest, and preparing in secret understanding with the faithful, to leave his place of exile and return to France.

He well knew that he could rely on his old army— on the army who loudly cried, " *Vive le roi !* " and then added, *sotto voce*, " *de Rome, et son petit papa !* " *

Hortense, the new Duchess of St. Leu, took but little part in all these things. She had, notwithstanding her youth and beauty, in a measure taken leave of the world. She felt herself to be no longer the woman, but only the mother; her sons were the objects of all her tenderness and love, and she lived for them only. In her retire-

* Cochelet, Mémoires sur la Reine Hortense, vol. iii., p. 121.

ment at St. Leu, her time was devoted to the arts, to
reading, and to study; and, after having been thus occupied throughout the day, she passed the evening in her
drawing-room, in unrestrained intellectual conversation
with her friends.

For she had friends who had remained true, notwithstanding the obscurity into which she had withdrawn
herself, and who, although they filled important positions
at the new court, had retained their friendship for the
solitary dethroned queen.

With these friends the Duchess of St. Leu conversed,
in the evening, in her parlor, of the grand and beautiful
past, giving themselves up entirely to these recollections,
little dreaming that this harmless relaxation could awaken
suspicion.

For the Duke of Otranto, who had succeeded in his
shrewdness in retaining his position of minister of police,
as well under Louis XVIII. as under Napoleon, had his
spies everywhere; he knew of all that was said in every
parlor of Paris; he knew also that it was the custom, in
the parlors of the Duchess of St. Leu, to look from the
dark present back at the brilliant past, and to console
one's self for the littleness of the present, with the recollection of the grandeur of departed days! And Fouché,
or rather the Duke of Otranto, knew how to utilize
everything.

In order to arouse Minister Blacas out of his stupid
dream of security, to a realizing sense of the grave
events that were taking place, Fouché told him that a

conspiracy against the government was being formed in the parlors of the Duchess of St. Leu; that all those who were secret adherents of Bonaparte were in the habit of assembling there, and planning the deliverance of the emperor from Elba. In order, however, on the other hand, to provide against the possibility of Napoleon's return, the Duke of Otranto hastened to the Duchess of St. Leu, to warn her and conjure her to be on her guard against the spies by whom she was surrounded, as suspicion might be easily excited against her at court.

Hortense paid no attention to this warning; she considered precaution unnecessary, and was not willing to deprive herself of her one happiness—that of seeing her friends, and of conversing with them in a free and unconstrained manner.

The parlors of the duchess, therefore, continued to be thrown open to her faithful friends, who had also been the faithful servants of the emperor; and the Dukes of Bassano, of Friaul, of Ragusa, of the Moskwa, and their wives, as well as the gallant Charles de Labedoyère, and the acute Count Regnault de Saint-Jean d'Angely, still continued to meet in the parlors of the Duchess of St. Leu.

The voice of hostility was raised against them with ever-increasing hostility; the reunions that took place at St. Leu were day by day portrayed at the Tuileries in more hateful colors; and the poor duchess, who lived in sorrow and retirement in her apartments, became an object of hatred and envy to these proud ladies of the old aristocracy, who were unable to comprehend how this woman could be thought of while they were near, although she had been the ornament of the imperial court, and who was considered amiable, intellectual, and beautiful, even under the legitimate dynasty.

Hortense heard of the ridiculous and malicious reports which had been circulated concerning her, and, for the sake of her friends and sons, she resolved to put an end to them.

"I must leave my dear St. Leu and go to Paris," said she. "There they can better observe all my actions. Reason demands that I should conform myself to circumstances."

She therefore abandoned her quiet home at St. Leu, and repaired with her children and her court to Paris, to again take up her abode in her dwelling in the Rue de la Victoire.

But this step gave fresh fuel to the calumnies of her enemies, who saw in her the embodied remembrance of the empire which they hated and at the same time feared.

The Bonapartists still continued their visits to her parlors, as before; and no appeals, no representations could induce Hortense to close her doors against her faithful friends, for fear that their fidelity might excite suspicion against herself.

In order, however, to contradict the report that adherents of Napoleon only were in the habit of frequenting her parlors, the duchess also extended the hospitalities of her parlors to the strangers who brought letters of recommendation, and who desired to be introduced to her. Great numbers hastened to avail themselves of this permission.

The most brilliant and select circle was soon assembled around the duchess. There, were to be found the great men of the empire, who came out of attachment; distinguished strangers, who came out of admiration; and, finally, the aristocrats of the old era, who came out of curiosity, who came to see if the Duchess of St. Leu was really so intelligent, amiable, and graceful, as she was said to be.

The parlors of the duchess were therefore more talked of in Paris than they had been at St. Leu. The old duchesses and princesses of the Faubourg St. Germain, with all their ancestors, prejudices, and pretensions, were enraged at hearing this everlasting praise of the charming queen, and endeavored to appease their wrath by renewed hostilities against its object.

It was not enough that she was calumniated, at court and in society, as a dangerous person; the arm of the press was also wielded against her.

As we have said, Hortense was the embodied remembrance of the empire, and it was therefore determined that she should be destroyed. *Brochures* and pamphlets were published, in which the king was appealed to, to banish from Paris, and even from France, the dangerous woman who was conspiring publicly, and even under the very eyes of the government, for Napoleon, and to banish with her the two children also, the two Napoleons;

"for," said these odious accusers, "to leave these two
princes here, means to raise in France wolves that would
one day ravage their country." *

Hortense paid but little attention to these reports and
calumnies. She was too much accustomed to being misunderstood and wrongly judged, to allow herself to be
disquieted thereby. She knew that calumnies were
never refuted by contradiction, and that it was therefore
better to meet them with proud silence, and to conquer
them by contempt, instead of giving them new life by
combating and contradicting them.

She herself entertained such contempt for calumny
that she never allowed anything abusive to be said in her
presence that would injure any one in her estimation.
When, on one occasion, while she was still Queen of
Holland, a lady of Holland took occasion to speak ill of
another lady, on account of her political opinions, the
queen interrupted her, and said : " Madame, here I am a
stranger to all parties, and receive all persons with the
same consideration, for I love to hear every one well
spoken of ; and I generally receive an unfavorable impression of those only who speak ill of others." †

And, strange to say, she herself was ever the object of
calumny and accusation.

"During twenty-five years, I have never been separated from Princess Hortense," says Louise de Cochelet,
" and I have never observed in her the slightest feeling

* Cochelet, Mémoires sur la Reine Hortense, vol. ii., p. 230.
† Cochelet, vol. i., p. 378.

of bitterness against any one ; ever good and gentle, she never failed to take an interest in those who were unhappy ; and she endeavored to help them whenever and wherever they presented themselves. And this noble and gentle woman was always the object of hatred and absurd calumnies, and against all this she was armed with the integrity and purity of her actions and intentions only." *

Nor did Hortense now think of contradicting the calumnies that had been circulated concerning her. Her mind was occupied with other and far more important matters.

An ambassador of her husband, who resided in Florence, had come to Paris in order to demand of Hortense, in the name of Louis Bonaparte, his two sons.

After much discussion, he had finally declared that he would be satisfied, if his wife would send him his eldest son, Napoleon Louis, only.

But the loving mother could not and would not consent to a separation from either of her children ; and as, in spite of her entreaties, her husband persisted in refusing to allow her to retain both of them, she resolved, in the anguish of maternal love, to resort to the most extreme means to retain the possession of her sons.

She informed her husband's ambassador that it was her fixed purpose to retain possession of her children, and appealed to the law to recognize and protect them,

* Cochelet, vol. i., p. 878.

and not allow her sons to be deprived of their rights as
Frenchmen, by going into a compulsory exile.

While the Duchess of St. Leu was being accused of
conspiring in favor of Napoleon, her whole soul was
occupied with the one question, which was to decide
whether one of her sons could be torn from her side or
not; and, if she conspired at all, it was only with her
lawyer in order to frustrate her husband's plans.

But the calumnies and accusations of the press were
nevertheless continued ; and at last her friends thought it
necessary to lay before the queen a journal that contained
a violent and abusive article against her, and to request
that they might be permitted to reply to it.

With a sad smile, Hortense read the article and returned the newspaper.

" It is extremely mortifying to be scorned by one's
countrymen," said she, " but it would be useless to make
any reply.   I can afford to disregard such attacks—they
are powerless to harm me."

But when on the following morning the same journal
contained a venomous and odious article levelled at her
husband, Louis Bonaparte, her generous indignation was
aroused, and, oblivious of all their disagreements, and
even of the process now pending between them, she remembered only that it was the father of her children
whom they had dared to attack, and that he was not pres-
sent to defend himself.   It therefore devolved upon her
to defend him.

" I am enraged, and I desire that M. Després shall reply to this article at once," said Hortense. "Although paternal love on the one side, and maternal love on the other, has involved us in a painful process, it nevertheless concerns no one else, and it disgraces neither of us. I should be in despair, if this sad controversy were made the pretext for insulting the father of my children and the honored name he bears. For the very reason that I stand alone, am I called on to defend the absent to the best of my ability. Therefore let M. Després come to me; I will instruct him how to answer this disgraceful article!"

On the following day, an able and eloquent article in defence of Louis Bonaparte appeared in the journal—an article that shamed and silenced his accusers—an article which the prince, whose cause it so warmly espoused, probably never thought of attributing to the wife to whose maternal heart he had caused such anguish. *

CHAPTER IX.

THE BURIAL OF LOUIS XVI. AND HIS WIFE.

THE earnest endeavors of the Bourbon court to find the resting-place of the remains of the royal couple who had died on the scaffold, and who had expiated the crimes of their predecessors rather than their own, were at last successful. The remains of the illustrious martyrs had

* Cochelet, vol. i., p. 303.

been sought for in accordance with the directions of persons who had witnessed their sorrowful and contemptuous burial, and the body of Louis XVI. was found in a desolate corner of the grave-yard of St. Roch, and in another place also that of Queen Marie Antoinette.

It was the king's wish, and a perfectly natural and just one, to inter these bodies in the royal vault at St. Denis, but he wished to do it quietly and without pomp; his acute political tact taught him that these sad remains should not be made the occasion of a political demonstration, and that it was unwise to permit the bones of Louis XVI. to become a new apple of discord.

But the king's court, even his nearest relatives, his ministers, and the whole troop of arrogant courtiers, who desired, by means of an ostentatious interment, not only to show a proper respect for the beheaded royal pair, but also to punish those whom they covertly called " regicides," and whom they were nevertheless now compelled to tolerate—the king's entire court demanded a solemn and ceremonious interment; and Louis, who, as he himself had said, "was king, but not master," was compelled to yield to this demand.

Preparations were therefore made for an ostentatious interment of the royal remains, and it was determined that the melancholy rites should take place on the 21st of January, 1815, the anniversary of painful memories and unending regret for the royal family.

M. de Chateaubriand, the noble and intelligent eulogist and friend of the Bourbons, caused an article to be in-

serted in the *Journal des Débats*, in which he announced
the impending ceremony. This article was then republished in pamphlet form; and so great was the sympathy of the Parisians in the approaching event, that
thirty thousand copies were disposed of, in Paris alone,
in one day.

On the 20th of January the graves of the martyrs
were opened, and all the princes of the royal house who
were present, knelt down at the edge of the grave to
mingle their prayers with those of the thousands who
had accompanied them to the church-yard.

But the king was right. This act, that appeared to
some to be a mere act of justice, seemed an insult to
others, and reminded them of the dark days of error and
fanaticism, in which they had allowed themselves to be
drawn into the vortex of the general delirium. Many of
those who in the Assembly had voted for the death of the
king, were now residing at Paris, and even at court, as
for instance Fouché, and to them the approaching ceremony seemed an insult.

"Are you aware," exclaimed Descourtis, as he rushed
into the apartment of Cambacérès, who was at that moment conversing with the Count de Pere, "have you
already been informed that this ceremony is really to take
place to-morrow?"

"Yes, to-morrow is the fated day. To-morrow we
are to be delivered over to the daggers of fanatics."

"Is this the pardon that was promised us?"

"As for that," exclaimed the Count de Pere (a good

18

royalist), "I was not aware that there was an article in
the constitution forbidding the reinterment of the mortal
remains of the royal pair. The proceeding will be perfectly lawful."

"It is their purpose to infuriate the populace," exclaimed Descourtis, pale with inward agitation. "Old
recollections are to be recalled and a mute accusation
hurled at us. But we shall some day be restored to
power again, and then we will remember also!"

Cambacérès, who had listened to this conversation in
silence, now stepped forward, and, taking Descourtis's
hand in his own, pressed it tenderly.

"Ah, my friend," said he, in sad and solemn tones,
"I would we were permitted to march behind the funeral-
car in mourning-robes to-morrow! We owe this proof of
repentance to France and to ourselves!"

The solemn funeral celebration took place on the following day. All Paris took part in it. Every one, even
the old republicans, the Bonapartists as well as the royalists, joined the funeral procession, in order to testify that
they had abandoned the past and were repentant.

Slowly and solemnly, amid the ringing of all the
bells, the roll of the drum, the thunders of artillery,
and the chants of the clergy, the procession moved onward.

The golden crown, which hung suspended over the
funeral-car, shone lustrously in the sunlight. It had
fallen from the heads of the royal pair while they still
lived; it now adorned them in death.

Slowly and solemnly the procession moved onward; it had arrived at the Boulevards which separates the two streets of Montmartre.   Suddenly a terrible, thousand-voiced cry of horror burst upon the air.

The crown, which hung suspended over the funeral-car, had fallen down, touching the coffins with a dismal sound, and then broke into fragments on the glittering snow of the street.

This occurred on the 21st of January; two months later, at the same hour, and on the same day, the crown of Louis XVIII. fell from his head, and Napoleon placed it on his own!

CHAPTER X.

NAPOLEON'S RETURN FROM ELBA.

A CRY of tremendous import reverberated through Paris, all France, and all Europe, in the first days of March, 1815.   Napoleon, it was said, had quitted Elba, and would soon arrive in France!

The royalists heard it with dismay, the Bonapartists with a delight that they hardly took the pains to conceal.

Hortense alone took no part in the universal delight of the imperialists.   Her soul was filled with profound sadness and dark forebodings.   "I lament this step," said she; "I would have sacrificed every thing to prevent his return to France, because I am of the belief that no good can come of it. Many will declare for, and many against him, and we shall have a civil war, of which the emperor himself may be the victim." *

In the meanwhile the general excitement was continually increasing; it took possession of every one, and at this time none would have been capable of giving cool and sensible advice.

Great numbers of the emperor's friends came to the Duchess of St. Leu, and demanded of her counsel, assist-ance, and encouragement, accusing her of indifference and want of sympathy, because she did not share their hopes, and was sad instead of rejoicing with them.

But the spies of the still ruling government, who lay in wait around the queen's dwelling, did not hear her words; they only saw that the emperor's former generals and advisers were in the habit of repairing to her parlors, and that was sufficient to stamp Hortense as the head of the conspiracy which had for its object the return of Napoleon to France.

The queen perceived the danger of her situation, but she bowed her head to receive the blows of Fate in silent resignation. "I am environed by torments and perplexities," said she, "but I see no means of avoiding them. There is no resource for me but to arm myself with courage, and that I will do."

The royal government, however, still hoped to be able to stem the advancing tide, and compel the waves of

* Cochelet, vol. ii., p. 348.

insurrection to surge backward and destroy those who had set them in motion.

They proposed to treat the great event which made France glow with new pulsations, as a mere insurrection, that had been discovered in good time, and could therefore be easily repressed.   They therefore determined, above all, to seize and render harmless the " conspirators," that is to say, all those of whom it was known that they had remained faithful to the emperor in their hearts.

Spies surrounded the houses of all the generals, dukes, and princes of the empire, and it was only in disguise and by the greatest dexterity that they could evade the vigilance of the police.

The Duchess of St. Leu was at last also compelled to yield to the urgent entreaties of her friends, and seek an asylum during these days of uncertainty and danger. She quitted her dwelling in disguise, and, penetrating through the army of spies who lay in wait around the house and in the street in which she resided, she happily succeeded in reaching the hiding-place prepared for her by a faithful servant of her mother.   She had already confided her children to another servant who had remained true to her in her time of trouble.

The Duke of Otranto, now once more the faithful Fouché of the empire, was also to have been arrested, but he managed to effect his escape.   General Lavalette— who was aware that the dwelling of the Duchess of St. Leu was no longer watched by the police, who had discovered that the duchess was no longer there—Lavalette took advantage of this circumstance, and concealed himself in her dwelling, and M. de Dandré, the chief of police, who had vainly endeavored to catch the so-called conspirators, exclaimed in anguish : " It is impossible to find any one ; it has been so much noised about that these Bonapartists were to be arrested, that they are now all hidden away."

Like a bombshell the news suddenly burst upon the anxious and doubting capital: " The emperor has been received by the people in Grenoble with exultation, and the troops that were to have been led against him have, together with their chieftain, Charles de Labedoyère, gone over to the emperor. The gates of the city were thrown open, and the people advanced to meet him with shouts of welcome and applause ; and now Napoleon stood no longer at the head of a little body of troops, but at the head of a small army that was increasing with every hour."

The government still endeavored, through its officials and through the public press, to make the Parisians disbelieve this intelligence.

But the government had lost faith in itself. It heard the old, the hated cry, "Vive l'empereur !" resounding through the air ; it heard the fluttering of the victorious battle-flags of Marengo, Arcola, Jena, and Austerlitz ! The Emperor Napoleon was still the conquering hero, who swayed destiny and compelled it to declare for him.

A perfect frenzy of dismay took possession of the

royalists ; and when they learned that Napoleon had
already arrived in Lyons, that its inhabitants had received
him with enthusiasm, and that its garrison had also declared for him, their panic knew no bounds.

The royalist leaders assembled at the ,house of Count
de la Pere, for the purpose of holding a last great discussion and consultation. The most eminent persons,
men and women, differing widely on other subjects, but
a unit on this point, assembled here with the same feelings of patriotic horror, and with the same desire to promote the general welfare. There were Madame de Staël,
Benjamin Constant, Count Lainé, and Chateaubriand ;
there were the Duke de Némours, and Count de la Pere,
and around them gathered the whole troop of anxious
royalists, expecting and hoping that the eloquent lips of
these celebrated personages who stood in their midst
would give them consolation and new life.

Benjamin Constant spoke first. He said that, to Napoleon, that is, to force, force must be opposed. Bonaparte was armed with the love of the soldiers, they must
arm themselves with the love of the citizens. His appearance was imposing, like the visage of Cæsar ; it
would be necessary to oppose to him an equally sublime
countenance. Lafayette should, therefore, be made com-
mander-in-chief of the French army.

M. de Chateaubriand exclaimed, with noble indignation, that the first step to be taken by the government
was to punish severely a ministry that was so short-
sighted, and had committed so many faults. Lainé de-

clared, with a voice tremulous with emotion, that all was lost, and that but one means of confounding tyranny remained ; a scene, portraying the whole terror, dismay, and grief of the capital at the approach of the hated enemy, should be arranged. In accordance with this plan, the whole population of Paris—the entire National Guard, the mothers, the young girls, the children, the old and the young—were to pass out of the city, and await the tyrant; and this aspect of a million of men fleeing from the face of a single human being was to move or terrify him who came to rob them of their peace !

In her enthusiastic and energetic manner, Madame de Staël pronounced an anathema against the usurper who was about to kindle anew, in weeping, shivering France, the flames of war.

All were touched, enthusiastic, and agitated, but they could do nothing but utter fine phrases ; and all that fell from the eloquent lips of these celebrated poets and politicians was, as it were, nothing more than a bulletin concerning the condition of the patient, and concerning the mortal wounds which he had received. This patient was France ; and the royalists, who were assembled in the house of Count de la Pere, now felt that the patient's case was hopeless, and that nothing remained to them but to go into exile, and bemoan his sad fate ! *

* Mémoires d'une Femme de Qualité, vol. i., p. 99.

CHAPTER XI.

LOUIS XVIII.'S DEPARTURE AND NAPOLEON'S ARRIVAL.

WHILE the royalists were thus considering, hesitating, and despairing, King Louis XVIII. had alone retained his composure and sense of security. That is to say, they had taken care not to inform him of the real state of affairs. On the contrary, he had been informed that Bonaparte had been everywhere received with coldness and silence, and that the army would not respond to his appeal, but would remain true to the king. The exultation with which the people everywhere received the advancing emperor found, therefore, no echo in the Tuileries, and the crowd who pressed around the king when he repaired to the hall of the *Corps Législatif* to hold an encouraging address, was not the people, but the royalists—those otherwise so haughty ladies and gentlemen of the old nobility, who again, as on the day of the first entrance, acted the part to which the people were not disposed to adapt themselves, and transformed themselves for a moment into the people, in order to show to the king the demonstrations of his people's love.

The king was completely deceived. M. de Blacas told the king of continuous reverses to Napoleon's arms, while the emperor's advance was in reality a continuous triumph. They had carried this deception so far that they had informed the king that Lyons had closed its gates to Napoleon, and that Ney was advancing to meet him, vowing that he would bring the emperor back to Paris in an iron cage.

The king was therefore composed, self-possessed, and resolute, when suddenly his brother, the Count d'Artois, and the Duke of Orleans, who, according to the king's belief, occupied Lyons as a victor, arrived in Paris alone, as fugitives, abandoned by their soldiers and servants, and informed Louis that Lyons had received the emperor with open arms, and that no resource had been left them but to betake themselves to flight.

And a second, and still more terrible, item of intelligence followed the first. Ney, the king's hope, the last support of his tottering throne, Ney had not had the heart to maintain a hostile position toward his old companion in arms. Ney had gone over to the emperor, and his army had followed him with exultation.

The king's eyes were now opened, he now saw the truth, and learned how greatly he had been deceived.

"Alas," cried he, sadly, "Bonaparte fell because he would not listen to the truth, and I shall fall because they would not tell me the truth!"

At this moment, and while the king was eloquently appealing to his brothers and relatives, and to the gentlemen of his court who surrounded him, to tell him the whole truth, the door opened, and the Minister Blacas, until then so complacent, so confident of victory, now stepped in pale and trembling.

The truth, which he had so long concealed from the king, was now plainly impressed on his pale, terrified countenance. The king had desired to hear the truth; it stood before him in his trembling minister.

A short interval of profound silence occurred; the eyes of all were fastened on the count, and, in the midst of the general silence, he was heard to' say, in a voice choked with emotion: "Sire, all is lost; the army, as well as the people, betray your majesty. It will be necessary for your majesty to leave Paris."

The king staggered backward for an instant, and then fastened an inquiring glance on the faces of all who were present. No one dared to return his gaze with a glance of hope. They all looked down sorrowfully.

The king understood this mute reply, and a deep sigh escaped his breast.

"The tree bears its fruit," said he, with a bitter smile; "heretofore it has been your purpose to make me govern for you, hereafter I shall govern for no one. If I shall, however, return to the throne of my fathers once more, you will be made to understand that I will profit by the experience you have given me!" *

A few hours later, at nightfall, supported on the arm of Count Blacas, without any suite, and preceded by a single lackey bearing a torch, the king left the once more desolate and solitary Tuileries, and fled to Holland.

Twenty-four hours later, on the evening of the 20th of March, Napoleon entered the Tuileries, accompanied

---

* The king's own words. Mémoires d'une Femme de Qualité, vol. i., p. 156.

by the exulting shouts of the people, and the thundering *"Vive l'empereur"* of the troops. On the same place where the white flag of the Bourbons had but yesterday fluttered, the *tricolore* of the empire now flung out its folds to the breeze.

In the Tuileries the emperor found all his old ministers, his generals, and his courtiers, assembled. All were desirous of seeing and greeting him. An immense concourse of people surged around the entrance on the stairways and in the halls.

Borne aloft on the arms and shoulders of the people, the emperor was carried up the stairway, and into his apartments; and, while shouts of joy were resounding within, the thousands without joined the more fortunate ones who had borne the emperor to his apartments, and rent the air with exulting cries of *"Vive l'empereur!"*

In his cabinet, to which Napoleon immediately repaired, he was received by Queen Julia, wife of Joseph Bonaparte, and Queen Hortense, who had abandoned her place of concealment, and hurried to the Tuileries to salute the emperor.

Napoleon greeted Hortense coldly, he inquired briefly after the health of her sons, and then added, almost severely: "You have placed my nephews in a false position, by permitting them to remain in the midst of my enemies."

Hortense turned pale, and her eyes filled with tears. The emperor seemed not to notice it. "You have accepted the friendship of my enemies," said he, "and have placed yourself under obligations to the Bourbons. I depend on Eugene; I hope he will soon be here. I wrote to him from Lyons."

This was the reception Hortense received from the emperor. He was angry with her for having remained in France, and at the same time the flying Bourbons, who were on their way to Holland, said of her : " The Duchess of St. Leu is to blame for all ! Her intrigues alone have brought Napoleon back to Paris."

CHAPTER XII.

THE HUNDRED DAYS.

The hundred days that followed the emperor's return are like a myth of the olden time, like a poem of Homer, in which heroes destroy worlds with a blow of the hand, and raise armies out of the ground with a stamp of the foot; in which nations perish, and new ones are born within the space of a minute.

These hundred days stand in history as a giant era, and these hundred days of the restored empire were replete with all the earth can offer of fortune, of magnificence, of glory, and of victory, as well as of all that the earth contains that is disgraceful, miserable, traitorous, and perfidious.

Wondrous and brilliant was their commencement. All France seemed to hail the emperor's return with ex-

ultation. Every one hastened to assure him of his unchangeable fidelity, and to persuade him that they had
only obeyed the Bourbons under compulsion.

The old splendor of the empire once more prevailed
in the Tuileries, where the emperor now held his glittering court again. There was, however, this difference:
Queen Hortense now did the honors of the court, in the
place of the Empress Marie Louise, who had not returned with her husband; and the emperor could not
now show the people his own son, but could only point
to his two nephews, the sons of Hortense.

The emperor had quickly reconciled himself to the
queen; he had been compelled to yield to her gentle and
yet decided explanations; he had comprehended that
Hortense had sacrificed herself for her children, in continuing to remain in France notwithstanding her reluctance. After this reconciliation had taken place, Napoleon extended his hand to Hortense, with his irresistible
smile, and begged her to name a wish, in order that he
might fulfil it.

Queen Hortense, who had been so bitterly slandered
and scorned by the royalists, and who was still considered
by the fleeing Bourbons to be the cause of their overthrow—this same queen now entreated the emperor to
permit the Duchess d'Orleans, who had not been able to
leave Paris on account of a broken limb, to remain, and
to accord her a pension besides. She told the emperor
that she had received a letter from the duchess, in which
she begged for her intercession in obtaining some assist-

ar.ce from the emperor, assuring her that it was urgently needed, in her depressed circumstances.

The emperor consented to grant this wish of his step-daughter Hortense; and it was solely at her solicitation that Napoleon accorded a pension of four hundred thousand francs to the Duchess d'Orleans, the mother of King Louis Philippe.*

A few days later, at Hortense's request, a pension of two hundred thousand francs was also accorded to the Duchess of Bourbon, who had also besought the queen to exert her influence in her behalf; and both ladies now hastened to assure Hortense of their everlasting gratitude. The fulfilment of her wish filled Hortense with delight; she was as proud of it as of a victory achieved.

"I considered it a sacred duty," said she, "to intercede for these ladies. They were as isolated and desolate as I had been a few days before, and I know how sad it is to be in such a state!"

But Hortense's present state was a very different one. She was now no longer the Duchess of St. Leu, but the queen and the ornament of the court once more; all heads now bowed before her again, and the high-born ladies, who had seemed oblivious of her existence during the past year, now hastened to do homage to the queen.

"Majesty," said one of these ladies to the queen, "unfortunately, you were always absent in the country when I called to pay my respects during the past winter."

* La Reine Hortense en Italie, en France, et en Angleterre. Ecrit par elle-même, p. 185.

The queen's only response was a gentle "Indeed, madame," which she accompanied with a smile.

Hortense, as has before been said, was now again the grand point of attraction at court, and, at Napoleon's command, the public officials now also hastened to solicit the honor of an audience, in order to pay their respects to the emperor's step-daughter. Each day beheld new *fêtes* and ceremonies.

The most sublime and imposing of all these was the ceremony of the *Champ de Mai*, that took place on the first of June, and at which the emperor, in the presence of the applauding populace, presented to his army the new eagles and flags, which they were henceforth to carry into battle instead of the lilies of the Bourbons.

It was a wondrous, an enchanting spectacle to behold the sea of human beings that surged to and fro on this immense space, and made the welkin ring with their "*Vive l'empereur!*"—to behold the proud, triumphant soldiers receiving from Napoleon the eagles consecrated by the priests at the altar that stood before the emperor. It was a wondrous spectacle to behold the hundreds of richly-attired ladies glittering with diamonds, who occupied the tiers of seats that stood immediately behind the emperor's chair, and on which Hortense and her two sons occupied the first seats.

The air was so balmy, the sun shone so lustriously over all this splendor and magnificence, the cannon thundered so mightily, and the strains of music resounded so sweetly on the ear; and, while all were applauding and rejoicing, Hortense sat behind the emperor's chair covertly sketching the imposing scene that lay before her, the grand ceremony, which, a dark foreboding told her, " might perhaps be the last of the empire." *

Hortense alone did not allow herself to be deceived by this universal delight and contentment.

The heavens still seemed bright and serene overhead, but she already perceived the gathering clouds, she already heard the mutterings of the storm that was soon, and this time forever, to hurl the emperor's throne to the ground. She knew that a day would suddenly come when all this brightness would grow dim, and when all those who now bowed so humbly before him, would turn from him again—a day when they would deny and desert the emperor as they had already done once before, and that, from that day on, the present period of grandeur would be accounted to her as a debt. But this knowledge caused her neither anxiety nor embarrassment.

The emperor was once more there; he was the lord and father left her by her mother Josephine, and it was her duty and desire to be true and obedient to him as long as she lived.

The sun still shone lustrously over the restored empire, and in the parlors of Queen Hortense, where the diplomats, statesmen, artists, and all the notables of the empire were in the habit of assembling, gayety reigned supreme. There music and literature were discussed, and homage done to all the fine arts.

* Cochelet, vol. iii., p. 97.

19

Benjamin Constant, who had with great rapidity transformed himself from an enthusiastic royalist into an imperial state-councillor, came to the queen's parlors and regaled her guests by reading to them his romance Adolphe; and Metternich, the Austrian ambassador, seemed to have no other destiny than to amuse the queen and the circle of ladies assembled around them, and to invent new social games for their entertainment.

Metternich knew how to bring thousands of charming little frivolities into fashion; he taught the ladies the charming and poetic language of flowers, and made it a symbolic means of conversation and correspondence in the queen's circle. He also, to the great delight of the court, invented the alphabet of gems; in this alphabet each gem represented its initial letter, and, by combinations, names and devices were formed, which were worn in necklaces, bracelets, and rings.

The little games with which the diplomatic Metternich occupied himself during the hundred days at the imperial court at Paris, were, it appears, of the most innocent and harmless nature.

CHAPTER XIII.

NAPOLEON'S LAST ADIEU.

THE storm, of the approach of which Queen Hortense had so long had a foreboding, was preparing to burst over France. All the princes of Europe who had once been Napoleon's allies had now declared against him. They all refused to acknowledge Napoleon as emperor, or to treat with him as one having any authority.

"No peace, no reconciliation with this man," wrote the Emperor Alexander to Pozzo di Borgo ; "all Europe is of the same opinion concerning him. With the exception of this man, any thing they may demand ; no preference for any one ; no war after this man shall have been set aside." *

But, in order to " set this man aside," war was necessary. The allied armies therefore advanced toward the boundaries of France ; the great powers declared war against France, or rather against the Emperor Napoleon ; and France, which had so long desired peace, and had only accepted the Bourbons because it hoped to obtain it of them, France was now compelled to take up the gauntlet.

On the 12th of June the emperor left Paris with his army, in order to meet the advancing enemy. Napoleon himself, who had hitherto gone into battle, his countenance beaming with an assurance of victory, now looked gloomy and dejected, for he well knew that on the fate of his army now depended his own, and the fate of France.

This time it was not a question of making conquests, but of saving the national independence, and it was the mother-earth, red with the blood of her children, that was now to be defended.

Paris, that for eighty days had been the scene of splen-

* Cochelet, vol. iii., p. 90.

dor and festivity, now put on its mourning attire. All rejoicings were at an end, and every one listened hopefully to catch the first tones of the thunder of a victorious battle.

But the days of victory were over ; the cannon thundered, the battle was fought, but instead of a triumph it was an overthrow.

At Waterloo, the eagles that had been consecrated on the first of June, on the *Champ de Mai,* sank in the dust; the emperor returned to Paris, a fugitive, and broken down in spirit, while the victorious allies were approaching the capital.

At the first intelligence of his return, Hortense hastened to the Elysée, where he had taken up his residence, to greet him. During the last few days she had been a prey to gloomy thoughts; now that the danger had come, now when all were despairing, she was composed, resolute, and ready to stand at the emperor's side to the last.

Napoleon was lost, and Hortense knew it; but he now had most need of friends, and she remained true, while so many of his nearest friends and relatives were deserting him.

On the twenty-second day of June the emperor sent in his abdication in favor of his son, the King of Rome, to the chambers ; and a week later the chambers proclaimed Napoleon's son Emperor of France, under the name of Napoleon II.

But this emperor was a child of four years, and was,

moreover, not in France, but in the custody of the Emperor of Austria, whose army was now marching on Paris with hostile intent!

Napoleon, now no longer Emperor of France, had been compelled to take the crown from his head a second time; and for the second time he quitted Paris to await the destiny to be appointed him by the allies.

This time he did not repair to Fontainebleau, but to Malmaison—to Malmaison, that had once been Josephine's paradise, and where her heart had at last bled to death. This charming resort had passed into the possession of Queen Hortense; and Napoleon, who but yesterday had ruled over a whole empire, and to-day could call nothing, not even the space of ground on which he stood, his own, Napoleon asked Hortense to receive him at Malmaison.

Hortense accorded his request joyfully, and, when her friends learned this, and in their dismay and anxiety conjured her not to identify in this manner herself and children with the fate of the emperor, but to consider well the danger that would result from such a course, the queen replied resolutely: "That is an additional reason for holding firm to my determination. I consider it my sacred duty to remain true to the emperor to the last, and the greater the danger that threatens the emperor, the happier I shall be in having it in my power to show him my entire devotion and gratitude."

And when, in this decision, when her whole future hung in the balance, one of her most intimate lady-friends

ventured to remind the queen of the disgraceful and malicious reports that had once been put in circulation with
regard to her relation to Napoleon, and suggested that
she would give new strength to them by now receiving
the emperor at Malmaison, Hortense replied with dignity:
" What do I care for these calumnies ?   I fulfil the duty
imposed on me by feeling and principle.   The emperor
has always treated me as his child ; I shall therefore ever
remain his devoted and grateful daughter ; it is my first
and greatest necessity to be at peace with myself." *

Hortense therefore repaired with the emperor to Malmaison, and the faithful, who were not willing to leave
him in his misfortune, gathered around him, watched
over his life, and gave to his residence a fleeting reflection
of the old grandeur and magnificence.   For they who
now stood around Napoleon, guarding his person from
any immediate danger that threatened him at the hands
of fanatic enemies or hired assassins, were marshals, generals, dukes, and princes.

But Napoleon's fate was already decided—it was an
inevitable one, and when the intelligence reached Malmaison that the enemy was approaching nearer and nearer,
and that resistance was no longer made anywhere, and
when Napoleon saw that all was lost, his throne, his crown,
and even the love which he imagined he had for ever
built up for himself in the hearts of the French people
by his great deeds and victories—when he saw this he
determined to fly, no matter whither, but away from the

* Cochelet, vol. iii., p. 149.

France that would no longer rally to his call, the France that had abandoned him.

The emperor resolved to fly to Rochefort, and to embark there in order to return to Elba. The provisional government that had established itself in Paris, and had sent an ambassador to Napoleon at Malmaison with the demand that he should depart at once, now instructed this ambassador to accompany the emperor on his journey, and not to leave him until he should have embarked.

Napoleon was ready to comply with this demand. He determined to depart on the afternoon of the 30th of June. He had nothing more to do but to take leave of his friends and family. He did this with cold, tearless composure, with an immovable, iron countenance; no muscle of his face quivered, and his glance was severe and imperious.

But, when Hortense brought in her two sons, when he had clasped them in his arms for the last time, then a shadow passed over his countenance; then his pale compressed lips quivered, and he turned away to conceal the tears that stood in his eyes.

But Hortense had seen them, and in her heart she preserved the remembrance of these tears as the most precious gem of her departed fortune. As the emperor then turned to her to bid her adieu in his former cold and immovable manner, Hortense, who well knew that a volcano of torments must be glowing under this cold lava, entreated him to grant her a last favor.

A painful smile illumined the emperor's countenance

for a moment. There was, it seemed, still something
that he could grant; he was not altogether powerless!
With a mute inclination of the head he signified his assent. Hortense handed him a broad black belt.

"Sire," said she, "wear this belt around your body
and beneath your clothing. Conceal it carefully, but in
the time of necessity remember it and open it."

The emperor took the belt in his hand, and its weight
startled him.

"What does it contain?" asked he: "I must know
what it contains!"

"Sire," said Hortense, blushing and hesitating: "Sire,
it is my large diamond necklace that I have taken apart
and sewed in this belt. Your majesty may need money
in a critical moment, and you will not deny me this last
happiness, your acceptance of this token."

The emperor refused, but Hortense entreated him so
earnestly that he was at last compelled to yield, and accept
this love-offering.

They then took a hasty and mute leave of each other,
and Hortense, in order to hide her tears, hastened with
her children from the room.

The emperor summoned a servant, and ordered that
no one else should be admitted; but at this moment the
door was hastily thrown open, and a national guard entered the room.

"Talma!" exclaimed the emperor, almost gayly, as
he extended his hand.

"Yes, Talma, sire," said he, pressing the emperor's

hand to his lips. "I disguised myself in this dress, in order that I might get here to take leave of your majesty."

"To take leave, never to see each other more," said the emperor, sadly. "I shall never be 'able to admire you in your great *rôles* again, Talma. I am about to depart, never to return again. You will play the emperor on many an evening, but not I, Talma! My part is at an end!"

"No, sire, you will always remain the emperor!" exclaimed Talma, with generous enthusiasm; "the emperor, although without the crown and the purple robe."

"And also the emperor without a people," said Napoleon.

"Sire, you have a people that will ever remain yours, and a throne that is imperishable! It is the throne that you have erected for yourself on the battle-fields, that will be recorded in the books of history. And every one, no matter to what nation he may belong, who reads of your great deeds, will be inspired by them, and will acknowledge himself to be one of your people, and bow down before the emperor in reverence."

"I have no people," murmured Napoleon, gloomily; "they have all deserted—all betrayed me, Talma!"

"Sire, they will some day regret, as Alexander of Russia will also one day regret, having deserted the great man he once called brother!" And, in his delicate and generous endeavor to remind Napoleon of one of his moments of grandeur, Talma continued: "Your majesty perhaps remembers that evening at Tilsit, when the Emperor of Russia made you so tender a declaration of his love, publicly and before the whole world? But no, you cannot remember it; for you it was a matter of no moment; but I—I shall never forget it! It was at the theatre; we were playing 'Œdipus.' I looked up at the box in which your majesty sat, between the King of Prussia and the Emperor Alexander. I could see you only—the second Alexander of Macedon, the second Julius Cæsar —and I held my arms aloft and saw you only when I repeated the words of my part: 'The friendship of a great man is a gift of the gods!' And as I said this, the Emperor Alexander arose and pressed you to his heart. I saw this, and tears choked my utterance. The audience applauded rapturously; this applause was, however, not for me, but for the Emperor Alexander!" *

While Talma was speaking, his cheeks glowing and his eyes flashing, a rosy hue suffused the emperor's countenance, and, for an instant, he smiled. Talma had attained his object; he had raised up the humiliated emperor with the recital of his own grandeur.

Napoleon thanked him with a kindly glance, and extended his hand to bid him adieu.

As Talma approached the emperor, a carriage was heard driving up in front of the house. It was Letitia, the emperor's mother, who had come to take leave of her son. Talma stood still, in breathless suspense; in his

* This scene is entirely historical. See Bossuet, Mémoires; Bourrienne, Mémoires; Cochelet and Une Femme de Qualité.

heart he thanked Providence for permitting him to witness this leave-taking.

"Madame mère" walked past Talma in silence, and without observing him. She saw only her son, who stood in the middle of the room, his sombre and flashing glance fastened on her with an unutterable expression. Now they stood face to face, mother and son. The emperor's countenance remained immovable as though hewn out of marble.

They stood face to face in silence, but two great tears slowly trickled down the mother's cheeks. Talma stood in the background, weeping bitterly. Napoleon remained unmoved. Letitia now raised both hands and extended them to the emperor. "Adieu, my son!" said she, in full and sonorous tones.

Napoleon pressed her hands in his own, and gazed at her long and fixedly; and then, with the same firmness, he said: "My mother, adieu!"

Once more they gazed at each other; then the emperor let her hand fall. Letitia turned to go, and at this moment General Bertrand appeared at the door to announce that all was prepared for the journey.*

* This leave-taking was exactly as above described, and Talma himself narrated it to Louise de Cochelet. See her Mémoires, vol. iii., p. 173.

BOOK IV.

THE DUCHESS OF ST. LEU.

CHAPTER I.

THE BANISHMENT OF THE DUCHESS OF ST. LEU.

FOR the second time, the Bourbons had entered Paris under the protection of the allies, and Louis XVIII. was once more King of France. But this time he did not return with his former mild and conciliatory disposition. He came to punish and to reward; he came unaccompanied by mercy. The old generals and marshals of the empire, who had not been able to resist their chieftain's call, were now banished, degraded, or executed. Ney and Labédoyère paid for their fidelity to the emperor with their blood; and all who were in any way connected with the Bonapartes were relentlessly pursued. The calumnies that had been circulated in 1814 against the Duchess of St. Leu were now to bear bitter fruit. These were the dragon's teeth from which the armed warriors had sprung, who now levelled their swords at the breast of a defenceless woman.

King Louis had returned to the throne of his fathers,

but he had not forgotten that he had been told on his flight: "The Duchess of St. Leu is to blame for all! Her intrigues have brought Napoleon back!" Now that he was again king, he thought of it, and determined to punish her. He requested it of Alexander, as a favor, that he should this time not call on the Duchess of St. Leu.

The emperor, dismayed by the odious reports in circulation concerning Hortense, and already enchained in the mystic glittering web with which Madame de Krüdener had enveloped him, and separated from the reality of the world, acceded to the wishes of the Bourbons, and abandoned the queen. This was the signal that let loose the general wrath of the royalists; they could now freely utter their scorn and malice. By low calumnies they could now compensate themselves for their humiliation of the past, for having been compelled to approach the daughter of Viscountess de Beauharnais with the reverence due to a queen.

They could pursue the step-daughter of the emperor with boundless fury, for this very fury proved their royalism, and to hate and calumniate Bonaparte and his family was to love and flatter the Bourbons.

Day by day these royalists hurled new accusations against the duchess, whose presence in Paris unpleasantly recalled the days of the empire, and whom they desired to remove from their sight, as well as the column on the *Place Vendôme.*

While the poor queen was living in the retirement of

her apartments, in sadness and desolation, the report was circulated that she was again conspiring, and that she was in the habit of leaving her house every evening at twilight, in order to incite the populace to rise and demand the emperor's return, or at least the instalment of the little King of Rome on the throne instead of Louis de Bourbon.

When the queen's faithful companion, Louise de Cochelet, informed her of these calumnies, Hortense remained cold and indifferent.

"Madame," exclaimed Louise, "you listen with as much composure as if I were reciting a story of the last century!"

"And it interests me as little," said Hortense, earnestly; "we have lost all, and I consider any blow that may still strike us, with the composure of an indifferent spectator. I consider it natural that they should endeavor to calumniate me, because I bear a name that has made the whole world tremble, and that will still be great, though we all be trodden in the dust. But I will shield myself and children from this hatred. We will leave France and go to Switzerland, where I possess a little estate on the Lake of Geneva."

But time was not allowed the duchess to prepare for her departure. The dogs of calumny and hatred were let loose upon her to drive her from the city. A defenceless woman with two young children seemed to be an object of anxiety and terror to the government, and it made haste to get rid of her.

On the morning of the 17th of July, an adjutant of the Prussian General de Müffling, the allied commandant of Paris, came to the dwelling of the Duchess of St. Leu, and informed her intendant, M. Deveaux, that the duchess must leave Paris within two hours, and it was only at the urgent solicitation of the intendant, that a further sojourn of four hours was allowed her.

Hortense was compelled to conform to this military command, and depart without arranging her affairs or making any preparations for her journey. Her only possession consisted of jewelry, and this she of course intended to take with her. But she was warned that a troop of enraged Bourbonists, who knew of her approaching departure, had quitted Paris to lie in wait for her on her road, "in order to rob her of the millions in her custody."

The queen was warned to take no money or articles of value with her, but only that which was absolutely necessary.

General de Müffling offered her an escort of his soldiers; Hortense declined this offer, but requested that an Austrian officer might be allowed to accompany her for the protection of herself and children on the journey. Count de Boyna, adjutant of Prince Schwartzenberg, was selected for this purpose.

On the evening of the 17th of July, 1815, the Duchess of St. Leu took her departure. She left her faithful friend Louise de Cochelet in Paris to arrange her affairs, and assure the safe-keeping of her jewelry. Accompanied

only by her equerry, M. de Marmold, Count Boyna, her
children, her maid, and a man-servant, she who had been
a queen left Paris to go into exile.

It was a sorrowful journey that Hortense now made
through her beloved France, that she could no longer call
her country, and that now seemed as ill-disposed toward
the emperor and his family as it had once passionately
loved them.

In these days of political persecution, the Bonapartists
had everywhere hidden themselves in obscure places, or
concealed their real disposition beneath the mask of Bour-
bonism. Those whom Hortense met on her journey were
therefore all royalists, who thought they could give no
better testimony to their patriotism than by persecuting
with cries of scorn, with gestures of hatred, and with loud
curses, the woman whose only crime was that she bore the
name of him whom France had once adored, and whom
the royalists hated.

Count Boyna was more than once compelled to protect Hortense and her children against the furious attacks
of royalists—the stranger against her own countrymen!
In Dijon, Count Boyna had found it necessary to call on
the Austrian military stationed there for assistance in
protecting the duchess and her children from the attacks
of an infuriated crowd, led by royal guards and beautiful
ladies of rank, whose hair was adorned with the lilies of
the Bourbons.*

Dispirited and broken down by all she had seen and

* Cochelet, vol. iii., p. 289.

experienced, Hortense at last reached Geneva, happy at the prospect of being able to retire to her little estate of Pregny, to repose after the storms of life. But this refuge was also to be refused her. The French ambassador in Switzerland, who resided in Geneva, informed the authorities of that city that his government would not tolerate the queen's sojourn so near the French boundary, and demanded that she should depart. The authorities of Geneva complied with this demand, and ordered the Duchess of St. Leu to leave the city immediately.

When Count Boyna imparted this intelligence to the duchess, and asked her to what place she would now go, her long-repressed despair found utterance in a single cry: "I know not. Throw me into the lake, then we shall all be at rest!"

But she soon recovered her usual proud resignation, and quietly submitted to the new banishment that drove her from her last possession, the charming little Pregny, from her "*rêve de chalet.*"

In Aix she finally found repose and peace for a few weeks—in Aix, where she had once celebrated brilliant triumphs as a queen, and where she was at least permitted to live in retirement with her children and a few faithful adherents.

But in Aix the most fearful blow that Fate had in store for her fell upon her!

Her action against her husband had already been decided in 1814, shortly before the emperor's return, and it

20

had been adjudged that she should deliver her elder son, Napoleon Louis, into the custody of his father. Now that Napoleon's will no longer restrained him, Louis demanded that this judgment be carried out, and sent Baron von Zuyten to Aix to bring back the prince to his father, then residing in Florence.

The unhappy mother was now powerless to resist this hard command; she was compelled to yield, and send her son from her arms to a father who was a stranger to the boy, and whom he therefore could not love.

It was a heart-rending scene this parting between the boy, his mother, and his young brother Louis, from whom he had never before been separated for a day, and who now threw his arms around his neck, tearfully entreating him to stay with him.

But the separation was inevitable. Hortense parted the two weeping children, taking little Louis Napoleon in her arms, while Napoleon Louis followed his governor to the carriage, sobbing as though his heart would break. When Hortense heard the carriage driving off, she uttered a cry of anguish and fell to the ground in a swoon, and a long and painful attack of illness was the consequence of this sorrowful separation.

CHAPTER II.

LOUIS NAPOLEON AS A CHILD.

THE Duchess of St. Leu was, however, not destined to find repose in Aix; the Bourbons—not yet weary of persecuting her, and still fearing the name whose first and greatest representative was now languishing on a solitary, inhospitable rock-island — the Bourbons considered it dangerous that Hortense, the emperor's step-daughter, and her son, whose name of Louis Napoleon seemed to them a living monument of the past, should be permitted to sojourn so near the French boundary. They therefore instructed their ambassador to the government of Savoy to protest against the further sojourn of the queen in Aix, and Hortense was compelled to undertake a new pilgrimage, and to start out into the world again in search of a home.

She first turned to Baden, whose duchess, Stephanie, was so nearly related to her, and from whose husband she might therefore well expect a kindly reception. But the grand-duke did not justify his cousin's hopes; he had not the courage to defy the jealous fears of France, and it was only at the earnest solicitation of his wife that he at last consented that Hortense should take up her residence at the extreme end of the grand-duchy, at Constance, on the Lake of Constance; and this permission was only accorded her on the express condition that neither the duchess nor her son should ever come to

Carlsruhe, and that his wife, Stephanie, should never visit her cousin at Constance.

Hortense accepted this offer with its conditions, contented to find a place where she could rest after her long wanderings, and let the bleeding wounds of her heart heal in the stillness and peace of beautiful natural scenery. She passed a few quiet, happy years in Constance, desiring and demanding nothing but a little rest and peace, aspiring to but one thing—to make of the son, whom Providence had given her as a compensation for all her sufferings, a strong, a resolute, and an intelligent man.

Her most tender care and closest attention were devoted to the education of this son. An excellent teacher, Prof. Lebas, of Paris, officiated as instructor to the young prince. She herself gave him instruction in drawing, in music, and in dancing; she read with him, sang with him, and made herself a child, in order to replace to her lonely boy the playmate Fate had torn from his side.

While reposing on her *chaise-longue* on the long quiet evenings, her boy seated on a cushion at her feet, she would speak to him of his great uncle, and of his heroic deeds, and of his country, of France that had discarded them, to be able to return to which was, however, her most ardent wish, and would continue to be while life lasted. She would then inspire the boy's soul with the description of the great battles which his uncle had won in Italy, on the Nile, on the Rhine, and on the Danube;

and the quiet, pale boy, with the dark, thoughtful eyes, would listen in breathless suspense, his weak, slender body quivering with emotion when his mother told him how dearly his uncle had loved France, and that all his great and glorious deeds had been done for the honor and renown of France alone.

One day, while he was sitting before her, pale and trembling with agitation, his mother pointed to David's splendid painting, representing Napoleon on the heights of the Alps, the genial conception of which painting is due to Napoleon's own suggestions.

"Paint me tranquilly seated on a wild horse," Napoleon had said to David, and David had so painted him— on a rearing steed, on the summit of a rock which bears the inscription "Hannibal" and "Cæsar." The emperor's countenance is calm, his large eyes full of a mysterious brilliancy, his hair fluttering in the wind, the whole expression thoughtful and earnest; the rider heedless of the rearing steed, which he holds firmly in check with the reins.

A beautiful copy of this great painting hung in the parlor of the duchess; and to this she now pointed while narrating the history of the emperor's passage over the Great St. Bernard with an army, a feat never before performed except by Hannibal and Cæsar, and perhaps never to be performed again.

As she concluded her narrative, an almost angry expression flitted across the young prince's countenance. Rising from his seat, and holding himself perfectly erect, he exclaimed: "Oh, mamma, I shall also cross the Alps some day, as the emperor did!"

And while thus speaking, a glowing color suffused his face; his lips trembled, and the feverish beating of his heart was quite audible.

Hortense turned in some anxiety to her friend Louise de Cochelet, and begged her in a low voice to soothe the child with the recital of some merry narrative. As Louise looked around the room thoughtfully and searchingly, a cup that stood on the mantel-piece arrested her gaze. She hastened to the mantel, took the cup, and returned with it to little Louis Napoleon.

"Mamma has been explaining a very grave picture to you, Louis," said she; "I will now show you a merry one. Look at it—isn't it charming?"

The prince cast a hasty, absent-minded look at the cup, and nodded gravely. Louise laughed gayly.

"You see, Louis," said she, "that this is the exact counterpart of the picture of the Emperor Napoleon, who, while riding over the Alps, encounters on their summit the great spirits of Hannibal and Cæsar. Here is a little Napoleon, who is not climbing up the Alps, but climbing down from his bed, and who, on this occasion, meets a black spirit, in the person of a chimney-sweep. This is the history of the great and of the little Napoleon; the great meets Hannibal, the little the chimney-sweep."

"Am I the little Napoleon?" asked the boy, gravely.

"Yes, Louis, you are, and I will now tell you the

story of this cup.   One day, when we were all still in Paris, and while your great uncle was still Emperor of France—one day, you met in your room a little Savoyard, who had just crept out of the chimney in his black dress, his black broom in his hand.   You cried out with horror, and were about to run away, but I held you back and told you that these chimney-sweeps were poor boys, and that their parents were so poor that they could not support their children, but were compelled to send them to Paris to earn their bread by creeping into and cleaning our hot and dirty chimneys, with great trouble, and at the risk of their lives.   My story touched you, and you promised me never to be afraid of the little chimney-sweeps again.   A short time afterward, you were awakened early in the morning by a strange noise, your brother still lay asleep at your side, and your nurse was absent from the room.   This noise was made by a chimney-sweep who had just come down the chimney and now stood in your room.   As soon as you saw him, you remembered his poverty, jumped out of bed in your night-clothes, and ran to the chair on which your clothes lay. You took out of your pocket the purse you were compelled to carry with you on your walks to give money to the poor, and you emptied its entire contents into the black, sooty hand of the young Savoyard.   You then tried to get back to bed, but it was too high for you; you could not climb over the railing.   Seeing this, the chimney-sweep came to your assistance, and took the little prince in his arms to help him into bed.   At this moment, your nurse entered the room, and your brother, who had just awakened, cried loudly when he saw Louis in the arms of a chimney-sweep.

" This is the story of little Napoleon and the chimney-sweep ! Your grandmother, the Empress Josephine, was so much pleased with this story, that your mother had the scene painted on a cup, and presented it to the empress, in order to afford her a gratification. And what do you think, Louis—this cup was also the cause of a punishment being remitted your cousin, the King of Rome, who now lives in Vienna ! "

" Tell me all about it, Louise," said the prince, smiling.

" You shall hear it ! Your mother had instructed me to take the cup to Malmaison to the empress. But before going, I endeavored to obtain some news about the little King of Rome for the empress. Your good grandmother loved him as though he had been her own child, although she had never seen him. I therefore went to the Tuileries to see the little King of Rome, with whose governess, Madame de Montesquieu, I was intimately acquainted. On entering the apartment, I saw the king cowering behind a chair in a corner of the room ; Madame de Montesquieu intimated by a look that he was undergoing a punishment ; I understood it, and first conversed with his governess for a short time. When I then turned and approached him, he concealed the tearful, flushed face, that his long blond curls covered as with a golden veil, whenever he moved behind the chair.

"'Sire,' said Madame de Montesquieu to him, 'sire, do you not intend to bid Mademoiselle de Cochelet good-morning? She came here expressly to see you.'

"'Your majesty does not recognize me,' said I, attempting to take his small hand in mine. He tore it from me, and cried in a voice almost choked with sobbing: 'She will not let me look at the soldiers of my papa!'

"Madame de Montesquieu told me that it was the little prince's greatest pleasure to see the Guards exercising on the *Place de Carrousel*, but that she had deprived him of this pleasure to-day, because he had been naughty and disobedient; that, when he heard the music and drums, his despair and anger had become so great that she had been forced to resort to severe means, and make him stand in the corner behind a chair. I begged for the young king's pardon; I showed him the cup, and explained the scene that was painted on it. The king laughed, and Madame de Montesquieu pardoned him for the sake of his little cousin, Louis Napoleon, who was so well behaved, and who was always held up to him as a model.* Now you have heard the whole story, are you pleased with it, Louis?"

"I like it very much," said the grave boy, "but I do not like my cousin's governess, for having intended to prevent him from looking at his father's soldiers. Oh, how handsome they must have been, the soldiers of the emperor! Mamma, I wish I were also an emperor, and had ever so many handsome soldiers."

* Cochelet, vol. i., p. 212.

Hortense smiled sadly, and laid her hand on the boy's head as if to bless him. "Oh, my son," said she, "it is no enviable fortune to wear a crown. It is almost always fastened on our head with thorns!"

From this day on, Prince Louis Napoleon would stand before his uncle's portrait, lost in thought, and, after looking at it to his satisfaction, he would run out and call the boys of the neighborhood together, in order to play soldier and emperor with them in the large garden that surrounded his mother's house, and teach the boys the first exercise.

One day, in the zeal of play, he had entirely forgotten his mother's command, not to go out of the garden, and had marched into the open field with his soldiers. When his absence from the garden was noticed, all the servants were sent out to look for him, and the anxious duchess, together with her ladies, assisted in this search, walking about in every direction through the cold and the slush of the thawing snow. Suddenly they came upon the boy barefooted and in his shirt-sleeves, wading toward them through the mud and snow. He was alarmed and confused at this unexpected meeting, and confessed that a moment before, while he had been playing in front of the garden, a family had passed by so poor and ragged that it was painful to look at them. As he had no money to give them, he had put his shoes on one child, and his coat on another.*

The duchess did not have the courage to scold him;

* Cochelet, vol. iv., p. 303.

she stooped down and kissed her son ; but when her ladies commenced to praise him, she motioned to them to be silent, and said in a loud voice that what her son had done was quite a matter of course, and therefore deserved no praise.

An ardent desire to gladden others and make them presents was characteristic of little Louis Napoleon. One day, Hortense had given him three beautiful studs for his shirt, and on the same day the prince transferred them to one of his friends who admired them.

When Hortense reproached her son for doing so, and threatened to make him no more presents, as he always gave them away again directly, Louis Napoleon replied, " Ah, mamma, this is why your presents give me double pleasure—once when you give them to me, and the second time when I make others happy with them." *

CHAPTER III.

THE REVOLUTION OF 1830.

FATE seemed at last weary of persecuting the poor Duchess of St. Leu. It at least accorded her a few peaceful years of repose and comfort ; it at least permitted her to rest from the weariness of the past on the bosom of Nature, and to forget her disappointments and sorrows. The Canton of Thurgau had had the courage to extend

* Cochelet, vol. i, p. 355.

permission to the duchess to take up her residence within its borders, at the very moment when the Grand-duke of Baden, who had been urged to the step by Germany and France, had peremptorily ordered Hortense to leave Constance and his grand-duchy without delay.

Hortense had thankfully accepted the offer of the Swiss canton, and had purchased, on the Swiss side of the Lake of Constance, an estate, whose beautiful situation on the summit of a mountain, immediately on the banks of the lake, with its magnificent view of the surrounding country, and its glittering glaciers on the distant horizon, made it a most delightful place of sojourn. Hortense now caused the furniture of her dwelling in Paris, that had been sold, to be sent to her. The sight of these evidences of her former grandeur awakened sweet and bitter emotions in her heart, as they were one after another taken out of the cases in which they had been packed— these sofas, chairs, divans, carpets, chandeliers, mirrors, and all the other ornaments of the parlors in which Hortense had been accustomed to receive kings and emperors, and which were now to adorn the Swiss villa that was outwardly so beautiful because of the vicinity, and inwardly so plain and simple.

But Hortense knew how to make an elegant and tasteful disposition of all these articles ; she herself arranged every thing in her house, and took true feminine delight in her task. And when all was at last arranged—when she walked, with her son at her side, through the suite of rooms, in which every ornament and piece of furniture reminded her of the past—when these things recalled the proud days of state when so many friends, relatives, and servants, had surrounded her—a feeling of unutterable loneliness, of painful desolation, came over her, and she sank down on a sofa and wept bitterly. But there was nevertheless a consolation in having these familiar articles in her possession once more ; these mute friends often awakened in the solitary queen's heart memories that served to entertain and console her. Arenenberg was a perfect temple of memory ; every chair, every table, every article of furniture, had its history, and this history spoke of Napoleon, of Josephine, and the great days of the empire.

In Arenenberg Hortense had at last found a permanent home, and there she passed the greater part of the year ; and it was only when the autumnal storms began to howl through her open and lightly-constructed villa, that Hortense repaired to Rome, to pass the winter months in a more genial climate, while her son Louis Napoleon was pursuing his studies at the artillery school at Thun.

And thus the years passed on, quiet and peaceful, though sometimes interrupted by new losses and sorrows. In the year 1821 the hero, the emperor, to whose laurel-crown the halo of a martyr had now also been added, died on the island-rock, St. Helena.

In the year 1824 Hortense lost her only brother, Eugene, the Duke of Leuchtenberg.

The only objects of Hortense's love were now **her**

two sons, who were prospering in mind and body, and
were the pride and joy of their mother, and an object of
annoyance and suspicion to all the princes of Europe.
For these children bore in their countenance, in their
name, and in their disposition, too plain an impress of
the great past, which they could never entirely ignore
while Bonaparte still lived to testify to it.

And they lived and prospered in spite of the Bourbons; they lived and prospered, although banished from
their country, and compelled to lead an inactive life.

But at last it seemed as though the hour of fortune
and freedom had come for these Bonapartes—as though
they, too, were to be permitted to have a country to which
they might give their devotion and services.

The thundering voice of the revolution of 1830 resounded throughout trembling Europe. France, on whom
the allies had imposed the Bourbons, arose and shook its
mane; with its lion's paw it overthrew the Bourbon
throne, drove out the Jesuits who had stood behind it,
and whom Charles X. had advised to tear the charter to
pieces, to destroy the freedom of the press, and to reintroduce the *autos da fé* of the olden time.

France had been treated as a child in 1815, and was
now determined to assert its manhood; it resolved to
break entirely with the past, and with its own strength
to build up a future for itself.

The lilies of the Bourbons were to bloom no more;
these last years of fanatical Jesuit tyranny had deprived
them of life, and France tore the faded lily from her

bosom in order to replace it with a young and vigorous plant. The throne of the Bourbons was overthrown, but the people, shuddering at the recollection of the sanguinary republic, selected a king in preference. It stretched out its hand after him it held dearest; after him who in the past few years had succeeded in winning the sympathy of France. It selected the Duke of Orleans, the son of Philippe Égalité, for its king.

Louis Philippe, the enthusiastic republican of 1790, who at that time had caused the three words "*Liberté, Égalité, Fraternité*," and the inscription "*Vive la République*," to be burnt on his arm, in order to prove his republicanism; the proscribed Louis Philippe, who had wandered through Europe a fugitive, earning his bread by teaching writing and languages—the same Louis Philippe now became King of France.

The people called him to the throne; they tore the white flag from the roof of the Tuileries, but they knew no other or better one with which to replace it than the *tricolore* of the empire.

Under the shadow of this *tricolore* Louis Philippe mounted the throne, and the people—to whom the three colors recalled the glorious era of the empire—the people shouted with delight, and in order to indulge their sympathies they demanded for France—not the son of Napoleon, not Napoleon II.—but the ashes of Napoleon, and the emperor's statue on the Palace Vendôme. Louis Philippe accorded them both, but with these concessions he thought he had done enough. He had accepted the *tricolore* of the empire; he had promised that the emperor should watch over Paris from the summit of the Vendôme monument, and to cause his ashes to be brought to Paris—these were sufficient proofs of love.

They might be accorded the dead Napoleon without danger, but it would be worse to accord them to living Napoleons; such a course might easily shake the new throne, and recall the allies to Paris.

The hatred of the princes of Europe against Napoleon was still continued against his family, and it was with them, as Metternich said, "a principle never to tolerate another Napoleon on the throne."

The European powers had signified to the King of France, through their diplomatic agents, their readiness to acknowledge him, but they exacted one condition—the condition that Louis Philippe should confirm or renew the decree of exile fulminated by the Bourbons against the Bonapartes.

Louis Philippe had accepted this condition; and the Bonapartes, whose only crime was that they were the brothers and relatives of the deceased emperor, before whom not only France, but all the princes of Europe, had once bent the knee—the Bonapartes were once more declared strangers to their country, and condemned to exile!

CHAPTER IV.

THE REVOLUTION IN ROME, AND THE SONS OF HORTENSE.

IT was a terrible blow to the Bonapartes, this new decree of banishment! Like a stroke of lightning it entered their hearts, annihilating their holiest hopes and most ardent desires, and their joy over the glorious and heroic revolution of July gave place to a bitter sense of disappointment.

▶ Nothing, therefore, remained for them but to continue the life to which they had become somewhat accustomed, and to console themselves, for their new disappointment, with the arts and sciences.

At the end of October, in the year 1830, Hortense determined to leave Arenenberg and go to Rome with her son, as she was in the habit of doing every year.

But this time she first went to Florence, where her elder son, Napoleon Louis, recently married to his cousin, the second daughter of King Joseph, was now living with his young wife. The heart of the tender mother was filled with anxiety and care; she felt and saw that this new French Revolution was likely to infect all Europe, and that Italy, above all, would be unable to avoid this infection. Italy was diseased to the core, and it was to be feared that it would grasp at desperate means in its agony, and proceed to the blood-letting of a revolution, in order to restore itself to health. Hortense felt this, and feared for her sons.

21

She feared that the exiled, the homeless ones, who had been driven from their country, and were not permitted to serve it, would devote their services to those who were unhappy and who suffered like themselves. She feared the enthusiasm, the generous courage, the energy of her sons, and she knew that, if a revolution should break out in Italy, it would gladly adorn itself with the name of Napoleon.

Hortense, therefore, conjured her sons to hold themselves aloof from all dangerous undertakings, and not to follow those who might appeal to them with the old word of magic power, "liberty;" that, in spite of the tears and blood it has already caused mankind, can never lose its wondrous power.

Her two sons promised compliance; and, much relieved, Hortense left Florence, and went, with her younger son, Louis Napoleon, to Rome.

But Rome, otherwise so aristocratic and solemn, assumed an unusual, an entirely new, physiognomy this winter. In society the topics of conversation were no longer art and poetry, the Pantheon and St. Peter, or what the newest amusement should be; but politics and the French Revolution were the all-engrossing topics, and the populace listened anxiously for the signal that should announce that the revolution in Italy had at last begun.

Even the populace of Rome, usually addicted to lying so harmlessly in the sunshine, now assembled in dense groups on the streets, and strange words were heard when the police cautiously approached these groups for the purpose of listening. But they now lacked the courage to arrest those who uttered those words; they felt that such a provocation might suffice to tear away the veil behind which the revolution still concealed itself.

The whole energy and watchfulness of the Roman government was therefore employed in endeavoring to avert the revolution, if possible; not, however, by removing the cause and occasion, but by depriving the people of the means. The son of Hortense, Louis Napoleon, seemed to the government a means which the revolution might use for its purposes, and it was therefore determined that he should be removed.

His name, and even the three-colored saddle-blanket of his horse, with which he rode through the streets of Rome, were exciting to the populace, in whose veins the fever of revolution was already throbbing. Louis Napoleon must therefore be removed.

The Governor of Rome first addressed the prince's great-uncle, Cardinal Fesch, requesting him to advise the Duchess of St. Leu to remove the young prince from Rome for a few weeks.

But the cardinal indignantly declared that his nephew, who had done nothing, should not be compelled to leave Rome merely on account of his name and his saddle-blanket, and that he would never advise the Duchess of St. Leu to do anything of the kind.

The Roman government therefore determined to adopt energetic means. It caused the dwelling of the duchess to be surrounded by soldiers, while a papal officer presented himself before Hortense, and announced that he had received orders to remove Prince Louis from the city at once, and to conduct him without the papal territory.

The fear of approaching evil caused the government to forget the respect due to nobility in misfortune, and the emperor's nephew was turned out of the city like a criminal !

Hortense received this intelligence almost with joy. Far from Rome, it seemed to her that he would be safer from the revolution, whose approach she so much dreaded ; and it therefore afforded her great satisfaction to send the prince to Florence, to his father, believing that he would there be shielded from the dangerous political calumnies that threatened him in Rome. She therefore permitted him to depart; and how could she have prevented his departure—she, the lone, powerless woman, to whom not even the French ambassador would have accorded protection ! No one interceded for her—no one protested against the violent and brutal course pursued toward Louis Napoleon—no one, except the Russian ambassador.

The Emperor of Russia was the only one of all the sovereigns of Europe who felt himself strong enough not to ignore the name of Napoleon, and the consideration due to the family of a hero and of an emperor.

The Emperor of Russia had, therefore, never refused his protection and assistance to the Bonapartes, and his -

ambassador was now the only one who protested against the violent course taken by the Roman government.

The revolution at last broke forth. Italy arose as France had done, resolved to throw off the yoke of tyranny and oppression, and be free! The storm first broke out in Modena. The duke saw himself compelled to fly, and a provisional government under General Menotti placed itself in his stead. But, while this was taking place in Modena, the populace of Rome was holding high festival in honor of the newly-chosen Pope Gregory XVI., who had just taken his seat in the chair of the deceased Pope Pius VIII., and these festivities, and the Carnival, seemed to occupy the undivided attention of the Romans; under the laughing mask of these rejoicings the revolution hid its grave and threatening visage, and it was not until *mardi-gras* that it laid this mask aside and showed its true countenance.

The people had been accustomed to throw confectionery and flowers on this day, but this time the day was to be made memorable by a shower of stones and bullets; this time they were not to appear in the harlequin jacket, but in their true form, earnest, grand, commanding, self-conscious, and self-asserting.

But the government had been informed of the intention of the conspirators to avail themselves of the drive to the Corso, to begin the revolution, and this procession was prohibited an hour before the time appointed for its commencement.

The people arose against this prohibition, and the revolution they had endeavored to repress by this means now broke out.

The thunder of cannon and the rattling of musketry now resounded through the streets of Rome, and the people everywhere resisted the papal soldiery with energy and determination.

The new pope trembled in the Quirinal, the old cardinals lost courage, and in dismay recoiled a step at every advancing stride of the insurgents. Gregory felt that the papal crown he had just achieved was already on the point of falling from his head, to be trodden in the dust by the victorious populace; he turned to Austria, and solicited help and assistance.

But young Italy, the Italy of enthusiasm, of liberty, and of hope, looked to France for support. Old Italy had turned to Austria for help; young Italy looked for assistance to the free, newly-arisen France, in which the revolution had just celebrated a glorious victory. But France denied its Italian brother, and denied its own origin; scarcely had the revolution seated itself on the newly-erected kingly throne and invested itself with the crown and purple robe, when, for its own safety, it became reactionary, and denied itself.

With all Italy, Rome was resolved to shake off the yoke of oppression; the whole people espoused this cause with enthusiasm; and in the streets of Rome—at other times filled with priests and monks and holy processions —in these streets, now alive with the triumphant youth of Rome, resounded exultant songs of freedom.

The strangers, terrified by this change, now quitted the holy city in crowds, and hastened to their homes. Hortense desired to remain; she knew that she had nothing to fear from the people, for all the evil that had hitherto overtaken her, had come, not from the people, but always from the princes only.* However, letters suddenly arrived from her sons, conjuring her to leave Rome and announcing that they would leave Florence within the hour, in order to hasten forward to meet their mother.

Upon reading this, Hortense cried aloud with terror —she, who knew and desired no other happiness on earth than the happiness of her children, she whose only prayer to God had ever been, that her children might prosper and that she might die before them, now felt that a fearful danger threatened her sons, and that they were now about to be swept into the vortex of the revolution.

They had left Florence, and their father, and were now on the way to Rome, that is, on the way to the revolution that would welcome them with joy, and inscribe the name Napoleon on its standards!

But it was perhaps still time to save them; with her prayers and entreaties she might still succeed in arresting them on the verge of the abyss into which they were hastening in the intoxication of their enthusiasm. As this thought occurred to her, Hortense felt herself strong, determined, and courageous; and, on the same day on which she had received the letters, she left Rome, and

* La Reine Hortense, p. 63.

hurried forward to meet her sons. She still hoped to be in time to save them; she fancied she saw her sons in every approaching carriage—but in vain !

They had written that they would meet her on the road, but they were not there !

Perhaps they had listened to. the representations of their father; perhaps they had remained in Florence, and were awaiting their mother's arrival there.

Tormented by fear and hope, Hortense arrived in Florence and drove to the dwelling in which her son Louis Napoleon had resided. Her feet could scarcely bear her up; she hardly found strength to inquire after her son—he was not there !

But he might be with his father, and Hortense now sent there for intelligence of her sons. The messenger returned, alone and dejected : her sons had left the city !

The exultant hymn of liberty had struck on their delighted ear, and they had responded to the call of the revolution.

General Menotti had appealed to them, in the name of Italy, to assist the cause of freedom with their name and with their swords, and they had neither the will nor the courage to disregard this appeal.

A servant, left behind by her younger son, delivered to the duchess a letter from her son Louis Napoleon, a last word of adieu to his beloved mother.

" Your love will understand us," wrote Louis Napoleon. " We cannot withdraw ourselves from duties that devolve upon us; the name we bear obliges us to listen to the appeal of unhappy nations. I beg you to represent this matter to my sister-in-law as though I had persuaded my brother to accompany me ; it grieves him to have concealed from her one action of his life." *

CHAPTER V.

THE DEATH OF PRINCE NAPOLEON.

THAT which Hortense most dreaded had taken place : the voice of enthusiasm had silenced every other consideration ; and the two sons of the Duchess of St. Leu, the nephews of the Emperor Napoleon, now stood at the head of the revolution. From Foligno to Civita Castellano, they organized the defence, and from the cities and villages the young people joyously hurried forth to enroll themselves under their banners, and to obey the Princes Napoleon as their leaders ; the crowds which the young princes now led were scarcely armed, but they nevertheless advanced courageously, and were resolved to attempt the capture of Civita Castellano, in order to liberate the state prisoners who had been languishing in its dungeons for eight years.

This was the intelligence brought back by the couriers whom Hortense had dispatched to her sons with letters entreating them to return.

It was too late—they neither would nor could return.

* La Reine Hortense, p. 78.

Their father wrung his hands in despair, and conjured his wife, he being confined to his arm-chair by illness and the gout, to do all in her power to tear their sons from the fearful danger that menaced them. For the revolution was lost; all who were cool and collected felt and saw this. But the youth refused to see it; they still continued to flock to the revolutionary banners; they still sang exultant hymns of freedom, and, when their parents endeavored to hold them back, they fled from the parental house secretly, in order to answer the call that resounded on their ear in such divine notes.

One of the sons of the Princess of Canino, the wife of Lucien Bonaparte, had fled from his father's castle in order to join the insurgents. They succeeded in finding, and forcing him to return, and as the family were under obligations to the pope for having created the principalities of Canino and Musignano, for Lucien Bonaparte and his eldest son, the most extreme measures were adopted to prevent the young prince from fighting against the troops of the pope.

The Princess of Canino, as a favor, requested the Grand-duke of Tuscany to confine her son in one of the state prisons of Tuscany; her request was granted, and her son taken to a prison, where he was kept during the entire revolution. It was proposed to the Duchess of St. Leu to adopt this same means of prevention, but, in spite of her anxiety and care, and although, in her restlessness and feverish disquiet, she wandered through her rooms day and night, she declined to take such a course. She was not willing to subject her sons to the humiliation of such compulsion ; if their own reason, if the prayers and entreaties of their mother, did not suffice, force should not be resorted to, to bring them back.   The whole family was, however, still employing every means to induce the two Princes Napoleon to withdraw from the revolution, which must inevitably again draw down upon the name Napoleon the suspicion of the angry and distrustful princes of Europe.

Cardinal Fesch and King Jerome conjured their nephews, first in entreating, and then in commanding letters, to leave the insurgent army.

With the consent of their father, Louis Bonaparte, they wrote to the provisional government at Bologna that the name of the two princes was injuring the cause of the revolution, and to General Armandi, the minister of war of the insurgent government, entreating him to recall the princes from the army.   Every one, friend and foe, combined to neutralize the zeal and efforts of the two princes, and to prove to them that they could only injure the cause to which they gave their names ; that foreign powers, considering the revolution a matter to be decided by Italy alone, would perhaps refrain from intervening ; but that they would become relentless should a Bonaparte place himself at the head of the revolution, in order perhaps to shake the thrones of Europe anew.

The two princes at last yielded to these entreaties and representations ; they gave up their commands, and re-signed the rank that had been accorded them in the insurgent army; but, as it was no longer in their power to serve the revolution with their name and with their brains, they were at least desirous of serving it with their arms: they resigned their commands, but with the intention of remaining in the army as simple soldiers and volunteers without any rank.

And when their father and their uncles, not yet satisfied with what they had done, urged them still further, the two princes declared that, if these cruel annoyances were continued, they would go to Poland, and serve the revolution there.*

Hortense had taken no part in these attempts and efforts of her family; she knew that it was all in vain; she understood her sons better than they, and she knew that nothing in the world could alter a resolution they had once formed. But she also knew that they were lost, that the revolution must be suppressed, that they would soon be proscribed fugitives, and she quietly prepared to assist them when the evil days should come. She armed herself with courage and determination, and made her soul strong, in order that she might not be overwhelmed by the misfortune that was so near at hand.

While all about her were weeping and lamenting, while her husband was wringing his hands in despair, and complaining of the present, Hortense quietly and resolutely confronted the future, and prepared to defy it.

That which she dreaded soon took place. An Austrian fleet sailed into the Adriatic; an Austrian army was

* La Reine Hortense, p. 93.

marching on the insurrectionary Italian provinces.   Modena had already been reconquered; the insurgents were already flying in crowds before the Austrian cannon, whose thundering salvos were destined to destroy once more the hopes of the youth of Italy.

Like an enraged lioness glowing with enthusiasm and courage, Hortense now sprang up. The danger was there, and she must save her sons! She had long considered how it was to be done, and whither she was to go with them. She had first resolved to go with them to Turkey, and to take up her residence in Smyrna, but the presence of the Austrian fleet which ruled the Adriatic made this plan impracticable. At this moment of extreme danger, a volume of light suddenly beamed in upon her soul, and pointed out the way to safety. " I will take them by a road," said she to herself, "on which they will be least expected. I will conduct them through France, through Paris. The death-penalty will there hang suspended over them, but what care I for that? Liberty, justice, and humanity, still exercise too much control over France to make me apprehend such severe measures. I must save my sons; the way through France is the way of safety, and I shall therefore follow it!"

And Hortense immediately began to carry her plan into execution. She requested an Englishman residing in Florence, to whose family she had once rendered important services in France, to call on her, and begged him to procure her a passport for an English lady and her two sons through France to England.

The lord understood her, and gladly consented to assist her and her two sons.

On the following day he brought her the required
passport, and Hortense, who well knew that the best way
to keep a secret was to have no confidants, now declared
to her husband, as well as to her family and her friends,
that she was resolved to find her sons, and to embark
with them from Ancona for Corfu!

For this purpose she demanded a passport of the government of Tuscany, and it was accorded her.

Her sons were still in Bologna, but it was known that
this city must fall into the hands of the Austrians in a
few days, and all was lost unless Hortense arrived there
before them. She sent a trusty servant to her sons to
announce her coming. Then, at nightfall, she herself
departed, accompanied by one of her ladies only. She
was courageous and resolute, for she knew that the safety
of her sons, her only happiness, was at stake.

Her rapidly-driven carriage had soon passed without
the city, and she now found herself in a part of the
country still occupied by the insurgents. Here all still
breathed courage, joyousness, and confidence. The entire population, adorned with cockades and three-colored
ribbons, seemed happy and contented, and refused to believe in the danger that threatened.

Festivals were everywhere being held in honor of the
revolution and of liberty, and those who spoke of the advancing Austrians and of dangers were ridiculed. Instead of making preparations for their defence, the insur-

gents folded their hands in contentment, rejoicing over that which they had already attained, and blind to the tide that was rolling down upon them.

In the mean while, the insurgent army was in position near Bologna, and also still occupied the two cities of Terni and Soleta, which they had courageously defended against the papal troops.   Every one expected that a decisive battle would soon take place, and every one looked forward to it with a joyous assurance of victory.

Hortense was far from participating in this general confidence.   In Foligno, where she had remained to await her sons, she passed several sorrowful days of expectancy and suspense, alarmed by every noise, and ever looking forward with an anxiously-throbbing heart to the moment when her sons should come to her as fugitives, perhaps covered with wounds, perhaps dying, to tell her that all was lost!   Her anxiety at last became so great, that she could no longer remain in Foligno; she must be nearer her sons, she must view the dangers that encompassed them, and, if need be, share them.   Hortense, therefore, left Foligno, and started for Ancona.

On her arrival at the first station, she saw a man descend from a carriage and approach her.   He was unknown to her, and yet she felt a dark foreboding at his approach.   The mother's heart already felt the blow that awaited her.

This man was a messenger from her sons.   " Prince Napoleon is ill," said he.

Hortense remembered that she had heard that a contagious disease was ravaging the vicinity. " Is he indeed ill ? " cried she, in dismay.

" Yes ; and he earnestly desires to see you, madame ! "

" Oh," exclaimed Hortense, in terror, " if he calls for me, he must be very ill indeed !—Forward, forward, with all possible speed ; I must see my son ! "

And onward they went with the speed of the wind from station to station, approaching nearer and nearer to their destination ; but as they neared their destination, the faces they met grew sadder and sadder. At every station groups of people assembled about her carriage and gazed at her sorrowfully ; everywhere she heard them murmur : " Napoleon is dead ! Poor mother ! Napoleon is dead ! " Hortense heard, but did not believe it ! These words had not been spoken by men, but were the utterances of her anxious heart ! Her son was not dead, he could not be dead. Napoleon lived, yes, he · still lived ! And again the people around her carriage murmured, " Napoleon is dead ! "

Hortense reclined in her carriage, pale and motionless. Her thoughts were confused, her heart scarcely beat.

At last she reached her destination ; her carriage drove up to the house in Pesaro, where her sons were awaiting her.

At this moment a young man, his countenance of a deathly pallor, and flooded with tears, rushed out of the door and to her carriage. Hortense recognized him, and stretched out her arms to him. It was her son Louis

Napoleon, and on beholding his pale, sorrowful countenance, and his tear-stained eyes, the unhappy mother learned the truth. Yes, it was not her heart, it was the people who had uttered the fearful words: "Napoleon is dead! Poor mother! Napoleon is dead!"

With a heart-rending cry, Hortense sank to the ground in a swoon.

CHAPTER VI.

THE FLIGHT FROM ITALY.

BUT Hortense now had no leisure to weep over the son she had so dearly loved; the safety of the son who remained to her, whom she loved no less, and on whom her whole love must now be concentrated, was at stake.

She still had a son to save, and she must now think of him—of Louis Napoleon, who stood in sorrow at her side, lamenting that Fate had not allowed him to die with his brother.

Her son must be saved. This thought restored Hortense to health and strength. She is informed that the authorities of Bologna have already tendered submission to the Austrians; that the insurgent army is already scattering in every direction; that the Austrian fleet is already to be seen in the distance, approaching, perhaps with the intention of landing at Sinigaglia, in order to surround the insurgen.. and render flight impossible.

This intelligence aroused Hortense from her grief
22

and restored her energy. She ordered her carriage and drove with her son to Ancona, in full view of the people, in order that every one should know that it was her purpose to embark with her son for Corfu at that seaport. At Ancona, immediately fronting the sea, stood her nephew's palace, and there Hortense descended from her carriage.

The waves of the storm-tossed sea sometimes rushed up to the windows of the room occupied by the duchess; from there she could see the port, and the crowds of fugitives who were pressing forward to save themselves on the miserable little vessels that there lay at anchor.

And these poor people had but little time left them in which to seek safety. The Austrians were rapidly advancing; on entering the papal territory, they had proclaimed an amnesty, from the benefits of which Prince Louis Napoleon, General Zucchi, and the inhabitants of Modena, were, however, excepted. The strangers who had taken part in the insurrection were to be arrested and treated with all the severity of the law.

The young people who had flocked from Modena, Milan, and from all Italy, to enroll themselves under the banner of the Roman revolution, now found it necessary to seek safety from the pursuing Austrians in flight.

Louis Napoleon also had no time to lose; each moment lost might render flight impossible! Hortense was weary and ill, but she now had no time to think of herself; she must first save her son, then she could die, but not sooner.

With perfect composure she prepared for her double (her feigned and her real) departure.

Outwardly, she purposed embarking with her son at Corfu; secretly, it was her intention to fly to England through France! But the English passport that she had received for this purpose mentioned two sons, and Hortense now possessed but one; and it was necessary for her to provide a substitute for the one she had lost.

She found one in the person of the young Marquis Zappi, who, compromised more than all the rest, joyfully accepted the proposition of the Duchess of St. Leu, promising to conform himself wholly to her arrangements, without knowing her plans and without being initiated in her secrets.

Hortense then procured all that was necessary to the disguise of the young men as liveried servants, and ordered her carriage to be held in readiness for her departure.

While this was being done in secret, she publicly caused all preparations to be made for her journey to Corfu. She sent her passport to the authorities for the purpose of obtaining the official *visa* for herself and sons, and had her trunks packed. Louis Napoleon had looked on, with cold and mute indifference, while these preparations were being made. He stood by, pale and dejected, without complaining or giving utterance to his grief.

Becoming at last convinced that he was ill, Hortense sent for a physician.

The latter declared that the prince was suffering from a severe attack of fever, which might become dangerous unless he sought repose at once. It was therefore necessary to postpone their departure for a day, and Hortense passed an anxious night at the bedside of her fever-shaken, delirious son.

The morning at last dawned, the morning of the day on which they hoped to fly; but when the rising sun shed its light into the chamber in which Hortense stood at her son's bedside, who can describe the unhappy mother's horror when she saw her son's face swollen, disfigured, and covered with red spots!

Like his brother, Louis Napoleon had also taken the same disease.

For a moment Hortense was completely overwhelmed, and then, by the greatest effort of her life, she summoned her fortitude to her aid. She immediately sent for the physician again, and, trusting to a sympathetic human heart, she confided all to him, and he did not disappoint her. What is to be done must be done quickly, immediately, or it will be in vain!

Hortense thinks of all, and provides for all. Especially, she causes her son's passport to Corfu to be signed by the authorities, and a passage to be taken for him on the only ship destined for Corfu now lying in the harbor. She instructs the servants, who are conveying trunks and packages to the vessel, to inform the curious spectators of her son's intended departure on this vessel. She at the same time causes the report to be circulated that she has suddenly been taken ill, and can therefore not accompany her son.

The physician confirms this statement, and informs all Ancona of the dangerous illness of the Duchess of St. Leu.

And after all this had been done, Hortense causes her son's bed to be carried into the little cabinet adjoining her room, and falling on her knees at his bedside, and covering her face with her hands, she prays to God to preserve the life of her child!

On the evening of this day the vessel destined for Corfu hoisted its anchor. No one doubted that Louis Napoleon had embarked on it, and every one pitied the poor duchess, who, made ill by grief and anxiety, had not been able to accompany her son.

In the mean while Hortense was sitting at the bedside of her delirious son. But she no longer felt weak or disquieted; nervous excitement sustained her, and gave her strength and presence of mind. Her son was at the same time threatened by two dangers—by the disease, which the slightest mistake might render mortal; and by the arrival of the Austrians, who had expressly excepted her son Louis Napoleon from the benefits of the amnesty. She must save her son from both these dangers—this thought gave her strength.

Two days had now passed; the last two vessels had left the harbor, crowded with fugitives; and now the advance-guard of the Austrians was marching into Ancona.

The commandant of the advance-guard, upon whom

the duty of designating quarters for the following army devolved, selected the palace of Princess Canino, where the Duchess of St. Leu resided, as headquarters for the commanding general and his staff. Hortense had expected this, and had withdrawn to a few small rooms in advance, holding all the parlors and large rooms in readiness for the general. When they, however, demanded that the entire palace should be vacated, the wife of the janitor, the only person whom Hortense had taken into her confidence, informed them that Queen Hortense, who was ill and unhappy, was the sole occupant of these reserved rooms.

Strange to relate, the Austrian captain who came to the palace to make the necessary preparations for his general's reception was one of those who, in the year 1815, had protected the queen and her children from the fury of the royalists. For the second time he now interested himself zealously in behalf of the duchess, and hastened forward to meet the general-in-chief, Baron Geppert, who was just entering the city, in order to acquaint him with the state of affairs. He, in common with all the world, convinced that her son, Louis Napoleon, had fled to Corfu, declared his readiness to permit the duchess to retain the rooms she was occupying, and begged permission to call on her. But the duchess was still ill, and confined to her bed, and could receive no one.

The Austrians took up their quarters in the palace; and in the midst of them, separated from the general's room by a locked door only, were Hortense and her sick son. The least noise might betray him. When he coughed it was necessary to cover his head with the bed-clothes, in order to deaden the sound; when he desired to speak he could only do so in a whisper, for his Austrian neighbors would have been astonished to hear a male voice in the room of the sick duchess, and their suspicions might have been thereby aroused.

At last, after eight days of torment and anxiety, the physician declared that Louis Napoleon could now undertake the journey without danger, and consequently the duchess suddenly recovered! She requested the Austrian general, Baron Geppert, to honor her with a call, in order that she might thank him for his protection and sympathy; she told him that she was now ready to depart, and proposed embarking at Livorno, in order to join her son at Malta, and go with him to England. As she would be compelled to pass through the whole Austrian army-corps on her way, she begged the general to furnish her with a passport through his lines over his own signature; requesting in addition that, in order to avoid all sensation, the instrument should not contain her name.

The general, deeply sympathizing with the unhappy woman who was about to follow her proscribed son, readily accorded her request.

Hortense purposed beginning her journey on the following day, the first day of the Easter festival; and, on sending her farewell greeting to the Austrian general, she informed him that she would start at a very early hour, in order to hear mass at Loretto.

During the night all necessary preparations for the journey were made, and Louis Napoleon was compelled to disguise himself in the dress of a liveried servant; a similar attire was also sent to Marquis Zappi, who had hitherto been concealed in the house of a friend, and in this attire he was to await the duchess below at the carriage.

At last, day broke and the hour of departure came. The horn of the postilion resounded through the street. Through the midst of the sleeping Austrian soldiers who occupied the antechamber through which they were compelled to pass, Hortense walked, followed by her son, loaded with packages, in his livery. Their departure was witnessed by no one except the sentinel on duty.

Day had hardly dawned. In the first carriage sat the duchess, with a lady companion, and in front, on the box, her son, as a servant, at the side of the postilion; in the second carriage her maid, behind her the young Marquis Zappi.

As the sun arose and shone down upon the beautiful Easter day, Ancona was already far behind, and Hortense knelt down at the side of Louis Napoleon to thank God tearfully for having permitted her to succeed so far in rescuing her son, and to entreat Him to be merciful in the future. But there were still many dangers to be overcome; the slightest accident might still betray them. The danger consisted not only in having to pass through all the places where the Austrian troops were stationed; General Geppert's pass was a sufficient protection against any thing that might threaten them from this quarter.

The greatest danger was to be apprehended from their friends—from some one who might accidentally recognize her son, and unintentionally betray them.

They must pass through the grand-duchy of Tuscany, and there the greatest danger menaced, for there her son was known to every one, and every one might betray them. This part of the journey must therefore be made, as far as possible, by night. The courier whom they had dispatched in advance had everywhere ordered the necessary relays of horses; their dismay was, therefore, great when they found no horses at the station Camoscia, on the boundary of Tuscany, and were informed that several hours must elapse before they could obtain any!

These hours of expectation and anxiety were fearful. Hortense passed them in her carriage, breathlessly listening to the slightest noise that broke upon the air.

Her son Louis had descended from the carriage, and seated himself on a stone bench that stood in front of the miserable little station-house. Worn out by grief and still weak from disease, indifferent to the dangers that menaced from all sides, heedless of the night wind that swept, with its icy breath, over his face, the prince sank down upon this stone bench, and went to sleep.

Thus they passed the night. Hortense, once a queen, in a half-open carriage; Louis Napoleon, the present Emperor of France, on a stone bench, that served him as a couch!

CHAPTER VII.

THE PILGRIMAGE.

HEAVEN took pity on the agony of the unhappy Duchess of St. Leu. It heard the prayer of her anxious mother's heart, and permitted mother and son to escape the dangers that menaced them at every step in Italy.

At Antibes they succeeded in crossing the French boundary without being recognized. They were now in their own country—in *la belle France*, which they still loved and proudly called their mother, although it had forsaken and discarded them. The death-penalty threatened the Bonapartes who should dare to set foot on French soil. But what cared they for that? Neither Hortense nor her son thought of it. They only knew that they were in their own country. They inhaled with delight the air that seemed to them better and purer than any other; with hearts throbbing with joy, they listened to the music of this beautiful language that greeted them with the sweet native melodies.

At Cannes they passed the first night. What recollections did this place recall to Hortense! Here it was that Napoleon had landed on his return from Elba to France; from Cannes he had commenced his march to Paris with a handful of soldiers, and had arrived there with an army. For the people had everywhere received him with exultation; the regiments that had been sent out against the advancing general had everywhere joyously gone over to his standard. Charles de Labédoyère, this enthusiastic adherent of the emperor, had been the first to do this. He was to have advanced against the emperor from Grenoble; but, with the exulting cry, "*Vive l'empereur!*" the entire regiment had gone over to its adored chieftain. Labédoyère had paid dearly for the enthusiasm of those moments; for, the for-the-second-time restored Bourbons punished his fidelity with death. Like Marshal Ney, Charles de Labédoyère was also shot; like the emperor himself, he paid for the triumph of the hundred days with his liberty and with his life!

Of all these names and events of the past, Hortense thought, while enjoying the first hours of repose in their room at an hotel in Cannes. Leaning back in her chair, her large eyes gazing dreamily at the ceiling above her, she told the attentive prince of the days that had been, and spoke to him of the days in which they were now living —of these days of humiliation and obscurity—of those days in which the French nation had risen, and, shaking its lion's mane, hurled the Bourbons from their ancestral throne, and out of the land they had hitherto proudly called their own. On driving out the Bourbons, the people had freely chosen another king—not the King of Rome, who, in Vienna, as Duke of Reichstadt, had been made to forget the brilliant days of his childhood—not the son of the Emperor Napoleon. The people of France had chosen the Duke of Orleans as their king, and Louis Philippe's first act had been to renew the decree of banishment which the Bourbons had fulminated against the Bonapartes, and which declared it to be a capital crime if they should ever dare to set foot on the soil of France.

"The people acted freely and according to their own will," said Hortense, with a sad smile, as she saw her son turn pale, and wrinkles gather on his brow. "Honor the will of the people, my son! In order to reward the emperor for his great services to the country, the people of France had unanimously chosen him their emperor. The people who give have also the right to take back again. The Bourbons, who consider themselves the owners of France, may reclaim it as an estate of which they have been robbed by the house of Orleans. But the Bonapartes must remember that they derived all their power from the will of the people. They must be content to await the future expression of its will, and then submit, and conform themselves to it." *

Louis Napoleon bowed his head and sighed. He must conform to the will of the people; cautiously, under a borrowed name, he must steal into the land of his longing and of his dreams; he must deny his nationality, and be indebted, for his name and passport, to the country that had bound his uncle, like a second Prometheus, to the rock, and left him there to die! But he did it with a sorrowful, with a bleeding heart; he wandered with his mother, who walked heavily veiled at his side, from place to place, listening to her reminiscences of the great past. At her

* The duchess's own words. See La Reine Hortense en Italie, Suisse, France, etc., p. 79.

relation of these reminiscences, his love and enthusiasm for the fatherland, from which he had so long been banished, burned brighter and brighter. The sight, the air of this fatherland, had electrified him; he entertained but one wish: to remain in France, and to serve France, although in the humble capacity of a private soldier.

One day Louis Napoleon entered his mother's room with a letter in his hand, and begged her to read it. It was a letter addressed to Louis Philippe, in which Louis Napoleon begged the French king to annul his exile, and to permit him to enter the French army as a private soldier.

Hortense read the letter, and shook her head sadly. It wounded her just pride that her son, the nephew of the great emperor, should ask a favor of him who had not hesitated to make the most of the revolution for himself, but had nevertheless lacked the courage to help the banished Bonapartes to recover their rights, and enable them to return to their country. In his ardent desire to serve France, Louis Napoleon had forgotten this insult of the King of France.

" My children," says Hortense, in her memoirs, " my children, who had been cruelly persecuted by all the courts, even by those who owed every thing to the emperor, their uncle, loved their country with whole-souled devotion. Their eyes ever turned toward France, busied with the consideration of institutions that might make France happy; they knew that the people alone were their friends; the hatred of the great had taught them

this. To conform to the will of the people with resignation was to them a duty, but to devote themselves to the
service of France was their hearts' dearest wish. It was
for this reason that my son had written to Louis Philippe,
hoping to be permitted to make himself useful to his
country in some way."

Hortense advised against this venturous step; and
when she saw how much this grieved her son, and observed his eyes filling with tears, she begged that he
would at least wait and reflect, and postpone his decision
until their arrival in Paris.

Louis Napoleon yielded to his mother's entreaties, and
in silence and sadness these two pilgrims continued their
wandering through the country and cities, that to Hortense seemed transformed into luminous monuments of
departed glory.

In Fontainebleau Hortense showed her son the palace
that had been the witness of the greatest triumphs and
also of the most bitter grief of his great uncle. Leaning on his arm, her countenance concealed by a heavy
black veil, to prevent any one from recognizing her, Hortense walked through the chambers, in which she had
once been installed as a mighty and honored queen, and
in which she was now covertly an exile menaced with
death. The servants who conducted her were the same
who had been there during the days of the emperor!
Hortense recognized them at once; she did not dare to
make herself known, but she nevertheless felt that she,
too, was remembered there. She saw this in the expres-

sion with which the servants opened the rooms she had once occupied; she heard it in the tone in which they mentioned her name! Every thing in this palace had remained as it then was! There was the same furniture in the rooms which the imperial family had occupied after the peace of Tilsit, and in which they had given such brilliant *fêtes*, and received the homage of so many of the kings and princes of Europe, all of whom had come to implore the assistance and favor of their vanquisher! There were also the apartments which the pope had occupied, once voluntarily; subsequently, under compulsion. Alas! and there was also the little cabinet, in which the emperor, the once so mighty and illustrious ruler of Europe, had abdicated the crown which his victories, his good deeds, and the love of the French people, had placed on his head! And, finally, there were also the chapel and the altar before which the Emperor Napoleon had stood god-father to his nephew Louis Napoleon! All was still as it had been, except that the garden, that Hortense and her mother had laid out and planted, had grown more luxuriant, and now sang to the poor banished pilgrim with its rustling tree-tops a melancholy song of her long separation from her home!

The sorrowing couple wandered on, and at last arrived before the gates of Paris. At this moment, Hortense was a Frenchwoman, a Parisian only, and, forgetting every thing else, all her grief and sufferings, she sought only to do the honors of Paris for her son. She ordered the coachman to drive them through the boulevards to the

Rue de la Paix, and then to stop at the first good hotel.
This was the same way over which she had passed sixteen
years before, escorted by an Austrian officer. Then she
had quitted Paris by night, driven out in a measure by
the allies, who so much feared her, the poor, weak woman,
with her little boys, that troops had been placed under
arms at regular intervals on her way, in order, as it was
given out, to secure her safe passage. Now, after sixteen
years, Hortense returned to Paris by the same route, still
exiled and homeless, at her side the son who was not only
menaced by the French decree of banishment, but also by
the Austrian edict of proscription.

But yet she was once more in Paris, once more at
home, and she wept with joy at beholding once more the
streets and places about which the memories of her youth
clustered.

By a strange chance, it was at the "*Hôtel de Hollande*" that the former Queen of Holland descended
from her carriage, and took up her residence, holding
thus, in a measure, her entrance into Paris, under the fluttering banner of the past. In the little *Hôtel de Hollande*, the Queen of Holland took possession of the
apartments of the first floor, which commanded a view
of the boulevard and the column of the *Place Vendôme.*
"Say to the column on the *Place Vendôme* that I am
dying, because I cannot embrace it," the Duke de Reichstadt once wrote in the album of a French nobleman, who
had succeeded, in spite of the watchful spies, who surrounded the emperor's son, in speaking to him of his

father and of the empire. This happiness, vainly longed for by the emperor's son, was at least to be enjoyed by his nephew.

Louis Napoleon could venture to show himself. In Paris he was entirely unknown, and could therefore be betrayed by no one. He could go down into the square and hasten to the foot of the *Vendôme* column, and in thought at least kneel down before the monument that immortalized the renown and grandeur of the emperor. Hortense remained behind, in order to perform a sacred duty, imposed on her, as she believed, by her own honor and dignity.

She was not willing to sojourn secretly, like a fugitive criminal, in the city that in the exercise of its free will had chosen itself a king, but not a Bonaparte. She was not willing to partake of French hospitality and enjoy French protection by stealth; she was not willing to go about in disguise, deceiving the government with a false pass and a borrowed name. She had the courage of truth and sincerity, and she resolved to say to the King of France that she had come, not to defy his decree of banishment by her presence, not for the purpose of intriguing against his new crown, by arousing the Bonapartists from their sleep of forgetfulness by her appearance, but solely because there was no other means of saving her son; because she must pass through France with him in order to reach England.

Revolution, which so strangely intermingles the destinies of men, had surrounded the new king almost en-

23

tirely with the friends and servants of the emperor and
of the Duchess of St. Leu. But, in order not to excite
suspicion against these, Hortense now addressed herself
to him with whom she had the slightest acquaintance,
and whose devotion to the Orleans family was too well
known to be called in doubt by her undertaking. Hortense therefore addressed herself to M. de Houdetot, the
adjutant of the king, or rather, she caused her friend
Mlle. de Massuyer to write to him. She was instructed
to inform the count that she had come to Paris with an
English family, and was the bearer of a commission from
the Duchess of St. Leu to M. de Houdetot.

M. de Houdetot responded to her request, and came
to the *Hôtel de Hollande* to see Mlle. Massuyer. With
surprise and emotion, he recognized in the supposititious
English lady the Duchess of St. Leu, who was believed
by all the world to be on the way to Malta, and for
whom her friends (who feared the fatigue of so long a
journey would be too much for Hortense in her weak
state of health) had already taken steps to obtain for her
permission to pass through France on her way to England.

Hortense informed Count Houdetot of the last
strokes of destiny that had fallen upon her, and expressed her desire to see the king, in order to speak with
him in person about the future of her son.

M. de Houdetot undertook to acquaint the king with
her desire, and came on the following day to inform the
duchess of the result of his mission. He told the duchess that the king had loudly lamented her boldness in

coming to France, and the impossibility of his seeing her. He told her, moreover, that, as the king had a responsible ministry at his side, he had been compelled to inform the premier of her arrival, and that Minister Casimir Perrier would call on her during the day.

A few hours later, Louis Philippe's celebrated minister arrived. He came with an air of earnest severity, as it were to sit in judgment upon the accused duchess, but her artless sincerity and her gentle dignity disarmed him, and soon caused him to assume a more delicate and polite bearing.

"I well know," said Hortense in the course of the conversation, "I well know that I have broken a law, by coming hither; I fully appreciate the gravity of this offence; you have the right to cause me to be arrested, and it would be perfectly just in you to do so!"—Casimir Perrier shook his head slowly, and replied: "Just, no! Lawful, yes!" *

CHAPTER VIII.

LOUIS PHILIPPE AND THE DUCHESS OF ST. LEU.

THE visit which Casimir Perrier had paid the duchess seemed to have convinced him that the fears which the king and his ministry had entertained had really been groundless, that the step-daughter of Napoleon had not come to Paris to conspire and to claim the still somewhat

* La Reine Hortense: Voyage en Italie, etc., p. 110.

unstable throne of France for the Duke de Reichstadt, or for Louis Napoleon, but that she had only chosen the way through France, in the anxiety of maternal love, in order to rescue her son.

In accordance with this conviction, Louis Philippe no longer considered it impossible to see the Duchess of St. Leu, but now requested her to call. Perhaps the king, who had so fine a memory for figures and money-matters, remembered that it had been Hortense (then still Queen of Holland) who, during the hundred days of the empire in 1815, had procured for the Duchess Orleans-Penthièvre, from the emperor, permission to remain in Paris and a pension of two hundred thousand francs per annum; that it had been Hortense who had done the same for the aunt of the present king, the Duchess of Orleans-Bourbon. Then, in their joy over an assured and brilliant future, these ladies had written the duchess the most affectionate and devoted letters; then they had assured Hortense of their eternal and imperishable gratitude.* Perhaps Louis Philippe remembered this, and was desirous of rewarding Hortense for her services to his mother and his aunt.

He solicited a visit from Hortense, and, on the second day of her sojourn in Paris, M. de Houdetot conducted the Duchess of St. Leu to the Tuileries, in which she had once lived as a young girl, as the step-daughter of the emperor; then as Queen of Holland, as the wife of the emperor's brother; and which she now beheld once more,

* La Reine Hortense: Voyage en Italie, etc., p. 185,

a poor, nameless pilgrim, a fugitive with shrouded countenance, imploring a little toleration and protection of those to whom she had once accorded toleration and protection.

Louis Philippe received the Duchess of St. Leu with all the elegance and graciousness which the "Citizen King" so well knew how to assume, and that had always been an inheritance of his house, with all the amiability and apparent open-heartedness beneath which he so well knew how to conceal his real disposition. Coming to the point at once, he spoke of that which doubtlessly interested the duchess most, of the decree of banishment.

"I am familiar," said the king, "with all the pains of exile, and it is not my fault that yours have not been alleviated." He assured her that this decree of banishment against the Bonaparte family was a heavy burden on his heart; he went so far as to excuse himself for it by saying that the exile pronounced against the imperial family was only an article of the same law which the conventionists had abolished, and the renewal of which had been so vehemently demanded by the country! Thus it had seemed as though he had uttered a new decree of banishment, while in point of fact he had only renewed a law that had already existed under the consulate of Napoleon. "But," continued the king with exultation, "the time is no longer distant when there will be no more exiles; I will have none under my government!"

Then, as if to remind the duchess that there had been

exiles and decrees of banishment at all times, also under the republic, the consulate, and the kingdom, he spoke of his own exile, of the needy and humiliating situation in which he had found himself, and which had compelled him to hire himself out as a teacher and give instruction for a paltry consideration.

The duchess had listened to the king with a gentle smile, and replied that she knew the story of his exile, and that it did him honor.

Then the duchess informed the king that her son had accompanied her on her journey, and was now with her in Paris ; she also told him that her son, in his glowing enthusiasm for his country, had written to the king, begging that he might be permitted to enter the army.

" Lend me the letter," replied Louis Philippe ; " Perrier shall bring it to me, and, if circumstances permit, I shall be perfectly willing to grant your son's request ; and it will also give me great pleasure to serve you at all times. I know that you have legitimate claims on the government, and that you have appealed to the justice of all former ministries in vain. Write out a statement of all that France owes you, and send it *to me alone*. I understand business matters, and constitute myself from this time on your *chargé d'affaires*.* The Duke of Rovigo," he continued, " has informed me that the other members of the imperial family have similar claims. It will afford me great pleasure to be of assistance to all of you, and I

---

* The king's own words. See Voyage en Italie, etc., p. 201.

shall interest myself particularly for the Princess de Mont-fort." *

Hortense had listened to the king, her whole face radiant with delight. The king's beneficent countenance, his friendly smile, his hearty and cordial manner, dis-pelled all doubt of his sincerity in Hortense's mind. She believed in his goodness and in his kindly disposition toward herself; and, in her joyous emotion, she thanked him with words of enthusiasm for his promised benefits, never doubting that it was his intention to keep his word.

"Ah, sire!" she exclaimed, "the entire imperial family is in misfortune, and you will have many wrongs to redress. France owes us all a great deal, and it will be worthy of you to liquidate these debts."

The king declared his readiness to do every thing. He who was so fond of taking in millions and of specu-lating, smilingly promised, in the name of France, to dis-burse millions, and to pay off the old state debt!

The duchess believed him. She believed in his pro-testations of friendship, and in his blunt sincerity. She allowed him to conduct her to his wife, the queen, and was received by her and Madame Adelaide with the same cordiality the king had shown. Once only in the course of the conversation did Madame Adelaide forget her cor-dial disposition. She asked the duchess how long she expected to remain in Paris, and when the latter replied that she intended remaining three days longer, Madame

† The Princess de Montfort was the wife of Jerome, the sister of the King of Wurtemberg, and a cousin of the Emperor of Russia.

exclaimed, in a tone of anxious dismay: "So long! Three days still! And there are so many Englishmen here who have seen your son in Italy, and might recognize you here!"

But Fate itself seemed to delay the departure of the duchess and her son. On returning home from her visit to the Tuileries, she found her son on his bed in a violent fever, and the physician who had been called in declared that he was suffering from inflammation of the throat.

Hortense was to tremble once more for the life of a son, and this son was the last treasure Fate had left her.

Once more the mother sat at the bedside of her son, watching over him, lovingly, day and night. That her son's life might be preserved was now her only wish, her only prayer; all else became void of interest, and was lost sight of. She only left her son's side when Casimir Perrier came, as he was in the habit of doing daily, to inquire after her son's condition in the name of the king, and to request the duchess to name the amount of her claims against France, and to impart to him all her wishes with regard to her future. Hortense now had but one ardent wish—the recovery of her son; and her only request was, that she might be permitted to visit the French baths of the Pyrenees during the summer, in order to restore her failing health.

The minister promised to procure this permission of the king, and of the Chambers, that were soon to be convened. "In this way we shall gradually become accustomed to your presence," observed Casimir Perrier. "As far as you are personally concerned, we shall be inclined to throw open the gates of the country to you. But with your son it is different, his name will be a perpetual obstacle in his way. If he should really desire at any time to take service in the army, it would be, above all, necessary that he should lay aside his name. We are in duty bound to consider the wishes of foreign governments: France is divided into so many parties, that a war could only be ruinous, and therefore your son must change his name, if—"

But now the duchess, her cheeks glowing, blushing with displeasure and anger, interrupted him. "What!" exclaimed she, "lay aside the noble name with which France may well adorn itself, conceal it as though we had cause to be ashamed of it?"

Beside herself with anger, regardless, in her agitation, even of the suffering condition of her son, she hastened to his bedside, to inform him of the proposition made to her by Louis Philippe's minister.

The prince arose in his couch, his eyes flaming, and his cheeks burning at the same time with the fever-heat of disease and of anger.

"Lay aside my name!" he exclaimed. "Who dares to make such a proposition to me? Let us think of all these things no more, mother. Let us go back to our retirement. Ah, you were right, mother: our time is passed, or it has not yet come!"

CHAPTER IX.

THE DEPARTURE OF THE DUCHESS FROM PARIS.

EXCITEMENT had made the patient worse, and caused his fever to return with renewed violence. Hortense was now inseparable from his bedside; she herself applied ice to his burning throat, and assisted in applying the leeches ordered by the physician. But this continuous anxiety and excitement, all these troubles of the present, and sad remembrances of the past, had at last exhausted the strength of the delicate woman; the flush of fever now began to show itself on her cheeks also, and the physician urged her to take daily exercise in the open air if she desired to avoid falling ill.

Hortense followed his advice. In the evening twilight, in plain attire, her face concealed by a heavy black veil, she now daily quitted her son's bedside, and went out into the street for a walk, accompanied by the young Marquis Zappi. No one recognized her, no one greeted her, no one dreamed that the veiled figure that walked so quietly and shyly was she who, as Queen of Holland, had formerly driven through these same streets in gilded coaches, hailed by the joyous shouts of the people.

But, in these wanderings through Paris, Hortense also lived in her memories only. She showed the marquis the dwelling she had once occupied, and which had for her a single happy association: her sons had been born there. With a soft smile she looked up at the proud *façade* of this building, the windows of which were brilliantly illumined, and in whose parlors some banker or ennobled provision-dealer was now perhaps giving a ball; pointing to these windows with her slender white hand, she said: "I wished to see this house, in order to reproach myself for having been unhappy in it; yes, I then dared to complain even in the midst of so much splendor; I was so far from dreaming of the weight of the misfortune that was one day to come upon me." *

She looked down again and passed on, to seek the houses of several friends, of whom she knew that they had remained faithful; heavily veiled and enveloped in her dark cloak she stood in front of these houses, not daring to acquaint her friends with her presence, contented with the sweet sense of being near them!

When, after having strengthened her heart with the consciousness of being near friends, she passed on through the streets, in which she, the daughter of France, was now unknown, homeless, and forgotten!—no, not forgotten!—as she chanced to glance in at a store she was just passing, she saw in the lighted window her own portrait at the side of that of the emperor.

Overcome by a sweet emotion, Hortense stood still and gazed at these pictures. The laughing, noisy crowd on the sidewalk passed on, heedless of the shrouded woman who stood there before the shop-window, gazing with tearful eyes at her own portrait. "It seems we are still remembered," whispered she, in a low voice. "Those

* The duchess's own words: see Voyage, etc., p. 225.

who wear crowns are not to be envied, and should not
lament their loss; but is it possible that the love of the
people, to receive which is so sweet, has not yet been
wholly withdrawn from us?"

The profound indifference with which France had
accepted the exile of the Bonapartes had grieved her
deeply.   She had only longed for some token of love and
fidelity in order that she might go back into exile consoled and strengthened.   And now she found it.   France
proved to her through these portraits that she was not
forgotten.

Hortense stepped with her companion into the store
to purchase the portraits of herself and of the emperor;
and when she was told that these portraits were in great
demand, and that many of them were sold to the people,
she hardly found strength to repress the tears of blissful
emotion that rose from her heart to her eyes.   She took
the portraits and hastened home, to show them to her
son and to bring to him with them the love-greetings of
France.   While the duchess, her thoughts divided between the remembrances of the past and the cares and
troubles of the present, had been sojourning in Paris for
twelve days, all the papers were extolling the heroism of
the duchess in having saved her son, and of her having
embarked at Malta in order to take him to England.

Even the king's ministerial council occupied itself
with this matter, and thought it proper to make representations to his majesty on the subject.   Marshal Sebas-
tiani informed the king that the Duchess of St. Leu, to

his certain knowledge, had landed at Corfu.   With lively interest he spoke of the fatiguing journey at sea that the duchess would be compelled to make, and asked almost timidly if she might not be permitted to travel through France.

The king's countenance assumed an almost sombre look, and he replied, dryly : "Let her continue her journey."   Casimir Perrier bowed his head over the paper that lay before him, in order to conceal his mirth, and minister Barthe availed himself of the opportunity to give a proof of his eloquence and of his severity, by observing that a law existed against the duchess, and that a law was a sacred thing that no one should be permitted to evade.

But the presence of the duchess, although kept a secret, began to cause the king and his premier Casimir Perrier more and more uneasiness.   The latter had already once informed her through M. de Houdetot that her departure was absolutely necessary and must take place at once, and he had only been moved to consent to her further sojourn by the condition of the prince, whose inflammation of the throat had rendered a second application of leeches necessary.

They were now, however, on the eve of a great and dangerous day, of the 5th of May.*   The people of Paris were strangely moved, and the new government saw with much apprehension the dawn of this day of such great memories for France.   There seemed to be some

* The anniversary of Napoleon's death.

justification for this apprehension. Since the break of
day, thousands of people had flocked to the column on
the *Place Vendôme*. Silently and gravely they approached the monument, in order to adorn with wreaths
of flowers the eagles, or to lay them at the foot of the
column, and then to retire mournfully.

Hortense stood at the window of her apartment, looking on with folded hands and tears of bliss at the impressive and solemn scene that was taking place on the
Place Vendôme beneath, when suddenly a violent knocking was heard at her door, and M. de Houdetot rushed
in, a pale and sorrowful expression on his countenance.

" Duchess," said he breathlessly, " you must depart
immediately, without an hour's delay! I am ordered to
inform you of this. Unless the life of your son is to be
seriously endangered, you must leave at once ! "

Hortense listened to him tranquilly. She almost
pitied the king—the government—to whom a weak
woman and an invalid youth could cause such fear.
How great must this fear be, when it caused them to
disregard all the laws of hospitality and of decency!
What had she done to justify this fear? She had not
addressed herself to the people of France, in order to
obtain help and protection for her son—for the nephew
of the emperor ; cautiously and timidly she had concealed herself from the people, and, far from being disposed to arouse or agitate her country, she had only made
herself known to the King of France in order to solicit
protection and toleration at his hands.

She was distrusted, in spite of this candor; and her presence, although known to no one, awakened apprehensions in those in authority. Hortense pitied them; not a word of complaint or regret escaped her lips. She sent for her physician at once; and, after informing him that she must necessarily depart for London, she asked him if such a journey would endanger her son's life. The physician declared that, while he could have desired a few days more of repose, the prince would nevertheless, with proper care and attention, be able to leave on the following day.

"Inform the king that I shall depart to-morrow," said Hortense; and, while M. de Houdetot was hastening to the king with this welcome intelligence, the duchess was making preparations for the journey, which she began with her son early on the following morning.

In four days they reached Calais, where they found the ship that was to convey them to England in readiness to sail. Hortense was to leave her country once more as a fugitive and exile! She was once more driven out, and condemned to live in a foreign country! Because the French people still refused to forget their emperor, the French kings hated and feared the imperial family. Under the old Bourbons, they had been hated; Louis Philippe, who had attained his crown through the people, felt that it was necessary to flatter the people, and show some consideration for their sympathies. He declared to the people that he entertained the most profound admiration for their great emperor, and yet he

issued a decree of banishment against the Bonapartes;
he ordered that the *Vendôme* column, with its bronze
statue of the emperor, should be adorned, and at the same
time his decree banished the daughter and the nephew
of the emperor from France, and drove them back into a
foreign country.

Hortense went, but she felt, in the pain it caused her,
that she was leaving her country—the country in which
she had friends whom she had not seen again; the country in which lay her mother's grave, which she had not
dared to visit; and, finally, the grave of her son! She
once more left behind her all the remembrances of her
youth—all the places she had loved; and her regret and
her tears made known how dear these things still were
to her; that the banished and homeless one was still
powerless to banish the love of country from her heart,
and that France was still her home!

CHAPTER X.

PILGRIMAGE THROUGH FRANCE.

The sojourn of the Duchess of St. Leu in England
where she arrived with her son after a stormy passage,
was for both a succession of triumphs and ovations. The
high aristocracy of London heaped upon her proofs of
esteem, of reverence, and of love; every one seemed
anxious to atone for the severity and cruelty with which

England had treated the emperor, by giving proofs of their admiration and respect for his step-daughter. All these proud English aristocrats seemed desirous of proving to the duchess and her son that they were not of the same disposition as Hudson Lowe, who had slowly tormented the chained lion to death with petty annoyances.

The Duchess of Bedford, Lord and Lady Holland, and Lady Grey, in particular, were untiring in their efforts to do the honors of their country to Hortense, and to show her every possible attention. But Hortense declined their proffered invitations. She avoided all publicity; she feared, on her own and her son's account, that the tattle of the world and the newspapers might once more draw down upon her the distrust and ill-will of the French government. She feared that this might prevent her returning with her son, through France, to her quiet retreat on the Lake of Constance, in Switzerland, to her charming Arenenberg, where she had passed so many delightful and peaceful years of repose and remembrance.

Hortense was right. Her sojourn in England excited, as soon as it became known, in every quarter, care, curiosity, and disquiet. All parties were seeking to divine the duchess's intention in residing in London. All parties were convinced that she entertained plans that might endanger and frustrate their own. The Duchess de Berri, who resided in Bath, had come to London as soon as she heard of the arrival of the Duchess of St. Leu, in order to inquire into Hortense's real intention. The bold and enterprising Duchess de Berri was preparing to go to France, in order to call the people to arms for herself and son, to hurl Louis Philippe from his usurped throne, and to restore to her son his rightful inheritance. They, therefore, thought it perfectly natural that Hortense should entertain similar plans for her son ; that she, too, should purpose the overthrow of the French king in order to place her own son, or the son of the emperor, the Duke de Reichstadt, on the throne.

On the other hand, it had been endeavored to persuade Prince Leopold, of Coburg, to whom the powers of Europe had just offered the crown of Belgium, that the Duchess of St. Leu had come to England in order to possess herself of Belgium by a *coup d'état*, and to proclaim Louis Napoleon its king. But this wise and magnanimous prince laughed at these intimations. He had known the duchess in her days of magnificence, and he now hastened to lay the same homage at the foot of the homeless woman that he had once devoted to the adored and powerful Queen of Holland. He called on the duchess, conversed with her of her beautiful and brilliant past, and told her of the hopes which he himself entertained for the future. Deeply bowed down by the death of his beloved wife, Princess Charlotte of England, it was his purpose to seek consolation in his misfortune by striving to make his people happy. He had therefore accepted the crown tendered him by the people, and was on the point of departing for Belgium.

While taking leave of the duchess, after a long and cordial conversation, he remarked, with a gentle smile :

" I trust you will not take my kingdom away from me on your journey through Belgium ? "

While the new government of France, as well as the exiled Bourbons, suspected the Duchess of St. Leu and her son of entertaining plans for the subversion of the French throne, the imperialists and republicans were hoping that Hortense's influence might be exerted upon the destinies of France. Everywhere in France as well as in England, the people were of the opinion that the new throne of Louis Philippe had no vitality, because it had no support in the heart of the people. The partisans of the Bourbons believed that France longed for the grandson of St. Louis, for its hereditary king, Henry V.; the imperialists were convinced that the new government was about to be overthrown, and that France was more anxious than ever to see the emperor's son, Napoleon II., restored. The republicans, however, distrusted the people and the army, and began to perceive that they could only attain the longed-for republican institutions under a Bonaparte. They therefore sent their secret emissaries as well to the Duke de Reichstadt as to Louis Napoleon.

The Duke de Reichstadt, to whom these emissaries proposed that he should come to France and present himself to the people, replied : " I cannot go to France as an adventurer ; let the nation call me, and I shall find means to get there."

To the propositions made to him, Louis Napoleon replied that he belonged to France under all circumstances ; that he had proved this by asking permission to serve

France, but he had been rejected. It would not become him to force to a decision by a *coup d'état* the nation whose decrees he would ever hold sacred.

Hortense regarded these efforts of the imperialists and of the republicans to win her son to their purposes with a sorrowful and anxious heart. She hoped and longed for nothing more than the privilege of living in retirement with her memories; she felt exhausted and sobered by the few steps she had already taken into the great world; she, who had ever felt the most tender sympathy for the misfortunes of others, and the most ardent desire to alleviate them—she had nowhere found in her misfortune any thing but injustice, indifference, and calumny.

Hortense longed to be back at Arenenberg, in her Swiss mountains. Thither she desired to return with her son, in order that she might there dream with him of the brilliant days that had been, and sing with him the exalted song of her remembrances! If the French government should permit her to journey with her son through France, she could easily and securely reach the Swiss Canton of Thurgau, where her little estate, Arenenberg, lay under the protection of the republic; the daughter of the emperor would there be certain to find peace and repose!

The duchess there wrote to M. de Houdetot, begging him to procure for her from the French government a passport, permitting her to travel through France under some assumed name. It was promised her after long hesitation, but under the condition that she should not commence her journey until after July, until after the first anniversary of the coronation of Louis Philippe.

Hortense agreed to this, and received on the first of August a passport, which permitted her, as Madame Arenenberg, to pass through France with her son in order to return to her estate in Switzerland.

It was at first the duchess's intention, notwithstanding the unquiet movements that were taking place in the capital, to journey through Paris, for the very purpose of proving, by her quiet and uninterested demeanor, that she had no share whatever in these movements and riots.

But, on informing Louis Napoleon of her intention, he exclaimed, with sparkling eyes: " If we go to Paris, and if I should see the people sabred before my eyes, I shall not be able to resist the inclination to place myself on its side ! " *

Hortense clasped her son anxiously in her arms, as if to protect him from all danger, on her maternal heart. " We shall not go to Paris," said she, " we will wander through France, and pray before the monuments of our happiness ! "

On the 7th of August the Duchess of St. Leu left England with her son, Louis Napoleon, and landed after a pleasant passage at Boulogne.

Boulogne was for Hortense the first monument of her happiness, at the foot of which she wished to pray ! There, during the most brilliant period of the empire,

* La Reine Hortense, p. 276.

she had attended the military *fêtes,* in the midst of which the emperor was preparing to go forth to encounter new dangers, and to reap, perhaps, new renown. A high column designated the place where these camp-festivals had once taken place. It had been erected under the empire, but under the restoration the name of Louis XVIII. had been inscribed on it.

Accompanied by the prince, the Duchess of St. Leu ascended this column, in order to show him from its summit the beautiful and flourishing France, that had once been her own and through which they must now pass with veiled countenances and borrowed names. From there she pointed out to him the situation of the different camps, the location of the imperial tent, then the place where the emperor's throne had stood, and where he had first distributed crosses of the legion of honor among the soldiers.

With a glowing countenance and in breathless attention, Louis Napoleon listened to his mother's narrative. Hortense, lost in her recollections, had not noticed that two other visitors, a lady and a gentleman, were now also on the platform and had listened to a part of her narrative. As the duchess ceased speaking, they approached to tell her with what deep interest they had listened to her narrative of the most glorious period of French history. They were a young married couple from Paris, and had much to relate concerning the parties who were now arrayed against each other in France, and who made the future of the country so uncertain.

In return for Hortense's so eloquent description of the past, they now told her of a *bon mot* of the present that was going the rounds of Parisian society. It was there said that the best means of satisfying everybody and all parties would be, to convert France into a republic and to give it three consuls, the Duke of Reichstadt, the Duke of Orleans, and the Duke of Bordeaux. "But," added they, "it might easily end in the first consul's driving out the other two, and making himself emperor."

Hortense found the courage to answer this jest with a smile, but she hastened to leave the place and to get away from the couple, who had perhaps recognized her, and told them of the *bon mot* with a purpose.

Sadly and silently, mother and son returned to their hotel, which was situated on the sea-side, and commanded a fine view of the surging, foaming waters of the channel and of the lofty column of the empire.

They both stepped out on the balcony. It was a beautiful evening; the setting sun shed its purple rays over the surface of the sea. Murmuring and in melodious *tace* the foaming waves rolled in upon the beach; on another side, the lofty column, glowing in the light of the setting sun, towered aloft like a pillar of fire, a memorial monument of fire!

Hortense, who for some time had been silently gazing, first at the column, then at the sea, now turned with a sad smile to her son.

"Let us spend an hour with recollections of the past," said she. "In the presence of this foaming sea and of this proud column, I will show you a picture of the past. Do you wish to see it ?"

His gaze fastened on the imperial column, Louis Napoleon silently nodded assent.

Hortense went to her room, and soon returned to the balcony with a book, bound in red velvet. Often, during the quiet days of Arenenberg, the prince had seen her writing in this book, but never had Hortense yielded to his entreaties and permitted him to read any part of her memoirs. Unsolicited it was her intention to unfold before him to-day a brilliant picture; in view of the sad and desolate present, she wished to portray to him the bright and glittering past, perhaps only for the purpose of entertaining him, perhaps in order to console him with the hope that all that is passes away, and that the present would therefore also come to an end, and that which once was, again become reality for him, the heir of the emperor.

She seated herself at her son's side, on a little sofa that stood on the balcony, and, opening her book, began to read.

CHAPTER XI.

FRAGMENT FROM THE MEMOIRS OF QUEEN HORTENSE.

" THE emperor had returned from Italy. The beautiful ceremony of the distribution of the crosses of the Legion of Honor had taken place before his departure, and I had been present on the occasion ; the emperor now repaired to Boulogne, in order to make a second distribution of the order in the army on his birthday. He had made my husband general of the army of the reserve, and sent him a courier, with the request that he should come with me and our son to the camp at Boulogne. My husband did not wish to interrupt the baths he was taking at St. Amand, but he requested me to go to Boulogne, to spend a week with the emperor.

" The emperor resided at Boulogne in a little villa called *Pont de Brigue*. His sister, Caroline, and Murat, lived in another little villa near by. I lived with them, and every day we went to dine with the emperor. During two years, our troops had been concentrating in full view of England, and every one expected an attack. The camp at Boulogne was erected on the sea-side, and resembled a long and regularly-built city. Each hut had a little garden, flowers, and birds. In the middle of the camp, on an elevation, stood the emperor's tent ; near by, that of Marshal Berthier. All the men-of-war on the water were drawn up in a line, only waiting the signal of departure. In the distance we could see England, and its beautiful ships that were cruising along the coast seemed to form an impenetrable barrier. This grand spectacle gave us for the first time an illustration of an unknown, hitherto not-dreamed-of power that stood opposed to us. Here every thing was calculated to excite the imagination. This boundless sea might soon transform itself into a battle-field, and swallow up the *élite* of the two greatest nations. Our troops, proud in the feeling that there were no obstacles for them, made impatient by two years' repose, glowing with energy and bravery, already imagined themselves to have attained the opposite coast. When one considered their bravery and confidence, success seemed certain ; but when the eye turned to the impenetrable forest of masts on the hostile ships, a feeling of anxiety and fear suddenly took possession of the heart. And yet nothing seemed to be wanting to the expedition but a favorable wind.

" Of all the homage that a woman can receive, military homage has in the highest degree the chivalrous character, and it is impossible not to feel flattered by it.

" There could not be any thing more delightful or imposing than the homage of which I was here the object, and it was only here that it made any impression on me.

" The emperor gave me as an escort his equerry, General Defrance. Whenever I approached a camp division, the guard was called out and presented arms.

" I had interceded for several soldiers who were undergoing punishment for breaches of discipline, and was on this account received everywhere with the liveliest enthusiasm. The entire mounted general staff escorted my carriage, and my approach was everywhere hailed by brilliant music. It was on such an occasion that I saw for the first time the urn which a grenadier wore attached to his belt ; I was told that the emperor, in order to do honor to the memory of the gallant Latour d'Auvergne,*

* Latour d'Auvergne, a descendant of the celebrated Turenne, was known and honored throughout the whole army on account of the

had caused his heart to be enclosed in a leaden casket, which he had intrusted to the oldest soldier of the regiment, commanding that his name should always be called at the roll-call, as though he were present. He who bore the heart replied : 'Dead on the field of honor.'

" One day, a breakfast was given me at the camp of Ambleteuse. I desired to go by water, and, notwithstanding a contrary wind, the admiral took me. I saw the English ships, and we passed so near them, that they might easily have captured our yacht. I also visited the Dutch fleet commanded by Admiral Versuelt, where I was received with great applause, the sailors little dreaming that I would be their queen within the space of a year.*

" On another occasion, the emperor ordered a review. The English, who felt disquieted, by the appearance of so many troops drawn up before them, approached nearer and nearer to our coasts, and even fired a few cannon-shots at us ; the emperor was at the head of his French columns when they replied to these shots, and was thus placed between two fires. As we had followed him, we

lion-hearted courage which he had exhibited on so many occasions. As he invariably declined the many advancements and honors that were tendered him, Napoleon appointed him first grenadier of the army. He fell in the action at Neuburg, and the Viceroy of Italy, Eugene Beauharnais, afterward caused a monument to be erected there in his memory.

* In order to reach the harbor of Ambleteuse to which they had been assigned, the Dutch had first been compelled to do battle with the English fleet, and in this combat they had acquitted themselves with the greatest honor.

were now compelled to remain at his side. To his uncle's
great joy, my son exhibited no symptom of fear whatever.
But the generals trembled at seeing the emperor exposed
to such danger. The ramrod of some awkward soldier
might prove as dangerous as a ball. In the midst of this
imposing spectacle, I was struck with astonishment at the
contrast presented by the troops under different circumstances. When drawn up in line of battle, they glowed
with gallantry and determination, but, in the days of repose, they resembled well-behaved children, who could
amuse themselves with a flower or a bird. The most
daring warrior was then often converted into the most
diligent and submissive scholar.

" For the breakfast which Marshal Davoust gave me
in his tent, the grenadiers had been preparing to entertain
us with several songs, and came forward to sing them
with the bashfulness of young girls. In the most embarrassed and timid manner, they sang a song full of the
fiercest and most daring threats against England.

" From the emperor's parlor we often saw the soldiers
of his guard assemble on the grass-plot before the castle ;
one of them would play the violin and instruct his com-
rades in dancing. The beginners would study the '*jétés*'
and '*assemblés*' with the closest attention ; the more advanced ones would execute a whole contre-dance. From
behind the window-blinds we watched them with the
greatest pleasure. The emperor, who often surprised us
at this occupation, would laugh with us and rejoice at the
innocent amusements of his soldiers.

"Was this project of a landing in England really intended? Or was it the emperor's purpose by these enormous preparations to divert attention from other points, and fix it on this one only? Even to-day this is a question which I cannot venture to decide; here, as elsewhere, I only report what I have seen.

"Madame Ney also gave me a brilliant festival at Montreuil, where her husband the marshal was in command. During the forenoon the troops were manœuvred before me, in the evening a ball took place. But this was suddenly interrupted by the intelligence that the emperor had just embarked.

"A number of young officers, who had been present at the ball, rushed out on the road to Boulogne; I followed them with the rapidity of lightning, escorted as usual by General Defrance, who burned with impatience to be again at the emperor's side. I myself felt unutterable emotion at the prospect of witnessing so great an occurrence. I imagined myself observing the battle from the summit of the tower that stood near the emperor's tent; beholding our fleet advance and sink down into the waves, I shuddered in anticipation.

"At last I arrived. I inquired after the emperor, and learned that he had actually attended the embarkation of all his troops during the night, but that he had just returned to his villa.

"I did not see him until dinner, at which he asked Prince Joseph, who was then colonel of a regiment, whether he had believed in this pretended embarkation, and what effect it had had on the soldiers. Joseph said that he, like all the world, had believed that a departure was really intended, and that the soldiers had doubted it so little that they had sold their watches. The emperor also often asked if the telegraph had not yet announced the approach of the French squadron ; his adjutant, Lauriston, was with the squadron, and the emperor seemed only to be awaiting Lauriston's arrival and a favorable wind, in order to set sail.

" The eight days' absence accorded me by my husband had expired, and I took leave of the emperor. I journeyed through Calais and Dunkirk. I saw troops defiling before me everywhere ; and with regret and fear I left this magnificent army, thinking that they might perhaps in a few days be exposed to the greatest dangers.

" At St. Amand we were every day expecting to hear of the passage of our fleet to England, when we suddenly saw the troops arriving in our neighborhood and passing on in forced marches toward the Rhine. Austria had broken the peace. We hastened at once to Paris, to see the emperor once more before his departure for Germany." *

* La Reine Hortense en Italie, France, etc., p. 278.

CHAPTER XII.

THE PILGRIM.

On the following morning the duchess left Boulogne with her son, in order to wander on with him through the land of her youth and of her memories.

It was a sad and yet heart-stirring pilgrimage; for, although banished and nameless, she was nevertheless in her own country—she still stood on French soil. For sixteen years she had been living in a foreign land, in a land whose language was unknown to her, and whose people she could therefore not understand. Now, on this journey through France, she rejoiced once more in being able to understand the conversation of the people in the streets, and of the peasants in the fields. It was a sensation of mingled bitterness and sweetness to feel that she was not a stranger among this people, and it therefore now afforded her the greatest delight to chat with those she met, and to listen to their *naïve* and artless words.

As soon as she arrived at her hotel in any city or village in which she purposed enjoying a day's rest, Hortense would walk out into the streets on her son's arm. On one occasion she stepped into a booth, seated herself, and conversed with the people who came to the store to purchase their daily necessaries; on another occasion, she accosted a child on the street, kissed it, and inquired after its parents; then, again, she would con-

verse with the peasants in the villages about their farms,
and the prospects of a plentiful harvest. The *naïve*,
strong, and healthy disposition of the people delighted
her, and, with the smiling pride of a happy mother,
she showed her son this great and beautiful family, this
French people, to which they, though banished and cast
off, still belonged.

In Chantilly, she showed the prince the palace of
Prince Condé. The forests that stood in the neighborhood had once belonged to the queen, or rather they had
been a portion of the appendage which the emperor,
since the union of Holland and France, had set apart
for her second son, Louis Napoleon. Hortense had
never been in the vicinity, and could therefore visit the
castle without fear of being recognized.

They asked the guide, who had shown them the castle
and the garden, who had been the former possessor of the
great forests of Chantilly.

"The step-daughter of the Emperor Napoleon, Queen
Hortense," replied the man, with perfect indifference.
"The people continued to speak of her here for a long
time; it was said that she was wandering about in the
country in disguise, but for the last few years nothing
has been heard of her, and I do not know what has become of her."

"She is surely dead, the poor queen," said Hortense,
with so sad a smile that her son turned pale, and his eyes
filled with tears.

From Chantilly they wandered on to Ermenonville

and Morfontaine, for Hortense desired to show her son all the places she had once seen in the days of fortune with the emperor and her mother. These places now seemed as solitary and deserted as she herself was. How great the splendor that had once reigned in Ermenonville, when the emperor had visited the owner of the place in order to enjoy with him the delights of the chase! In the walks of the park, in which thousands of lamps had then shone, the grass now grew rankly; a miserable, leaky boat was now the only conveyance to the Poplar Island, sacred to the memory of Jean Jacques, on whose monument Hortense and Louis Napoleon now inscribed their names. Morfontaine appeared still more desolate; the allies had sacked it in 1815, and it had not been repaired since then. In Morfontaine, Hortense had attended a magnificent festival given by Joseph Bonaparte, then its owner, to his imperial brother.

In St. Denis there were still more sacred and beautiful remembrances for Hortense, for here was situated the great college for the daughters of high military officers, of which Hortense had been the protectress. She dared not show herself, for she well knew that she was not forgotten here; here there were many who still knew and loved her, and she could only show herself to strangers. But she nevertheless visited the church, and descended with Louis Napoleon into the vaults. Louis XVIII. alone reposed in the halls which the empire had restored for the reception of the new family of rulers, adopted by France. Alas! he who built these halls, the Emperor

25

Napoleon, now reposed under a weeping-willow on a desolate island in the midst of the sea, and he who had deposed him now occupied the place intended for the sarcophagus of the emperor.

While wandering through these silent and gloomy halls, Hortense thought of the day on which she had come hither with the emperor to inspect the building of the church. And that time she had been ill and suffering, and with the fullest conviction she had said to her mother that she, Queen Hortense, would be the first that would be laid to rest in the vault of St. Denis. Now, after so many years, she descended into it living and had hardly a right to visit it.

But there was another grave, another monument to her memories, beside which Hortense desired to pray. This was the grave of the Empress Josephine, in the church at Ruelle.

With what emotions did she approach this place and kneel down beside the grave-mound! Of all that Josephine had loved, there remained only Hortense and her son, a solitary couple, who were now secretly visiting the place where Hortense's mother reposed. The number of flowers that adorned the monument proved that Josephine was at least resting in the midst of friends, who still held her memory sacred, and this was a consolation for her daughter.

From Ruelle and its consecrated grave they wandered on to Malmaison. Above all, Hortense wished to show this palace to her son! It was from this place that Na-

poleon had departed to leave France forever! Here
Hortense had had the pleasure of sweetening for him,
by her tender sympathy, the moment when all the world
had abandoned him—the moment when he fell from the
heights of renown into the abyss of misfortune. But,
alas! the poor queen was not even to have the satisfaction of showing to her son the palace, sacred to so many
memories that had once been her own! The present
owner had given strict orders to give admission to the
palace only upon presentation of permits that must be
obtained of him beforehand, and, as Hortense had none,
her entreaties were all in vain.

She was cruelly repelled from the threshold of the
palace in which in former days she had been so joyfully
received by her devoted friends and servants!

Sorrowfully, her eyes clouded with tears, she turned
away and returned to her hotel, leaning on her son's arm.

In silence she seated herself at his side on the stone
bench that stood before the house, and gazed at the palace in which she had spent such happy and momentous
days, lost in the recollections of the past!

" It is, perhaps, natural," she murmured in a low
voice, "that absence should cause those, who have the
happiness to remain in their homes, to forget us. But,
for those who are driven out into foreign lands, the life
of the heart stands still, and the past is all to them ; to
the exiled the present and the future are unimportant.
In France every thing has progressed, every thing is
changed, I alone am left behind, with my sentiments of

unchangeable love and fidelity! Alas! how sorrowful and painful it is to be forgotten! *   How—"

Suddenly she was interrupted by the tones of a piano, that resounded in her immediate vicinity. Behind the bench on which they were sitting, were the windows of the parlor of the hotel. These windows were open, and each tone of the music within could be heard with the greatest distinctness.

The playing was now interrupted by a female voice, which said: "Sing us a song, my daughter."

"What shall I sing?" asked another and more youthful voice.

"Sing the beautiful, touching song your brother brought you from Paris yesterday. The song of Delphine Gay, set to music by M. de Beauplan."

"Ah, you mean the song about Queen Hortense, who comes to Paris as a pilgrim? You are right, mamma, it is a beautiful and touching song, and I will sing it!"

And the young lady struck the keys more forcibly, and began to play the prelude.

Outside on the stone bench sat she who was once Queen Hortense, but was now the poor, solitary pilgrim. Nothing remained to her of the glorious past, but her son, who sat at her side! Hand in hand, both breathless with emotion, both pale and tearful, they listened until the young girl concluded her touching song.

* The duchess's own words. See Voyage en Italie, etc., p. 305.

CHAPTER XIII.

CONCLUSION.

THIS sorrowful pilgrimage was at last at an end. Hortense was once more in her mountain-home, in the charming villa overlooking the Lake of Constance, and commanding a lovely view of the majestic lake, with its island and its surrounding cities and villages.

Honor to the Canton Thurgau, which, when all the world turned its back on the queen upon whom all the governments and destiny alike frowned—when even her nearest relatives, the Grand-duke and the Grand-duchess Stephanie of Baden, were compelled to forbid her residence in their territory—still had the courage to offer the Duchess of St. Leu an asylum, and to accord her, on the free soil of the little republic, a refuge from which the ill-will and distrust of the mighty could not drive her!

In Arenenberg, Hortense reposed from her weariness. With a bleeding breast she returned home, her heart wounded by a fearful blow, the loss of a noble and beloved son, broken in spirit, and bowed down by the coldness and cruelty of the world, which, in the cowardly fear of its egoism, had become faithless, even to the holiest and most imperishable of all religions, the religion of memory!

How many, who had once vowed love and gratitude, had abandoned her! how many, whom she had benefited had deserted her in the hour of peril!

In the generosity and kindliness of her heart, she forgave them all; and, instead of nursing a feeling of bitterness, she pitied them! She had done with the outer world! Arenenberg was now her world—Arenenberg, in which her last and only happiness, her son, the heir of the imperial name, lived with her—Arenenberg, which was as a temple of memory, in which Hortense was the pious and believing priestess.

At Arenenberg Hortense wrote the sad and touching story of her journey through Italy, France, and England, which she undertook, in the heroism of maternal love, in order to rescue her son. The noblest womanhood, the most cultivated mind, the proudest and purest soul, speaks from out this book, with which Hortense has erected a monument to herself that is more imperishable than all the monuments of stone and bronze, for this monument speaks to the heart—those to the eyes only. Hortense wrote this book with her heart often interrupted by the tears that dimmed her eyes; she concludes it with a touching appeal to the French people, which it may well be permitted us to repeat here; it is as follows:

"The renewal of the law of exile, and the assimilation made between us and the Bourbons, testify to the sentiments and fears that are entertained respecting us. No friendly voice has been raised in our behalf; this indifference has doubled the bitterness of our banishment! May they, however, still be happy—those who forget! May they, above all, make France happy! This is my prayer!

" As for the people, it will, if it remembers its glory, its grandeur, and the incessant care of which it was the object, ever hold our memory dear. This is my firm conviction, and this thought is the sweetest consolation of an exile, the sweetest consolation he can take with him to the grave ! " *

Hortense still lived a few years of peaceful tranquillity ; far from all she loved—far also from the son who was her last hope, never dreaming that destiny had so brilliant a future in store for him, and that Louis Napoleon, whom the Bourbons had banished from France as a child, and the Orleans as a youth—that Louis Napoleon would one day be enthroned in Paris as emperor, while the Bourbons and Orleans languish in foreign lands as exiles !

In the year 1837, Hortense, the flower of the Bonapartes, died !

Weary, at last, of misfortune, and of the exile in which she languished, she bowed her head, and went home to her great dead—home to Napoleon and Josephine !

* Voyage en Italie, etc., p. 324.

(40)

THE END.

www.ingramcontent.com/pod-product-compliance
Lightning Source LLC
Chambersburg PA
CBHW030901270326
41929CB00008B/530